Jay Landesman

Rebel Without Applause

BLOOMSBURY

For my brother Alfred

First published in Great Britain 1987
Copyright © 1987 by Jay Landesman

Bloomsbury Publishing Ltd, 4 Bloomsbury Place, London WC1A 2QA

British Library Cataloguing in Publication Data

ISBN 0–7475–0035–5

Printed in Great Britain by
Butler & Tanner Ltd, Frome and London

came from Mrs. Pankhurst. It was no fault of her highly prized Singer sewing machine, whose hum was the most familiar sound of my early years. I sometimes thought that if it ever came down to a choice between me and the Singer, she'd have picked the Singer. I couldn't blame her, it was much more reliable.

Each summer, Cutie would take the whole family off to remote parts of Missouri's Ozarks, where running water and electricity were still novelties. She liked to keep us in touch with nature, leading us down to the creek every morning to plunge into the icy waters, thanking the Lord for giving her such a "big, wide, wonderful world to play in" at such remarkable low summer rates. She encouraged us to run around naked, but we had to wear shoes. She said that 'everything in nature is beautiful' but she was never without her fly swatter, her patent medicines, her jars of Mum, vaseline and the family enema bag. She gave us daily warnings about poisonous snakes, poison ivy and constipation, and she lived in fear that nature was out to destroy us in spite of its wonders.

Country life had charms for us that Cutie never imagined. The outhouse was one of them; it prevented her from checking up on our bowels. But to us it was a little temple of contemplation with the sexiest pin-ups in the world torn from the pages of the Sears Roebuck catalogue. By summer's end, there was nothing about women's underwear that I didn't know the price of, or range of size. The food we ate in the country was positively exotic compared to Cutie's kosher cooking in the city. Everything tasted fresher and cleaner; even pork was allowed us as long as it was cooked to a cinder.

Every day was spent trying to get away from her organized recreations, preferring to follow the farmer's children as they went about their chores. These summers gave me the feeling that I was part of a bigger family than just Landesmans. When father came out to visit us on the weekends and we were all together again, we behaved as we did in the city. We couldn't wait for him to leave so we could get back to nature's follies. But by the end of the summer we were glad to get back to the city.

City life had its charms for a skinny kid like me with an insatiable curiosity. Our house on the corner of Arlington Avenue and Minerva fronted US Highway 40. Everybody travelling west had to pass our modest two-family brick dwelling with its front porch, sloping lawn and a wild hedge that always needed trimming. The stop sign at the intersection gave us a chance to say hello or exchange insults with the children from far-away places with exotic license plates. Being first to spot what state they came from was a fascinating game we never tired of.

Cutie's warnings to stay away from the caravans that passed our house only added to the excitement when the gypsies came to town. Stories of kidnapped children fascinated me. Sometimes I wondered if I wasn't really a gypsy prince stolen by a middle class Jewish family. Whenever I had a fight with her, I thought I would get even by hitching a ride with the gypsies to some enchanted encampment. I would do anything to get away from the rules and regulations of home life.

Opposite our house was a city block of fenced property belonging to the St. Anne's Orphanage. Cutie always pointed out to me that I was lucky not to be behind the barbed wire with those poor orphans, but to me they looked like the lucky ones, running free, being attended to by pretty young women with bright wet lips and big breasts. We never understood that these women were there to have their own babies born out of wedlock, the fate of good Catholic girls gone bad. We were never allowed inside, but we were playmates all the same, throwing balls to one another over the fence, often holding hands through the wire. What mother could disapprove of being friendly to an orphan? Sometimes Cutie gave us brownie cookies to share with them.

At the other end of our block was Emerson school, where I spent my formative years in misery. The only comfortable place was the furnace room; I was on intimate terms with all the janitors. I respected them more than the teachers and had the impression that they knew more about a child's educational needs. Sometimes in winter I would do my homework next to a warm boiler; it was a lot better than doing it under Cutie's cold eyes. Not that I did a lot of homework. Instead, I developed a sense of irreverence with back issues of *Bally-Hoo,* an early mass market satirical magazine.

Being smaller and dumber than most of the children at school—my Sanford-Binet intelligence quotient was so low I thought it was my room number—I had to develop new skills to overcome my handicap. I became a part-time comic and full-time exhibitionist, appreciated by my fellow classmates but persecuted by the teachers. My imitations of Al Jolson and Eddie Cantor would have gotten me an *A* in any drama course, but because I performed them in Geography class I was penalized. School was a battle ground of wills that I emerged from scarred, but victorious. There wasn't a subject I took to which I didn't add a new dimension of juvenile peccadillos, including physical education and basket-weaving. If only the teachers had accepted my sense of humor, years of battling with their authority would have paid off.

Accused of harbouring general principles against the best interests of the school, I pleaded guilty with pride. Suspensions from school came as regular as clockwork, but Cutie forced the teachers to reinstate me; as the treasurer of the Parents Teachers Association she carried a lot of weight. Towards the end of my sentence I acquired a miraculous insight: *school is one big joke.*

What grown-ups in the 30s called a Depression, I called fun. The sidewalks and alleys were free and they were my stage. When my cousin, recently sacked from his job as a felt-presser in a men's hat factory, set up his apple stand on a busy intersection, I joined him in entertaining the tired men and women going home from work. While he sold his apples for a nickel and wisecracked about the shortcomings of capitalism, I set up a shoe-shine stand next to his and made up my first singing commercial in the style of Bing Crosby and the Mills Brothers:

Shine, shine, shine 'em up Mister
Only five cents per shine
(Ba bo bobo bo bo bobo)
I will shine your shoes
To satisfy you
And to keep you smiling all the time.
Black or brown, blue or white
I shine your shoes with all my might
So shine, shine, shine 'em up Mister
They're only five cents per shine.
(Ba bobo ba, bo ba bo)

The sidewalks were note books for the poor. I wrote some of my finest lines on them in chalk; "Irving HATES school," enclosed by a heart with an arrow through the word hate. They were our tennis courts, our exercise grounds and about the only thing we really owned. I remember it as a lifetime spent sitting on the curb watching the Fords go by.

What valuables lay in the gutter! King size cigarette butts, embossed cigar bands, silver foil from cigarette packages that you could sell if you could only collect a ton; or if you happened to get the lucky number from a pack of Lucky Strikes (or was it Camels?) you won a brand new Chevrolet. There were unused street car transfers and picture cards of baseball players, circulars for free home inspections, used postage stamps and leaflets for the Rosicrucians. Once in a while a soiled Irish linen handkerchief would be abandoned, and what was an almost new sanitary napkin doing next to it?

The alleys were the diamond mines of our street life. What treasures could be recycled in the ashpits of the alleyways: slightly used condoms and almost new batteries, Dixie paper cups by the score, cracked Bakelite household appliances, radio tubes, chipped crockery with years of life left in them. And the magazines that people threw away! Were they disgusted with themselves because they couldn't beat the time it took to read a *Liberty* magazine feature: 'THIS ARTICLE CAN BE READ IN FOUR MINUTES AND 32 SECONDS? It was their editor's brilliant contribution to journalism at the time.

Like millions of other good Americans during the Depression, our house displayed the New Deal's blue eagle in the window. My father, who by now was eking out a living as a part-time antique dealer, was invited by the Public Works project to join a distinguished group of unemployed muralists brightening up Federal Post Offices and children's hospitals with murals of nymphs and cherubs. Everyone was expected to do his bit for the country and at seventy-five dollars a week it was no hardship for Benjamin C. to pick up his brushes again. Cutie took over the running of the antique shop and once more he was wearing his artist's smock. Historians would have to say that the Depression was the best thing that happened to our family; under Cutie's reign the antique shop became a thriving enterprise. When my father returned to the business he was never again his own boss.

I remained fiercely independent having a whole string of jobs after school and on Saturdays. My success as a door to door salesman for the Curtis Publishing Company (*Saturday Evening Post, The Ladies Home Journal* and *House and Garden*) was inspired by all the salesmen that came to our house during the Depression selling Fuller brushes, large-size Hershey bars not-to-be-had in regular stores, and suits made to order at amazing low prices. A travelling violin lessons salesman was a particular source of inspiration. His great stroke was choosing my brother, Gene, to be the lucky candidate.

"Look, madame," he said to Cutie, "this boy has the hands of a virtuoso." Thrusting the violin under Gene's chin, he grabbed his right hand to place over the bow— when he noticed the deformed fingers of Gene's left hand. By no stretch of the imagination could they possibly do a simple fingering exercise, much less an intricate run, but he didn't crack a smile or show a sign of surprise. Placing Gene's gnarled fingers across the neck of the violin into a fingering position, he asked: "How does that feel, son?" He looked at Cutie. "Madame, this boy could be another Yehudi Menuhin." Gene was almost as surprised as the salesman when Cutie signed up for a full course.

My Saturday job was to light the furnaces of our Orthodox Jewish neighbors, who were forbidden to light fires on the Sabbath. My being Jewish didn't seem to matter to them; rather I got the impression they were secretly pleased that such a nice Jewish boy was so ambitious. One Christmas, taking advantage of the Christian spirit, I collaborated with Fred and Gene in a sure fire promotion. Gene stole the Christmas seals from Woolworth, Fred repackaged them with hand-drawn 'Greetings from St. Anne's Orphanage', and I, dressed in ill-fitting clothes in freezing weather, sold the packages door to door in rich districts. When the maid or butler appeared, I'd put the package of seals on their little silver tray and ask them to take it to their mistress. I never failed to make a sale or be served a cup of hot chocolate, frequently both.

Then I became interested in collecting stamps. In a few months I had accumulated enough from other dealers' stamp approval books to start my own stamp company. One of the antique shop's customers owned a big stamp company, and I got a job sweeping up the place on Saturdays. I swept up so many good stamps that I had deliberately dropped on the floor that I handed in my broom before I was caught.

I was approaching the age when a boy's thoughts turn from stamps to cars. I loved the smell of gasoline and the look of a really beautiful dash board. I learned to drive at a very early age, so when I had the opportunity to buy a model T Ford coupe with a rumble seat for twenty-eight dollars, I sold my stamp company to Fred to raise the money. It was hard to convince Cutie that it was a smart move; she saw the car as a hearse that would carry me to my funeral.

"It could be a money-maker, Cutie." I explained my plan for charging my friends to take them to school. A deal with father to advertise the antique shop on the doors and rumble seat brought in a dollar a week, putting the whole operation into profit. Cutie was only convinced when she got a call from the advertisement on the car. The stamp collection was worth about two hundred dollars—which proved I knew nothing about business, but knew a lot about how to handle Cutie.

I started High School in 1934, but I already knew that my education lay in the direction of the Show Boat Ball-room. Twice a week, rain or shine, found me gliding through twelve sets of dances with the finesse of a young Fred Astaire. I discovered being a good dancer was more important than being smart or good-looking. I never had any trouble getting a good partner, but Rita, the funny-looking Greek girl with the frizzy hair turned me down. She preferred an older man, usually Max, who was old enough to be her father. But Max was a great dancer, with the reputation of St. Vitus. It was rumored he seduced all his partners in a strange way, which eventually earned him the title of 'the Tongue'. I was good enough for Rita during the slow numbers, but she chose Max for the fast lane. By the time the last dance came around and the house lights dimmed I could have taken home any girl in the place, except Rita.

Beginning what I felt was a promising career in High School, I should have known by its name that it was going to be a mess. The school was named after the most boring man in the history of education, Ben Blewett. His main contribution to the learning process was the introduction of music appreciation concerts into the classroom. We were subjected to a steady barrage of Walter Damrosch pho-nograph records and opera singers who doubled on the piano, playing arias from Madame Butterfly. It only in-creased my appreciation of the Lucky Strike Hit Parade. The building itself was a huge remnant of Victorian times, with teachers to match. The only thing that gave the place any real class was the principal, Miss Lily Ernst. A lapsed mother superior transvestite-type, she was impressive in a flowing, pleated skirt which travelled to the top of her high-button shoes. Her man's ruffled shirt, adorned with a string tie beneath a single-breasted man's navy blue jacket, simply couldn't hide her enormous tits. Miss Ernst wore her hair in a smart pompadour that complemented her steel rim glasses and pink cheeks. I loved her. Every time I was sent to her office for provocative behavior we would look into each other's eyes long enough to establish a real rapport. She gave me the nick-name Butch, which I thought at the time was very cheeky, but I liked it; it was certainly a step up from 'Bird Legs'.

I tried to brighten school up with creative cheer-leading, but soon gave up. Ben Blewett was last in sports, last in educational standards, and last in the hearts of its students. Nobody had a good word for the school. When the time came to leave and enter college, dear Miss Ernst saw to it that my records were falsified enough to gain entrance to the University of Missouri.

Did I mention that I had a black front tooth when I arrived on campus in January, 1938? Funny how teeth play such a large role in one's freshman year. Students with perfect teeth seldom make perfect students; they tend to become, instead, very popular on campus. I had to thank Lefty O'Doyle, who hit me when I was drinking a coke, for whatever little academic success I had that first year. I survived not being invited to join the Jewish fraternity. When I wasn't asked to the informal tea or the Independent Students' League, though, I wondered if I could handle the social consequences. Luckily I lived in a boarding house with seven other students whose teeth were worse than mine. There was no way I was going to be a big man on campus with my smile, so I drifted towards a course in boxing where a black front tooth was a definite asset.

My interest in literature was kindled by browsing through the shelves of my cousin Julius's second-hand book shop. I wasn't looking for any serious relationship with books, just a brief affair with a dust jacket. I fell in love with blurbs and quotes. It was much more informative than reading the book.

From the first day I walked into Mr. McMurray's Psychology One course, I knew I had a promising future as a heavyweight neurotic. I had been in training for the role since birth, having as a manager one of the best in the business—Cutie. I was familiar with Freud through the book review section of my sister's *Nation*, got to know about Adler in the Encyclopedia Britannica. I was fairly well read on the subject of psychology. Mr. McMurray brought it alive—too alive some students claimed. He had a way of looking at me during his discussion of a case history of a famous Jewish hysteric that gave me the shivers. I knew he liked me when he asked me to join him for a drink in his study after school. He knew a potential case history when he saw one. I told him I was hoping to become a successful bourgeois antique dealer disguised as a playboy. I gave him a *Readers Digest* version of my life and hard times as son of Cutie; he cautioned me that playboy was a dangerous occupation.

"Did you ever think of becoming a bourgeois playboy disguised as a successful antique dealer?" he asked. His advice gave me a lot to think about in later life. By the end of the term, I felt qualified to go straight into Psychoanalysis Two.

Social life, incidentally, was not the disaster I imagined it would be. I made contact with a sorority girl at a meeting of the campus chapter of the Anti-Defamation League of the B'nai Brith. She was short and overweight, but when she got up to confess how ashamed she was to be Jewish, in addition to being ugly, my heart went out to her. There was a lot of dating between Jew and Gentile on campus, but little between fraternity and independents. When we started going together, it meant something: she was putting her sorority pin on the line! We discovered the only thing we had in common was the fact that both our parents were in the antique business. Under close questioning she confessed that hers were more second-hand furniture dealers, "but the only ones in Marshall, Illinois". After that our discussions revolved around Roosevelt's chances for a third term, and seeing how successful we were in reaching climax through mutual aid. I was a perfect gentleman: when the affair was over, I gave her back her sorority pin.

My relationship with the seven other students in my residence revolved around who left the dirty socks in the hall and whose turn it was to make a pass at the house-mother, a dangerous widow. There was one desperate intellectual from a small fishing village in Maine who tried to get a discussion going on Conrad's *Heart of Darkness* but gave up in despair when another student insisted that Thomas Wolfe's *Look Homeward Angel* was a more significant work. There was the usual excitement about our football team and talk of Babe Nadowitz and Bob Christian making All-American that year, but since dropping my cheerleader role I wasn't really involved.

The only activity outside of the academic curriculum that interested me was R.O.T.C. I looked quite stunning in the military uniform. I wore it as often as I could, preferring it to the one suit that I was rapidly outgrowing. The leather puttees were not made with Bird Legs in mind; I had to stuff the extra space around my calf with old newspapers that rustled when I walked. I enjoyed the drilling and carrying of guns. There was talk of the war with the Third Reich. Military life was a totally new experience for me, brought up in a family that voted for Eugene Debs and Norman Thomas's peace platforms. When I wore the full military uniform home one weekend, Cutie thought I looked "too Gentile."

I managed to pass all the courses with flying colors with the help of several secreted ponies and liberal glances at fellow students' answers. It came as a shock to several of my teachers, who were surprised to see me show up for the tests since I hadn't attended any of the lectures. I won't say that my first term was a success, but I did manage to do well considering my short attention span. I looked forward to returning the following season.

The summer holiday would have been welcome if a crisis had not arisen in the family. The B. Landesman antique shop was at the center of the problem. It turned out that it was impossible for Cutie and Benjamin C. to be in business together. It was worrisome enough to discover that though they slept in the same bed, their heads were at opposite ends! And now there was talk of separate antique shops!

The idea of them separating was too traumatic for me to handle although their different approaches to the running of a successful antique shop made life a non-stop argument. Her idea was to make profits while his aim was to make friends, a source of great anxiety to her.

The problem was solved when he decided to open up a shop in Houston, a booming town where his sister, Molly, and her son, Paul, lived. It was looked upon as a business decision, nothing to do with their personal life. I spent that summer working with Cutie in the antique shop, trying my best to take my father's place. After a few weeks, I understood perfectly why he'd left. She was a difficult woman to please. If I wanted to go across the street for a Coke, she'd make a big deal out of it. "It'll only rust your stomach. You'll probably get run over, too." If I waited on a customer, she would hover over me and then butt in to make sure the sale was not lost. If I started to wrap up the object sold, she'd take it away and wrap it herself, claiming I was using too much paper. Should I show some initiative in buying something while she was out, which happened rarely, she invariably bawled me out for paying too much. When I sold it the price I got was too low. An apprenticeship under Cutie was a no-win situation, but I managed to distract her attention from any inadequacies in business and focus her attention on my personal ones. I would deliberately lose money around the store for her to find. Money had a magic effect on Cutie; it raised her spirits enormously when she found it. I discovered that summer the only way to survive with Cutie was to keep her employed worrying about her inadequate son.

It was quite a different freshman that returned to the University that fall. I dropped out of the boxing team, my last link with organized college activity. Football, fraternities and classes seemed to be a waste of valuable time. If there had been a branch of the Young Communist League on campus I would have preferred it to anything that was going on in college. The military uniform that I had been so proud to wear now seemed like a terrible joke. Popularity was no longer a goal. Controversy seemed much more rewarding.

The students I lived with came from families that had made great sacrifices to get the knowledge that would enable them to fit into a slot after graduation. They did not take kindly to my making fun of Monsanto Chemical and IBM recruiters on campus. As a result, the little annoyances of whose turn it was to do the dishes and clean up became major ones. I was accused of not doing my share. When they decided amongst themselves to teach me a lesson by refusing me my morning portion of prunes, my reaction was swift, dramatic and final. I got up from the breakfast table and in my best Chinese accent said, "No prunes, no washie, I'm leaving!" They thought it funny, but not serious. One of them came into my room afterwards to apologize for the misunderstanding. When I told him I was fed up with college, he laughed.

"I've heard of some droll excuses for leaving college, but to leave over a bowl of prunes is bizarre. I must congratulate you, Landesman." He invited me out to have a beer with him and talk it over. "Stick it out," he warned, "it's safe here in college. There's a war coming up and I reckon this is the best place to be."

I told him I'd prefer war. "You know, the irony of it all is that I really hate prunes. I just eat them out of a deep respect for my mother's concern with my bowels."

It was no surprise to Cutie that I didn't stick it out. All

the years she spent going to the principal's offices to get me out of trouble with teachers prepared her for some-thing like this. I was surprised how sympathetic she was to the prune fiasco. In her books, avoiding constipation was as important as anything I could learn in college, and since I wasn't going to amount to much I might as well be healthy and dumb.

When my father heard that I had quit, he invited me to come and live with him in Houston. It occurred to me, as I wrote to tell him I was accepting his invitation, that I hardly knew him. I grew up under the impression that Cutie was both my parents; my father was more like a lodger who contributed a handsome sum for the upkeep of the house. I knew he was there, but his presence was taken for granted.

He was a handsome figure, sitting in his comfortable chair, reading his newspaper, smoking his Muriel cigar, occasionally getting up to change the record of his favorite opera, *Die Fledermaus*. His soft German accent was a source of constant embarrassment to me in front of my friends, but he was always charming with them. I don't remember him ever raising his voice to anyone, even Cutie who gave him every reason to do so. Like me, he had learned to keep Cutie busy worrying about his minor inadequacies, like over-tipping waitresses when we went out to Sunday din-ners at the Hotel Colorado. At Christmas time he was the Santa Claus that brought us antique toys which made us cry because they weren't new. He was the man who got dressed up to take Cutie to the Ethical Society lectures every week. He was the man who enjoyed his comforts and went to Friday night services at Temple Israel to thank God that he had found such a good life in America. Everybody who did business with him liked his polite way of asking about their well being first, details later. When he played pinochle with his friends, he never addressed them by their Christian names. He had no hobbies. He considered his work his pleasure, not a duty. His main concern was to keep up his life insurance payments and his car in good working order. Moderation in all things was his motto. He never drank anything stronger than an occasional beer. He was never envious of other people. The world suited Benjamin Landesman.

Houston, Texas, in 1939 was small, clean and hospitable to new enterprises like B. Landesman's antique shop. This was on Main Street in an almost-new hacienda type building that was all out of character with his European stock of treasures. Under the beautiful old-gold lettering on the front window was the classy touch: St. Louis and Houston. I was astonished at how romantic his shop was. It was a theatre setting depicting a series of tableaux that represented his idea of the way life should be lived with chaise longues, winged chairs, richly-inlaid library tables, ottomans, and paintings that told a story. The Italian cupid candlesticks converted into lamps cast a warm glow throughout the store and made any customer feel a little more extravagant, browsing among such exotic furnishings. B. Landesman's in St Louis was never like that.

There were more surprises. The store had a balcony where he recreated his early days as an artist in Berlin. Large Japanese vases filled with dried flowers and a mahogany artist's easel dominated the space. On a Tudor oak library table there were vases of old paint brushes and a dusty pallet that hadn't seen any fresh paint for fifty years. There was no sign that he had any desire to paint again; they were the artifacts he felt comfortable with. He looked as handsome as ever, even though his once bright red hair was turning slightly grey at the temples. He made no concessions to Texas-style dressing, preferring his woolen slacks and heavy worsted blazer to the lightweight man-made fibres of a seersucker suit. He had a couch draped with beautiful old materials where he took his daily naps, and a stove to make a cup of coffee on. He could have lived in that charming room, and so could I, for the rest of our lives.

Good old Benjamin, flowering in exile, creating for himself a little corner of the old world he felt at home with. He had spent the best part of his life decorating other people's rooms, and now he did one for himself. I was proud of him for putting on such a great show. I watched him handle his customers with exquisite charm and old world manners. He greeted a browser like an old friend, inquiring after the health and welfare of the whole family. It was a genuine concern and if it so happened the browser was going to New Orleans for the Mardi Gras, my father would volunteer to go along with him so he wouldn't feel lonely. A great believer in the sanctity of the home, he convinced the browser that beautiful things around the house were the foundations of a happy family life. I learned a great deal watching him make the antique business a way of life, and felt sorry for Cutie who took it all so seriously.

There was a spirit in Houston that I found in no other city. Part eagerness to show off, part greed, everything had a sense of a new adventure. New businesses with names like El Rancho Auditing blossomed overnight and nothing seemed to fail. Failure was the one word I never heard throughout my entire stay in Houston. Even my cousin Paul, who despite leaving a brilliant academic career to work for an oil-prospecting company as a physicist, never thought of himself as compromised. Houston was changing him from a brooding intellectual into a friendly cousin who had a lot to teach me. I was hungry for some intellectual overspill so we exchanged some tips on life. He introduced me to Beethoven and I caught him listening to my Benny Goodman records.

He subscribed to *Fortune* magazine, the mouthpiece of success, and I read it occasionally to find out what it was all about. In one of the issues I read an article on the state of Cafe Society in America. The article fascinated me, particularly a picture of an elegant couple in a nightclub with the caption: THEY WANT TO BE AMUSED. The woman was beautiful, but bored. I thought at the time that if I didn't go into the antique business I'd like to go into the business of amusing the bored, especially if they all looked like the woman in the photograph. If only I lived in New

York and dined at the El Morroco every night, I was sure I could talk her into being my first client. Her name meant nothing to me then, but I shared Mrs. William Rhinelander Stewart's fear of boredom. I cut the picture out to pin up in my room to remind me of my mission in life.

Houston was a town where you had to make up your own entertainment. One of my first attempts was to enroll in a course on the 18th Century Novella at Rice Institute, a college renowned for its beautiful campus. Since my interests were mainly literary, it sounded right. As it turned out, the course was extremely academic, requiring a wider background in literature than I had. Rapidly losing ground, I dropped out of class and began to seek other opportunities for amusement, this time in politics. Through Paul, I met the handful of radicals centered around the National Maritime Union's legal representative in Houston. He and his wife were an attractive couple who livened up union business with great social parties, but always in aid of the oppressed. After the collection for Harry Bridge's defense fund, after the folk singers, after the subscription drive for the *New Masses* magazine and the third bourbon and soda, the strange assortment of young women with horn-rim glasses didn't look too bad. It was very appealing to a young man from out of town looking to get laid.

Back in St. Louis my sense of humour had been unappreciated under the best of conditions, but in Houston it was totally misunderstood. My always making light of the serious didn't endear me to many of my new acquaintances, yet I did manage to impress one Googie Finkelstein, a delightfully uncomplicated girl with a stunning case of acne. Riding top down in a Ford V-8, her long, blonde hair blowing in the wind, my hand resting firmly between her thighs, on an open stretch of highway that led to a small road house where whiskey was served in coffee cups and the band played *The Yellow Rose of Texas,* it seemed like the right time to ask her what she wanted most in life.

18

"Well, sugar, I like you, but you're too technical," was her philosophical put-down.

I knew my time in Houston was drawing to a close. I had gotten to know my father better, and we had grown closer than I ever dreamed we could. He taught me a lot about the antique business, but what I carried away with me was his great sense of style. I realized that he no longer looked upon me as just a part of his inventory. I was a son who had found a lost father. When I hitched a ride to St. Louis in a van with a Jewish travelling antique salesman, Willie Teiber, I pulled my father's line:

"Wait! I'll go with you to keep you company."

2

After finding a father, my return to St. Louis was like losing a mother. Compared to the world of Benjamin C. that I had grown so fond of, she seemed to live in an alien world of crass commercialism. She controlled every aspect of the business, performing with a shrewdness that had sharpened considerably since I last worked with her. I took my revenge by telling her how successful the Houston operation was.

"He's got a real antique shop, not like the junk shop you have." She listened to my glowing descriptions of how her husband had blossomed out on his own, how close we'd become, and how I respected his way of doing business. To accept praise of others graciously was not one of Cutie's characteristics; I suspected she hadn't listened to a word I was saying.

"I do believe he's enjoying himself." I wanted it to sting.

"I'm glad to hear he's attending to business at last," was her only comment. The idea of anybody having any pleasure from business was beyond her comprehension.

My brother Gene had been the only one around for her to control in my absence. He successfully eluded all her attempts to draw him into the business. Instead, he set up a successful china and glass repair operation in the store. He invented a new way of fusing glass under extreme heat that made the crack invisible. People came into the shop from all over the country with their broken objects and Cutie would try to sell them something else. He had a workshop in the basement employing three very skilled, young, black ladies, and he seldom left his underground world. He became known as 'the Landesman Cutie never let out of the basement.' He was living in the back of it on a platform of old doors hung from the ceiling with chains. It was a Robinson Crusoe kind of existence, cooking his food on a Bunsen burner, and doing little entertaining. It was difficult to find a girl with the agility to climb the rope ladder to his floating island. Gene had problems with Cutie and for good reason. She was charging him rent for the air space. In retaliation, he charged her for every job he did for the shop, from changing light bulbs to fetching her a glass of water for her medicine. He kept track of these figures in a little black book that never left his person.

Fred was in California growing tomatoes in a hot house with chemicals instead of soil. It was an experimental project that had limited appeal to a person with artistic temperament, but he too had to get away from Cutie at any cost. Gertrude was living in New York, working as a psychiatric social worker. She had managed to escape Cutie early in life, but not unscarred. Cutie was paying for her analysis, as well she should. If it helped Gertrude to get married, there was no price too high for Cutie to pay. There was nothing worse in Cutie's book than to be an old maid. Any energy Cutie had left over from the business was devoted to overseeing Gert's virginity, while preparing her at the same time to make a good catch on the marriage market. As a result, the three of us had relative freedom from her advice on all social and career activity. Cutie was always proud of herself for not interfering in our lives, allowing us to bring girls home, throw parties, ignore school homework, as long as we did nothing that would land us in jail. On her deathbed, I asked her if she was disappointed in the way life had turned out for her. "I stayed out of jail, didn't I," she said grimly.

In spite of the closeness of family life, none of us children had anything in common with each other. Gertrude was intent upon a career. Fred, even at an early age, did everything possible to avoid committing himself to anything so mundane. He knew he was destined to become an artist, and that wasn't work. His teachers compared him to the Young Holbein, but the actual painting of pictures was not considered by him to be a necessary step in becoming an artist. Instead, he spent all his time in formulating an elaborate theory of æsthetics that proved that the actual painting was superfluous. He led a solitary existence, wasting no time on useless friendships, preferring to stay in his room, working out his theories, and keeping them to himself.

Gene was the inventor in the family, an early Do-It-Yourself mechanical genius. One of his first attempts at bypassing the use of gasoline as a fuel for the combustion engine was a brilliant success. We drove to Chicago's Century of Progress exhibition on a tankful of kerosene. Like Fred, he avoided useless friendships, preferring machines to relationships. We called him Mr. Fixit, but he always charged us for any little jobs he did for the family and put it down in his little black book.

Having no talent for anything that might be called useful, I was the one who specialised in making friends. Our house was always filled with my pals, providing an early training ground for crowd control tactics and my future as a brilliant party-giver. One of the reasons we got on so well as brothers was the fact that none of us were interested in what the others were doing. It eliminated the competition that ruins many a family.

By 1940, the threat of war and the registration for the draft prevented me from taking anything too seriously. Cutie wanted me to join her in the business, but I decided that it would be more practical to have my own antique shop. I found an empty store on Bed Bug Row, the name of a section of bizarre, run down shops that was an eyesore to the more respectable elements in the neighborhood. It was my favorite section of town, the source of many colorful stories. Above the shops there used to be brothels regularly visited by Babe Ruth and Tony Lazzari when they were in town. The whores were gone, but there remained a sense of camaraderie among the few artists, ex-pimps, interior decorators and antique dealers that inhabited the area. The antique dealers were a special breed of eccentric men and women, fiercely independent, congenially lazy, hustling in a relaxed atmosphere that suited me perfectly.

My shop was on the side of the street with a wide sidewalk that enabled me to display my stock al fresco. It was hardly worth bringing in at the close of the day, and frequently I didn't bother. Cutie had given me all her junk and what she considered unsaleable items to start me off, enough to fill a small size warehouse. Everything I sold was clear profit. I called the shop JAY IRVING'S, having added the name Jay after reading Fitzgerald's *The Great Gatsby*. It was the perfect name for a night club, and that's the way I ran the business. I always had a drink ready for any patron or friend who happened to drop by because they had no other place to go in the middle of the day. I conducted most of my business from a reclining position on a decrepit chaise longue on the sidewalk, providing a visual treat for the passing motorist and passengers on the University street car line. It was a happy time, lying in the sun with a cold drink in hand, reading *Remembrance of Things Past* to the music of the juke box of the sleazy tavern next door.

Inside the store, I created a studio atmosphere, a private workshop where I could entertain my growing circle of friends. I had the reputation of attracting interesting people; word got around that Jay Irving's was the place to go for some good jazz, a good martini, and some lively conversation. As the tempo for entertaining increased, my stock dwindled and the studio space became larger. The store became the center of my life. I gradually moved my books and some personal belongings there, until it looked like a respectable pied-a-terre. The only stock I had left by the end of the year was a double student lamp that I put in the window with a sign: NOT FOR SALE. Jay Irving's was unsuccessfully out of business by the time Uncle Sam was setting up for war.

The experience of combining business with pleasure proved so compatible with my temperament that I was totally committed to it as a way of life. Naturally, I withheld this information from Cutie, who was insisting I rejoin her in the growing business, promising a partnership if things went well. I capitulated, expecting my draft call-up any day.

If I couldn't handle the simple authority problems of school, how was I to accept the regimentation of army life? There was a part of me that wanted to get drafted, if only to get away from Cutie. I went into the induction center convinced that I was going to be accepted. Cutie, as always, didn't think much of my chances. My father, deep in the heart of Texas, bought a flag with one star to hang in the window of his shop, proud that he was about to have a son in service.

What would the Army do with a one-hundred-and-twelve-pound, six-foot weakling with a certifiable Oedipus complex? I was immediately classified 4-F, unfit for military duty. In quick succession, Gene and Fred were called for physicals. Gene actually looked forward to army life, where he thought his knowledge of machines would be invaluable. His scars and disfigured hands, especially his stiff trigger-finger, would never be accepted, but he was convinced that if he had mastered the violin with those hands, he could do anything. I wrote to my father not to count on putting out any flags. Knowing how Fred hated crowds, I added a P.S.: "Gert is the Landesmans' best bet for the army". Cutie was delighted she had raised her sons to be unfit; didn't she always claim we were an unhealthy lot? The rejection of all of us nearly broke my father's heart. He never got a chance to hang out the flag.

After Pearl Harbor, I had an attack of delayed patriotism. I left Cutie to take a job in a defense plant as an electrical expediter. My job was to dissect faulty cable sockets with a knife sharper than any surgeon's blade; it was an autopsy requiring a great deal of skill if I was to avoid cutting off my fingers. Life in the factory was not like the news reel's version of smiling Rosie the Riveter. It was incredibly boring and the pay was fifty cents an hour, less than I got at the Hussman Stamp Co. for sweeping the floor. When word got around that I had once been to college, the work mysteriously piled up and I could hardly take a toilet break if I wanted to keep up with those hundreds of unskilled workers who had never been in college.

When a union organizer handed out leaflets at the gate, I was immediately sympathetic. About time, I thought, to do something about the exploitation of the masses. He was thrilled at the chance to talk to anyone. It didn't surprise me that his efforts to unionize the place hadn't been well received. He was the most unlikely-looking union organiser I'd ever seen. He had the build of a model for a starving Armenian poster. Ordinarily that would be acceptable for a victim of the class war, but everything else about him was wrong. He had a rich growth of moustache that you could hide a bomb under and a smile that displayed a number of missing teeth that suggested the bomb might have exploded. His hound's tooth sport's jacket and the paisley silk scarf around his neck gave him the look of a proletarian Noel Coward. The high-heeled, pointed shoes didn't match his working class image. There were bags under his eyes that held a ten-year supply of tears. I took an immediate liking to him, accepting his invitation to join him for a strategy discussion over a drink. I was really curious to find out how this dude chose to be a protector of the working class.

He turned out to be a former New York news photographer. This job was his first union assignment. Like me, he had a delayed attack of social consciousness and patriotism. Union organizers were scarce, so they turned a blind eye to his peculiar appearance. Over dinner he told me his life story, impressing me with his range of failed careers. Would I help him? If there was one thing I liked, it was a challenge. He proceeded to outline his plan to get the workers interested: he would hold a mass meeting at the local roller-skating rink thus combining business with working class pleasure. I had doubts when he confessed he didn't know how to skate, but I shared his basic philosophy.

"You could fall down a lot and get their sympathy," I said, slapping him on the back. It was a nice touch, he agreed.

I didn't enhance my image among my fellow workers by handing out leaflets announcing the forthcoming event. From the response we got, I suggested that maybe an intimate, back-yard barbecue would be more appropriate. It was too late. He had rented the largest roller-skating rink in Missouri. Needless to say, no one showed up at the party. The sight of us roller-skating arm-in-arm—I had to support him all the way—was too sad even for me to appreciate. The result of my effort was to be marked as a trouble maker by the foreman, and I was taken off the socket work and put on the labor force, stacking heavy cables in the warehouse.

I decided that the war effort would best be served by my joining Cutie in the antique business to raise the morale on the decorative home front. It was time to take Cutie's business seriously and out of her control. Since there was nothing any of us ever did that satisfied her, we decided to satisfy ourselves. Under Fred's skillful guidance, we offered Cutie a contract that made Gene, Fred and I equal partners in exchange for a promissory note for her equity in the business and a life-time job, without pay, of course. We gave her car fare to and from work and small expenses, but we had to be careful not to give her the impression we were squeezing her out of her own shop.

Like the good sons we'd been raised by her to be, we explained that times had changed. Her nickel and dime philosophy in business was through. We saw a boom ahead for antiques.

Under Fred's artistic supervision, Gene's construction

skills, and my knowledge of genuine antiques, the shop was transformed into a show place. Poor Cutie wandered around its exquisitely decorated rooms, lost and confused.

She retaliated by pouring out her scorn with ironic comments on our up-market methods. Her favorite stock was relegated to a small area in the rear of the galleries, but little did anyone suspect that her collection of 19th century utilitarian cut-glass that we had such disdain for would be the basis of Landesman Galleries' greatest success.

During the war, lighting fixtures were no longer manufactured. Crystal chandeliers, one of our specialities, could not be found. The demand was enormous and Fred rose to the occasion with an ingenious piece of ad hoc designing. Since glass was the main ingredient of a chandelier, he used Cutie's collection of cut-glass carafes, water tumblers, flower vases, dessert dishes, hair receivers, finger bowls, and lamp bases, inverting them to disguise their original purpose. The Landesman chandelier was a masterpiece of ingenuity in a war-torn world.

To keep up the quality of our stock, I began taking buying-trips to New York to pick up collector's pieces of porcelain that were becoming so popular. I would walk into New York's finest shops and ask them what they had in the basement that was flawed. The sight of Meissen figurines with fingers chopped off, epergnes with centerpieces missing, exquisite vases with scars, chipped Dr. Wall Worcester tea-caddies, rare Jacob Petit clocks with their porcelain bases cut out from under them set my heart beating faster than if they had been perfect. Little did they know or care, in their eagerness to get rid of them, that I had a brother who could bring them back to life.

On those trips I stayed with Gert in her Greenwich Village apartment, getting my first taste of Village life. Visiting all the historic places with Gert during the day left me free at night to discover a whole new world where people enjoyed themselves in dark cellars listening to jazz, or having a drink at a bar next to real Bohemians quoting Baudelaire. The small shops specialising in hand-designed products of the artist-owner were like miniature Aladdin's caves, filled with surprises. Just walking the streets of Greenwich Village was a treat.

I felt more at home in the Village than I did in St. Louis, where everything looked so grey. I began to collect flawed people just to liven things up. The war was draining off all the normal ones, leaving me with a rich collection of eccentrics to play with. My best friend at that time was Bob Lazarus, who had been left an old-fashioned tailoring business in the black ghetto. Bob was rapidly turning it into an empire by creating custom-made zoot suits that the new fashion-conscious blacks demanded. His family warned him against exchanging their good reputation for fine conservative tailoring for a passing fad. He ignored his mother's advice like I ignored Cutie's, and we were both doing well as a result.

Discovering that being rebellious paid off, we began to flaunt our flair for outrage. What might have seemed eccentric during peace time was outrageous during a war. With everybody being so serious, we took delight in giving the solemn society something to talk about. One of our rituals was to meet at the most fashionable barber shop in midday and liven it up. From adjoining chairs we would vie with each other to see who could make the most demands. I would order a drink; he would send the shoeshine boy out for a bottle of champagne. While he had his facial, I had a massage that went so deep, the blackheads came out of hiding just to escape the heat. We each had our favorite manicurist and made bets on the side which one we would get into bed first. In between the blow-drying of the hair and the shave, we would order smoked salmon and caviar canapes from the gourmet restaurant. Cigars would follow. After the barbers were exhausted with their labors, we would send out for the racing form and make plans to attend the races that afternoon. The barbers and assorted personnel would queue up for the tipping ceremony, always a crowd-pleasing event. Of

that lasted more than two minutes, and that was usually about how difficult Cutie was. When we began to work together in the Galleries, everything changed between us. I became his number one fan. I admired his style and the way he used to walk into the Galleries as if it was his club, say hello to Cutie, check out a few things, and then split to his study to work on his real projects.

One of the many benefits of his marriage was my inheriting a collection of Paula's girl friends from Wisconsin U, who finished off my education. Let's see: I got a degree in Reichian Theory from Geraldine, who introduced me, in the nicest ways, to the glorification of the orgasm as the solution to all social and bodily ailments. With Dorothy, I took a post-graduate course in the development of the Democratic Neurosis, a theory that required my forgetting everything I learned from Geraldine.

Fred's marriage started a chain reaction in the Landesman family. Gene found Eleanor, a girl who managed to climb the rope ladder to his lair with such agility he proposed on the spot. Gert's analysis was drawing to a close, leaving her vulnerable to the proposal of a promising young lawyer. All Cutie had left to control was me and the little man who did the Galleries furniture refinishing. She made his life miserable with her demands. "If you don't keep that woman out of my workshop," he'd cry to me, "I'll quit. She upsets my hernia, and if that goes, you don't get anything out of me."

The only pleasures left for Cutie were criticizing me and Benjamin C., on his visits to St. Louis. He was considerably cheered up when Cutie confessed she missed him, but it was short-lived—she accused him of leaving her to the mercies of his ungrateful children who never listened to her anymore. He would cheer her up by being a good customer, buying from her without bargaining, while she scolded him for being such an easy mark. It still seemed that neither he nor I could do anything right.

The Landesman Galleries were too high class for her now. "You think you all are so smart," she'd say to us, "but let me tell you, when the war is over you'll lose your business and then you'll be thankful for my regular nickel and dime customers."

It was obvious that Benjamin C. missed his family. His affection for the new wives was touching, publicly hugging and kissing them more, I thought, than he ever did with us. And the Galleries were a source of great pride to him. He congratulated Fred and me for giving such prestige to the Landesman name.

"There's always a place for you here if you ever decide to come back," Fred told him. I could see father and Cutie as prisoners at the back of the Galleries, wondering what they'd done to their children to be treated so shabbily.

With Gene and Fred having such a good time, I was stuck with Cutie. I managed to defend myself by being busy; my main obsession was collecting jazz records and discovering places where jazz was still being played. Many of the old musicians who'd come up the 'riber' from New Orleans were still to be found playing in black dives and sleazy white bars. Once in a while I'd come across a fine piano player doing a solo stint in a local brothel. Have you ever tried going into a whore house with four other guys and telling the Madame, "we've just come for the music"?

I discovered John Arnold, an obscure musician who turned out to be a contemporary of Jelly Roll Morton, playing at my local cat house. I took him into a recording studio to lay down his version of a classic, *The Pearls,* and talk about the old days of St. Louis jazz. Bunk Johnson had recently been discovered in a rice paddy in Louisiana and recorded by the Library of Congress. Why not John Arnold? I formed the St. Louis Jazz Society for the preservation and promotion of the music and its performers with plans to issue bulletins and records.

When Billie Holliday came to St. Louis for a stint at the Mafia-controlled Plantation Club, I planned to interview her for the Club's newsletter. It proved to be a harrowing experience. Watching her perform on opening night, I was disappointed at her performance. Whether it was the drink, drugs, lack of rehearsal or just that she was out-of-place in such a big, commercial venue, she was erratic and lack-lustre. She finished her set to indifferent applause. The band had drowned out her subtle phrasing, causing her to strain her voice beyond recognition.

It was a distraught Lady Day I found pacing her dressing-room like a caged tiger when I went for an interview between sets. It was going to be hard to tell her how wonderful she was. After explaining my reason for being there, she said:

"Not now, honey, I've got to get out of here. Take me someplace where I can get a drink, you know what I mean?"

I knew a black club, actually the Baker Hotel, nearby, that would be perfect. On the way out, the manager of the club pulled me aside.

"Where are you goin' with the nigger?"

I told him I was from the local paper doing a story.

"O.K. Bring her back in half-an-hour, get it?" he said letting go of my suit front. Once in the car, she told me that they had made her use the back entrance, which really pissed her off.

"Where can I get something to smoke?" I offered her one of my Chesterfields but it wasn't what she had in mind. Walking into the lobby of the Baker Hotel with the star on my arm didn't bring any smiles from the flash cats hanging out there. A quick drink at the bar, surrounded by a host of new friends led to a journey upstairs to a private room. Their attempts to elbow me out of the scene didn't work. I had to bring her back on time.

Billie flopped on the bed, twisting and moaning in a tuneful agony. "Anybody got a joint?" she asked. Once they broke out the pot and brandy, Billie calmed down. I left the room for a minute just in case Billie wanted to be alone with this entourage. When I came back she was in even better shape. Against the protests of all the people around her, I hustled her out of the place with a determination that even surprised me. On the ride back, I tried to get my interview.

"Who were your early influences, Billie?" She looked at me as if I was some kind of nut. "What was the name of that bar we were just in? That's the kind of influence I like." She showed little interest in continuing the interview. "Are you planning to write any more songs?" I tried to sound intelligent and grown-up.

"Honey, just let me off at the front entrance. I'm going to show them mean fuckers a lesson." I jumped out of the car to open her door, but she had sprung out and was already running up the steps without even saying good-bye. When I tried to follow her in, the manager pulled me up short.

"That's it, kid, scram." I saw Billie walk past him as if he never existed.

I played a lot of Billie that week, basking in the knowledge that I had actually been in on an historic occasion, probably the most important event of my life. I certainly got a lot of attention when I repeated the story to my circle of jazz friends. I tried hard not to dramatise it out of recognition.

The Baldwin Piano Company's record department wasn't the place to find any good jazz, but one of my friends from the club suggested I go down there to have a look at the girl behind the counter.

"She's worth knowing and likes jazz," I was told. Her name was Carmen.

"Do you have any Billie Holliday?" I asked.

"I wish I did have," she answered smartly. "This is Andre Kostelanetz territory. Try Doubleday's record department, they're a little more jazzy." She turned to wait on other customers while I toyed with an RCA sheet of recent releases, sneaking a look at the girl who treated me so indifferently. She was quite good-looking, the kind of shiksa that a nice Jewish boy would bring home to mother if he wanted to give her a heart attack. I was interested; she moved like a good dancer. She was built like one too: small breasts, long legs, graceful neck, and a good gentile nose. Her smile wasn't as generous as it should have been; I discovered the reason why when I asked her for a date. She had a gum line that made her self-conscious when she showed teeth.

After a couple of evenings together, she began to look more Jewish to me. We discovered we liked doing everything together more than we liked doing it alone. She was fun to take along on explorations, contributing knowledge of music that impressed the executive board of the St. Louis Jazz Society. In appreciation of her talent in that department, I made her the official Sweetheart of the club, pinning a wooden cut-out of a trumpet on her blouse as an engagement present.

She introduced me to her mother and step-father, uncomplicated people, satisfied with their role in life. Her mother was a cashier at the YMCA and he was a clerk in a wholesale fruit and vegetable company. They were particularly pleased about her going with me. They were the kind of people I didn't have to impress; anything I did or said was perfectly acceptable. After Paula's problem-ridden girlfriends, Pat, as Carmen preferred to be called, was a refreshing tonic, a pure all-American model. Pat didn't know a Freud from a fraud, but she danced like Pan, following my most eccentric choreography without missing a step.

There were other things I liked about her: those long goodnight kisses and smooth caresses in the car outside her house. She knew how to move her body around a gearshift in a way that made retreating to the back seat of the car unnecessary. When I brought her around to meet Cutie at a family dinner, she got mixed reviews. Paula said I could do better, but I put that down to prejudice: she had her girl friend's interest at heart. Fred seldom criticized anything I did, preferring to withhold judgement on anything as sensitive as a boy-girl relationship. I wanted Fred's approval more than Cutie's. When I pressed him for an opinion, he said she was "interesting." Gene and Ellie liked her way of being at ease with the family, an important trait.

Pat complimented Cutie on her matzo ball soup and boiled brisket. She was familiar with the scene from all the books and movies of warm-hearted Jewish family life. She scored heavily when she gushed over Cutie's antique Singer sewing machine, mentioning in the same breath that she made her own clothes. I suppose I got serious when she told me *Casablanca* was her favorite movie.

NEUROTICA

I proposed the day the bomb dropped on Hiroshima.
The idea of getting married was considerably less dramatic. Like they were saying about the bomb: 'something
good may come out of it.' If there was ever a time in
history when a light touch was necessary, it was then. Our
honeymoon in New Orleans provided the combination of
comedy and pathos that was later to characterise the marriage. Her real father, who had deserted her when she was
a baby, was living in a trailer camp with his young wife, a
few years older than Pat. He was working in a strip joint on
Bourbon Street as a singing master of ceremonies. He was
perfect for the part; tall, greasy, with a pencil thin
moustache that dated him as early Ramon Navarro. I liked
him at first sight. His reminiscences of his days as a promising tenor with a travelling musical stock company, when
he'd lived with Pat's mother in a little house with a garden
and dog, was music to my ears. I admired people who had
fallen from grace and were still willing to talk about it.

"It's only temporary, honey," he told Pat. "I'll be going to
Las Vegas next winter where they recognise real class."

He announced the strippers at the club with florid introductions, tinged with a slight malice to please the rowdy
customers. "And now, Ladies and Gentlemen, Club Royal
takes great pleasure in presenting the international star,
Trixie La Toure, direct from Cairo—Cairo, Illinois, that
is." I could see he was uneasy during blue joke time, a bit
embarrassed because we were sitting at a table in the back

of the club. Pat was cringing with embarrassment while I loved every moment.

"He's a real professional. I dig him," I told her. When he started singing in a very pleasing tenor, I took Pat's hand and said, "The guy can really sell a song," but I was not prepared for his next move.

"Ladies and Gentlemen, tonight there's a little girl in the audience that I knew many years ago. She's here on her honeymoon with her fine husband. I want to dedicate the next song to her and hope she'll always remain"—he actually touched his breast pocket—"my little girl." He broke into *Because* as Pat slumped in her seat.

"That was touching," I told him when he came around to join us. Pat gave him a little kiss on the cheek. He took out his handkerchief and blew his nose to avoid his tears.

"I hope I didn't make you feel uncomfortable, honey. You're such a lovely woman."

It gave me the feeling that even if I hadn't chosen the right girl for a wife, I had at least chosen the right father-in-law.

We spent the rest of our honeymoon looking for the legendary jazzmen who were supposed to be still around. We were told that they were all playing in a club in nearby Algiers, but when we got there we were told they had just left for Chicago. I never did catch any live jazz in New Orleans that meant anything. By the time the honeymoon was over, I had fallen out of love with mouldy fig music. I decided it was time to start a new life based on the future rather than the past.

We had decided to set up housekeeping in Fred's warehouse, a few doors down from the Galleries. His wedding present to us was the choice of anything we wanted to use. We were like a couple of kids in a candy store, choosing all the fruity pieces that nobody would ever want to buy. No one in their right mind would ever have picked the Cardinal Richelieu bed to start out a married life upon. It was a monstrous piece of medieval fantasy, with dwarfs holding up the canopy and a mattress that could sleep six

Cardinals, if they happened to be very much in love. Every act of love-making could have been our last. Unsafe as it was, I insisted that all marriages needed an element of danger.

Once we were settled, our open house hospitality attracted the best collection of rejects St. Louis literary, artistic and musical life had to offer. The only price of admission was a healthy maladjustment to society; an interesting neurosis was an added bonus. 'Square' was the dreaded word. To be 'serious' was to leave yourself open to attack without chance of survival.

When someone brought ex-paratrooper-turned-artist, Stanley Radulovich around for the first time, he was wearing his veteran's discharge button in his lapel. Richard Rubinstein, who had spent the war in the front line of many a literary battle, was offended by such a cheap, patriotic gesture. "Take that corny medal off, soldier. You'll never get laid with that on." Everybody laughed except Radulovich, who was about to deck Rubenstein when he realised how out of place his gesture would have been in such a congenial surrounding. To Radulovich's credit, he took the button and flushed it down the toilet to tumultuous applause.

"Welcome to the club of the New, Forgotten Men." Rubenstein put one arm around him and poured him a drink with the other.

Rubenstein was a full-time neurotic and part-time poet from a rich family that had never heard of Rimbaud. He could quote him in French by the yard and did so for the benefit of many a bartender or waitress. He vetted any new number of our growing circle of malcontents by checking out their knowledge of French symbolist poets. He was seldom without a drink or a seconal, claiming that both were the elixir of life.

In all the talk about Art versus Life, there were still practical things someone had to do. Keeping the place fairly clean of the previous night's debris was a full-time job and Pat was elected. Preparing food and seeing that there was drink for a small army of freeloaders, meeting trains, taking messages, soothing wounded feelings, and the administration of raw eggs and Worcestershire sauce to hungover guests were endless tasks. Pat sometimes grew weary of the role. She once complained that she felt she was in a troop of strolling actors who never gave her a chance to play anything but the maid. While I was busy cultivating my own fan club with effortless hospitality and deft ego massaging, her growth was stunted by a natural inclination to be helpful.

Getting pregnant was her way of solving the problem. Initially, I thought it was a terrible solution, but when I saw how happy she was preparing for her new role, I conceded she might have a point. Why not? Fred and Gene had already started a family. Motherhood was fashionable. The family was in. Fred was creating his own base of operation. He had bought a Victorian mansion on Westminster Place, behind the Galleries, that was big enough for any baby boom. It had belonged to a millionaire steel magnate who had spared no expense in creating an environment befitting the social aspirations of a nouveau riche Victorian. The style of the house had been labelled 'Bad Taste' long before Fred and Paula bought it. It was a perfect example of the Richardson Romanesque style, with a tower, ballroom, organ, rathskellar and a three-car garage. All that was missing was a dungeon.

Gene and Ellie moved in with Fred and Paula, maintaining separate cooking facilities but sharing everything else. My cousin Paul, whom I lived with in Houston, now married, brought his family which included a retarded child and a precocious one, to join our growing family and growing chandelier business. The house was big enough for another two couples, but Fred enjoyed keeping it in the family, hoping someday I'd join them.

Benjamin C., on one of his visits, realizing what he was missing, decided to retire from the antique business and return to Cutie and the bosom of the growing family. We all agreed with his decision except Cutie, who practically forbade him to set foot in the Galleries during business hours.

He had a regular routine: first, a cup of coffee at Fred's, look in on the children, then up the next flight of stairs for another cup with Ellie, then a quick visit to Paul and Betty whose retarded child was a favorite of his. He was a family-proud man in his retirement, doting on the grand-children. His generous praise of us now that we were successful was genuine, but when he gave too much credit to the wives, we had to remind him we were successes 'in spite of them'. After his family visits, he started on the rounds of the Street, dropping in to say hello and ex-change gossip with Arman, the shoe rebuilder, Weber, the florist, Mr. Goldwasser, the druggist, and on the way home he would have still another cup of coffee at the Rex cafe.

The fruits of his retirement ended in a massive stroke. Cutie called me up, crying. I rushed over in time to see him being carried down on a stretcher, face contorted, his arms paralyzed and his false teeth missing. He was trying to talk, but Cutie and I never deciphered the message. She stayed by his side in the ambulance, holding his hand, wiping the drool from his sunken, purple lips. She couldn't resist scolding him for drinking too much coffee.

Cutie remained loyal to him at the hospital. Establishing her command post, she worried doctors, nurses, interns, and supervisors constantly, by checking on every move they made to save him. The end came in a few days. All of us were at the bedside. He never regained his speech but recognized us all, saying "goodbye" with his eyes. Cutie tried to tell him that Gertrude was going to have a baby, but it was too late.

It was touching to see Cutie break down and cry. Al-though she missed him when he moved to Houston, she always knew he'd be coming back. This time he wouldn't.

For Pat, it was a happy time. She flourished. For the first time we spent evenings together, alone, planning what to do when the baby came. We talked of moving in with Fred, but decided to get our own home. It was not to be. After seven months, she miscarried. We were alone, listening to some new Billie Holliday records when she mentioned she felt wet. I panicked more than she did. I called the doctor. While we were waiting for the ambulance, Rubenstein and Radulovich were calling me frantically from the sidewalk to tell me that they had found a place to open a bar, a project we had often discussed.

"Hey, fellows, I've got a little problem of my own here. Pat is having a miscarriage." It didn't stop them from pleading with me to let them in for just a minute. The bar was something I always said I'd go along with, but couldn't that wait?

Pat's miscarriage was so unexpected. She was considered such a healthy girl. Now she felt that she had let me down. Cutie was disappointed, and Paula and Ellie were sad that she wouldn't be joining them on their morning stroll with the babies, always a special time of day for them. Pat tried not to be depressed when she returned from the hospital. She began to go to evening classes in ceramics, she resumed her painting and designed a new spring wardrobe. For her birthday I bought her a pedigree afghan to keep her company. He was a beautiful specimen, highly nervous, not very bright, but ridiculously affectionate. She spent hours grooming it, lavishing the kind of love on it that she would have given the baby. She'd take it on long walks through the neighborhood with the girls pushing their prams, trying to keep a brave face, with only a dog on a leash. She knew in her heart it was no substitute but she had no other way of expressing her grief.

"Don't you feel anything?" she would ask me as we sat across from each other in our grotesquely furnished place where we had so much fun shocking people with. How could I tell her what I was thinking? It's not good form to say, "I think it was for the best."

We went into self-imposed exile. Reading, listening to music, and seeing Fred and Paula occasionally, we had little to say to each other. Paula joined Pat in some night classes and together they worked on a project that brought them closer together. Paula apologised to me for being so hard on Pat in the beginning.

"She's really quite talented, Jay, you should encourage her more."

I took her advice and noticed how much it raised her spirits. She began to invite people over for quiet, intimate dinners where she had a chance to talk about her new interests. We were well on the way to becoming a domesticated couple.

Radulovich's art gallery-bar changed all that. He had taken a store a block away from the old Mississippi riverfront, transforming it into the most atmospheric environment St. Louis had ever seen. He talked Thomas Hart Benton into exhibiting his paintings on the walls of the saloon, something that Benton always threatened to do someday. The publicity that resulted ensured the place immediate success. It wasn't only the paintings on the wall or the red-checkered table cloths with wine bottles and candles that people flocked to see; the real attraction was the people.

The poet, writer, radical, non conformist were no longer threatening outsiders in Little Bohemia, they were the star attraction, and the Establishment came to soak up the artistic atmosphere. Rubenstein and Stuart Perkoff read their poems; the audience listened. Writers made passes at secretaries, artists argued with students, strangers introduced themselves to strangers. Before the night was over, everyone felt a little less isolated, a little more a part of a special crowd. Business was so brisk that Radulovich seldom had time to get out from behind the bar, but the money was rolling in; art had to wait.

Pat and I went down to the place about three or four times a week. Being a part-owner of the hottest place in town attracted people to our table—nothing better for curing Pat's blues than attention. Anyone seeing us sitting at our regular table surrounded by people eager to know us, would have thought us the luckiest couple in town. We weren't though. The party mood adopted at Little

Bohemia lasted for about two blocks of the drive home. Once we got into bed, I was usually too tired or too drunk to be good company. Since the miscarriage, we weren't really making it sexually. There were so many things to distract me, it became a natural excuse to let a month go by without it. When we did have sex, it was of the perfunctory kind, always accompanied by a sense of obligation that produced a low-grade guilt in me.

On those nights we didn't go out, Pat invited a few of her old friends over for an evening of low-level conversation. I frequently retired before it was over, causing acute embarrassment among the guests. One of her friends, a beautiful girl, interested me. She was something of an expert on Doris Day movies, having based her life on Miss Day's screen image. She had just left her husband and Pat was her staunch ally. One day she dropped by when Pat was visiting her mother. If you can imagine Doris Day, a bit sad but hanging in there, sure that Rock Hudson was going to rescue her any minute, you'll understand how I slipped into an affair. Even Doris Day needs someone to tell her how beautiful and desirable she is after she's walked out on the man in her life. The guilt I assumed would go with adultery never surfaced; I began to enjoy sex with Pat again. If being bad made me feel so good, I had a brilliant future as an adulterer.

When a couple who were regular customers invited Rubenstein, Radulovich me and back to their house after the bar closed, we were delighted to accept. He was a successful advertising executive; she was a beautiful woman, obviously devoted to him and a den scout mother. Even though her children were in bed, she insisted we tip-toe in their room and have a look at them sleeping so peacefully. She obviously wanted to let us know she loved her children, no matter what games her husband played outside the nursery. After some tasteful, preliminary social amenities, she took us all to her bed, with her husband complimenting us on finding his wife so attractive. We did not disappoint either of them. On the way home, we asked ourselves the big question: *What is happening in America when you can't trust a scout den mother anymore?*

The next day, Rubenstein showed up with a copy of W. H. Auden's *Age of Anxiety.*

"The poet is the first to recognize the rot, the first to celebrate the glory, and the last to be appreciated." I didn't know if it was a quote from Auden or one of Rubenstein's rationalizations.

"Let's cure the ills of America by starting a poetry magazine."

I broke up.

"Your rejection slips are showing," I told him. "You'll never get laid with a poetry magazine." I knew he was serious when he didn't laugh.

"You ought to read Auden. It's a big book. He's got his finger on the pulse of the times. The new look is going to be the anxious look." I was fond of Rubenstein, but poetry was something I thought you got over when you left high school. Yet I was jealous of him; he at least knew he was a poet. I was a success but I didn't know who I was. Somewhere within me was a lost cause trying to break out. I was suffering from a disease not yet in the medical books: *Lack of Identity Blues.*

I began my search for a cure at the most superficial level—I grew a beard. I hid the upper half of my face behind dark glasses. My clothes sense deserted me. I longed for those hand-downs that had made my life so miserable. I put the two-tone saddle shoes at the back of the closet and slipped into a pair of dirty sneakers. The crew cut look had to go. Long hair was the mark of the Wild West, and the pioneer look was what I was after. Instead of a covered wagon, I bought a convertible Model A Ford with a roof so patched and torn it looked like something out of *Grapes of Wrath.* I did some serious thinking about Rubenstein's idea of starting a magazine. Restless on my Cardinal Richelieu bed, it occurred to me that my life lacked decent stationery. Nobody was going to be impressed with answers to the major themes of life written

45

on a letterhead that proclaimed to the world that I bought and sold antiques.

When ordering some new stationery for the Galleries, as a joke, I had some cards printed up announcing the existence of a new magazine: *NEUROTICA,* a Quarterly Journal; Publisher and Editor, JAY IRVING LANDESMAN. The catchy title came to me when I asked myself what was the most typical characteristic of all my friends. The word, neurotic, popped into my head; adding the 'a' was an afterthought. Just to annoy Cutie, I put some of the cards on the tray where the Landesman Galleries' cards were kept. Within a few days, I noticed that they were all gone. At first I thought that Cutie might have removed them, but she denied seeing them. When I explained my dilemma to Cutie and showed her one of my new cards, her explanation was interesting.

"Looking at you these days, they probably thought it was the name of the shop. You certainly look like Mr. Neurotica."

Drinking with Rubenstein the next night, he brought up the subject of a poetry magazine again. I let him go through his reasons.

"All of the poetry rags are so goddam academic, it's time for something radical," etc. With perfect timing, I pulled out a *Neurotica* card and threw it over to him.

"Would you put some money in a mag with a name like that?"

His mouth fell off his face. He sat there, staring at the card, mouthing the syllables of NEU-RO-TI-CA as if it was some kind of new catechism. "I like it. I like it."

The title said it all. A magazine for and about neurotics, written by neurotics. He held out his shaky hand to seal the deal. For the next month we looked at all the little magazines we could lay our hands on. We agreed they were all dead wood.

Convinced that there was a need for a little mag with a definite point of view, we decided that the time had come for the neurotic personality to defend himself against a hostile world. In various psychiatric magazines we found articles analysing the neurotic's influences in art and literature, going back to Freud. The relationship between art and neurosis was well documented; it was up to us to put it into language that readers of *Neurotica* could understand. We wanted the neurotic writer, artist, etc. to share his vision with other neurotics. We began to write manifestos that would explain our purpose in publishing, but with each attempt we failed to come to terms with the problem. It was either too technical, like the practitioners' journals, or too pseudo like *Popular Psychology*. Finally we hit the right note:

> *NEUROTICA* is a literary explosion, defense, and correlation of the problems and personalities that in our culture are defined as neurotic. It is said that if you tie a piece of red cloth to the gull's leg its fellow gulls will peck it to pieces.

> *NEUROTICA* wishes to draw an analogy between this observation and the plight of today's creative anxious man. We are interested in exploring the creativeness of this man who has been forced to live underground, and yet lights an utter darkness with his music, poetry, painting, and writing.

> *NEUROTICA* will present, in as non-technical language as possible, the authoritative scientists' approach to all aspects of neuroticism.

We sent out about a hundred letters to all the writers, psychiatrists, poets, artists and anybody we thought would contribute something interesting, enclosing a list of titles we thought would catch their interest.

THE NEW LOOK IS THE ANXIOUS LOOK

PSYCHIATRIST—GOD OR DEMI-TASSE?

PARTIES - PATHOLOGICAL OR OTHERWISE.

AMERICAN SEXUAL IMPERIALISM.

ALL THE GOOD ROLES HAVE BEEN TAKEN: THE PLIGHT OF THE TALENTED UNTALENTED.

THE UNIQUE MORES OF THE BAR AND TAVERN SO-
CIAL MILIEU.

THE THEATRE AS SUBLIMATED SUICIDE.

THE CASTRATION COMPLEX IN ANIMALS.

THE DRIVE TO BE A MISFIT AND ITS REWARD.

THE THERAPEUTIC NATURE OF EVIL ACTS.

LOVE FOUNDED ON MUTUAL MISUNDERSTANDING.

CAN YOU SLAP YOUR MOTHER? A SEMANTIC PROB-
LEM.

THE ART OF MOCK SUICIDE.

ART AS CATHARSIS: THE 'LAXATIVE THEORY' AS AN
EXPLANATION FOR VALUELESS ART.

CHOOSING A PSYCHIATRIST WITH CARE: THE NEED
OF AN AGENCY FOR HELPING THE INDIVIDUAL IN
THE MOST APPROPRIATE SELECTION.

We weren't counting on the scientific community to
write for us; they had their own journals, yet I thought we
could catch a couple of big fish with the sheer *chutzpah* of
the titles. Rubenstein contacted his friends in New York. I
put small ads in the *Saturday Review of Literature* and little
magazines announcing the project, requesting either contributions or subscriptions. The response was encouraging; manuscripts, poetry, and subscriptions began flowing
in at a brisk pace. When I got a letter from Dr. Karl
Menninger and the eminent psychoanalyst, Gregory
Zilboorg, in response to mine, I knew we were on the right
track even though they didn't contribute anything but
advice.

"It's a brave project," wrote Dr. Menninger, "don't expect too much from the profession; they're a stuffy lot . . .
I'm too busy at the moment to write anything for you, but I
am intrigued by the title *The Castration Complex in Animals*."

Dr. Zilboorg invited me to visit him the next time I came
to New York. He added:

"I doubt if any analysts would be interested in writing for *Neurotica*. They are much too neurotic to be associated with anything so neurotic as *Neurotica*. Best of luck."

With material flowing in, there was no doubt that we had enough for the first two issues. Turning my attention to practical matters like distribution, I contacted college town bookshops throughout America. The response was terrific, with orders for over 1500 copies of the first issue! I arranged for distribution in St. Louis of over 500 copies and subscriptions were reaching the 500 mark. With confidence, I ordered a first printing of 3000 copies. You would have thought the magazine's name was *Erotica*.

Time did a feature on the little magazine scene the month *Neurotica* came out, March, 1948. To my delight it was among the new mags featured. They quoted the first line of Rudolph Friedmann's lead article, *The End of Feeling:* 'Getting married is the best way of taking regular exercise.' They gave it enough space to make it look like one of the more significant new publications. I was convinced I had received top billing.

A nice touch was a feature in the *St. Louis Post-Dispatch* on *Neurotica* and me that enabled me to get more outlets locally. A cover story in *Writers Journal* showed a picture of Pat and me behind the wheel of my scruffy Ford, looking determined. All the publicity sold out the first issue and I had to reprint another two thousand to take care of the daily re-orders from shops all over the country. That first issue contained an article on why American homosexuals marry, an hour by hour account of the new anxious man called, "The New Look is the Anxious Look", written by Rubenstein, anonymously, of course, fiction by Marc Brandel and Douglas Rodewald, poetry by Kenneth Patchen, Henri Michaux, David Cornel DeJong, Rubenstein and the conductor-composer, Leonard Bernstein, who confessed that he was a dabbler in psychoanalysis and wrote a little poetry in between symphonies.

Rubenstein and I were pleased with our debut into the world of Little Mags. He hawked the first issue at Little

Bohemia as though it were a newspaper extra. "READ ALL ABOUT IT: LOW SCROTAL MOON NUDGES GREEN CORDUROY COAT OF ARTIST IN BROAD DAYLIGHT. EXTRA! EXTRA! ANXIOUS MAN SUPPRESSES SCREAM. GET YOUR COPY HERE." His self esteem rose considerably now that he was a published poet.

My life changed dramatically after the launch. I shaved off the beard and returned to my well-groomed look. Since *Neurotica* was a success, why not dress like one? Even Cutie was impressed. When she didn't ask for a commission for the copies of the mag I sold in the Galleries, I knew she was secretly pleased that it had gone over so well. As editor and publisher of America's first lay-psychiatric magazine, I gained a new status in the Galleries, qualifying me to discuss my customers' psychological needs as well as their decorative ones. There were some who sorely needed both; the psychological problems were 'on the house'. Without a couch in the office, it was amazing how successful I was in helping people with their domestic problems. I began to refer to customers as 'clients', just like a doctor, until Cutie warned me: "You'll get arrested for practicing without a license."

I continued to be active in the running of the Galleries despite the heavy work schedule of the magazine. Every day was full of surprises, but nothing as bizarre as what happened when my fantasy collided with reality. Eight years after I first saw the picture in *Fortune* of Janet Rhinelander Stewart, the woman who wanted to be amused walked into Landesman Galleries. I recognised her immediately.

"Can you help me?" she asked. Help her? I had to stop myself from quoting Tyrone Power's famous line in *Nightmare Alley:* "Lady, I was born for the job." She was standing there with a medium-size cigarette holder, looking a trifle impatient, waiting for a reply. Her voice was deeper than Power's, but she was much more beautiful.

I heard my voice going into a high castrato pitch when I

said, "I think I can." It wasn't a particularly funny answer, but she laughed. She was wearing a veil, a black dress, a million dollars worth of pearls, and a curious smile.

"I've just moved into a house on Lindell Boulevard and I need some chandeliers. I'm told you have the most interesting ones."

I took her on a guided tour of the Galleries, pointing out the more expensive ones. I saw Cutie eyeing me from behind the office door, rubbing hands in anticipation of a big sale. Mrs. Stewart liked my act, but didn't buy anything that day.

"I have some things I brought down from New York I no longer need. Perhaps we can do some bartering."

I suggested that I come over to the house to take a look.

After she left, Cutie came out from behind a screen, like something in an old silent movie. "You didn't close the deal, you smart Alec. I should have taken over. I would have sold her something, if only an ashtray. She smokes like a chimney."

There was nothing that Cutie could have said that would possibly bring me down from the high just experienced.

"Don't rush me, Cutie. That woman is going to be my best client."

"You didn't even sell her a subscription to your magazine, Mr. Neurotica."

True, but I knew that I was going to be very good at keeping her amused.

On the day of our appointment I appeared too early and overdressed. She was in a pongee silk dressing gown, although it was three o'clock in the afternoon. She introduced me to her daughters, two well-groomed teenagers, and a respectable-looking, middle-aged woman she called Nanny. Somewhat surprised, I asked if the girls weren't a little too old for one.

"Who said anything about Noonie being their nanny? That's quite absurd. She's mine." That laugh again, deep, rich and uninhibited. There was nothing predictable about this woman. Her soft blonde hair was parted down the middle and drawn in the back in an old-fashioned bun. Large, curious eyes, high, unlined forehead, and red, sensational lips complemented a flawless complexion. I remembered she was one of the American society women who had endorsed Ponds Cold Cream in a series of famous ads. It evidently worked in her case.

After a quick tour around the house, she asked if I would like to see the things she had to barter. I reminded her that history had credited the Rhinelanders of New York with bartering Manhattan away from the Indians.

"Nothing's changed," she said, by way of warning me not to expect any bargains.

She led the way up to the top floor and into a storage area almost as big and as crowded with china and glass as a Parke-Bernet auction preview. Together we unwrapped her past. Her running commentary on what life was like with servants, butlers, footmen, nannies, and cooks was a reaffirmation of conspicuous consumption theories. Gracious entertaining seemed to be the main occupation of the rich.

"It must have been fun in those days," I said.

There was a mischievous quality in her stories of her attempts at escaping boredom of that world. She had tried the usual charity volunteer work: sponsoring balls, appearing at benefits, without much enthusiasm. During the war she was attached to a medical hospital corps that was doing urine analysis for some government project. She considered that a very constructive period in her life. I must say, I was a bit shocked at that revelation. I pictured her with two Borzoi dogs, walking down Park Avenue, stopping traffic. She seemed to have spent her time between the El Morroco and Palm Beach, with occasional late night forays into Harlem to see the Duke. Even the fact that George Gershwin composed some of *Rhapsody in Blue* on her Steinway was passed on to me as something that happened all the time.

"Did you really say to *Fortune Magazine* that you want to be amused?"

She denied it, adding that the article was silly.

"Don't kill a young man's fantasy." I told her the story of cutting out her picture for my pin-up girl during the war.

"You'd have done better with Betty Grable."

Sitting on the floor with this strange woman, I warned her that she was going to find St. Louis a little dull unless she hung out in the right places with the fun people.

"And who would they be, excluding yourself, of course?" Then I told her about Jimmy Massucci, the Picker, who was always coming up with little gems of the past and about Mrs. Cunningham Walls, an impoverished dowager who opened an antique shop in Bed Bug Row to sell off her last possessions. I invited her down to Little Bohemia and promised to take her around to the more interesting country and western bars where she could still hear the early American guitar pickers, adding, "It'll be a change from the St. Louis Country Club."

"I'm sure it will," she agreed. I told her if it ever got too boring, she could always come by the Galleries and I'd buy her a cup of coffee at the Rex Cafe. I left her with the impression that I was the one to walk on the wild side with, but that I wasn't very good at bartering.

"You've taken advantage of me," I claimed as we concluded the business side of our relationship. Pointing to a collection of art deco cigarette holders, I suggested she throw those into the deal.

"I have a brother who collects useless artifacts". She hesitated. "I'll throw in a life time subscription to *Neu-rotica*".

"Don't send me that magazine of yours. I've seen a copy. It's too silly for words", she said, handing me the collection. I left with the feeling that even if I hadn't made a good deal, I certainly kept her amused.

4

I received a letter from my old friend, Dorothy, who now worked at the Four Seasons Bookshop in Greenwich Village, urging me to come to New York and promote the second issue of *Neurotica*. "There is a jockeying for window space that recognizes the power of personality more than the content of the issue," she wrote. In other words, if the boss likes you, you get the window. If they don't know you, you'll end up on a shelf underneath *the Rocky Mountain Review of Poetry*. "A visit to every shop that handles *Neurotica* is an absolute must—you don't have to go to bed with everyone, but make your presence felt." In a P.S. she added: "Be careful what you wear in this town. Your business background is already against you and you could well destroy your credibility if you showed up in a three piece suit." I took her advice about the clothes seriously, but took Pat along for a much needed holiday.

I arrived in New York in a black, button-down shirt, a yellow, hand-painted tie and wearing a crumpled seersucker suit with a new pair of Clark's desert boots. It didn't matter that our reservation at the Marlton Hotel, in the heart of the Village, turned out to be a converted elevator shaft, with the soot of a hundred parties still on the walls. The room began to look good once I'd stocked it with a few bottles of gin, a tray of pastrami sandwiches, and some people that could help me make my blitz on New York's literary scene a success.

The first person I called was John Clellon Holmes, who

contributed a short story to the second issue. I believe it was the first piece of published fiction that utilized the language of the hipster:

> This is a local fable and the boy is Beeker. This guy was a Peko-man, and he blew himself out of the coils of a trumpet every night. He came on for culture, not for loot; so he passed the marijuana to his cohorts when the need was near. This tea-dispensing on the cuff brought in enough for bills, and lad was living in a new era.'

Holmes, I thought, would be some far-out looking cat, shifty, probably strung out on the weed. Imagine my surprise to meet a quiet, almost shy, tall, thin, professorial type, with a magnificent Bobby Darin wave of blond hair. His thick, horn rim glasses slipping off his Bob Hope nose added a casual touch that prevented my saying, "What's a nice kid like you doing hanging out with all those hipsters?" He laughed easily and once we got drinks in our hands we both relaxed. He filled me in on what kind of impact *Neurotica* was having on the New York scene.

"It's going over big in the colleges; people are talking about it—some love it and the establishment hates it. You've done a brilliant job of distribution; I see it everywhere. How do you do it, man?" Explaining that I wasn't happy with the content of *Neurotica* yet, I said that I hoped he would help me get in touch with the writers that I was really after.

"Writers like yourself who know what's really going down on the scene." Holmes wasn't too encouraging; most of his contacts were too straight for what I was looking for.

While we talked about the need for some fresh outlooks, a call came in from Beka Dougherty, a friend from St. Louis who was working for *Time* magazine.

"I think *Neurotica* is terrific," she said in her cool, *Time* manner. "I put them on to you for the feature on Little Mags. You owe me a dinner." When I told her what I was looking for in New York, she said she knew the perfect man to write for *Neurotica*.

"He's absolutely unprintable, but exactly what you need." It turned out his name was Legman, which I thought was a joke name, but she assured me that he was no joke.

"Mention my name—he'll remember me." Excited at the prospect of meeting someone who was so good he was unprintable, I asked Holmes if he had ever heard of G. Legman.

"Sounds phoney," he said, "but if he's as good as she says, this is your lucky day."

I made a quick call to check it out. After I introduced myself as the editor of *Neurotica,* he cut me short.

"It's a piece of garbage." I laughed at the nerve of the guy.

He didn't sound enthusiastic about meeting me but said I could come up to the Bronx and talk to him.

"There's nothing here to eat or drink," he added, "so bring your own refreshments."

I knew at once that I was going to get along with Legman—he didn't mince words. His put-down was a challenge that I liked; he sounded just like Cutie. Holmes decided to come along, and by the time we left for the Bronx, I'd collected quite a party, including Herb Benjamin, who was writing the article for me on psychiatrists called *God or Demi-Tasse?,* and a very attractive young student who was spending her summer getting arrested to gather material for a thesis she was doing on the American penal system. Everybody was in good spirits. Armed with a bottle of whiskey, we caught the A train to the Bronx Zoo, where we were to meet up with a literary tiger.

We embarked, en masse, a noisy, playful bunch, as if we were going to a picnic. In the shadows stood a lonely figure; I knew immediately who it was.

"Are you Landesman? I'm Legman." The tone of the voice was sinister. As he stepped out of the shadows, I saw a heavily-moustached, portly figure, with a wild shock of hair that made me think of a young Balzac. I knew immediately there weren't going to be any laughs in the Bronx that night. By the light of the platform, I saw the lines of thwarted ambition around his mouth, making it seem in a permanent state of rage. He was surprised to see such an entourage, but rose to the occasion by taking us on a Grey Line bus tour of the delights of the Bronx on the way to his house.

"This is the butcher's where I buy my sheep lung. Oh, you've never eaten lung? Very nourishing, you must try it sometime when you're broke and *starving*." He let the words sink in. "That's the grocer, a generous man who gives my wife the vegetables that he ordinarily throws out with the garbage. Amazing what my wife can do with rotten greens and bruised tomatoes." He was doing his best to prepare us for the assault he had in mind for a bunch of city slickers intent on picking his brains. Holmes and I exchanged a quick, foreboding look and the rest of the group were cowed into silence.

Legman's house was a little cottage, possibly the only one left in the Bronx, with a distressed pickett fence going all around the place, trying to hide the shoddy patches of grass. The cottage itself was rather romantic looking, but he wasn't going to let us off that easily. He gave us a quick run down on the previous occupant, the chronicler of unexplained phenomenon, the legendary Charles Forte.

"A lot of unexplained things are still happening around here—ghosts and all that crap." Inside, it reeked of old herring bones. I noticed that Legman himself smelled of musty books. Books were everywhere; stacked in the halls, used as furniture, and what little furniture there was, was upholstered in books. Books were marching menacingly out of the closets, trickling out of the toilet, and from the smell of the place, I suspected they were being cooked on a back burner for a late night snack of glue pudding.

Legman introduced his wife, Beverly, who was administering what looked like mouth-to-mouth resuscitation to one of the dozen cats loitering in the kitchen, waiting, as far as I could figure, to be read to. Beverly was more shy than the cats, but much plainer.

For the next two hours, Legman gave us a whirlwind tour of his one man fight against censorship and social and sexual repression. He had been compiling evidence for years and it was all stored in files or staring at us from every nook and cranny. He started out with comic books, disappearing from time to time to throw examples of them on the table to prove how insidious they were.

"The generation of children born since 1930 cannot read! You don't believe it?" He threw some comics on the table with horrible illustrations of brutality. "Sex has been replaced by violence. Millions of comic books with nothing but violence! Where is the sex? Comics are only the tip of the iceberg. Debasement of women, murder movies, murder magazines, murder books—writers have created a whole new generation of children brought up on violence. Is it any wonder that there's no place for a decent, healthy emotion?"

Clarence Darrow could not have given a more eloquent performance. His indictment made us, the jury, cringe with guilt for ever having read a comic book or a murder mystery. In a brilliant summing up, he began to read from his manuscript:

"Murder having replaced sex in the popular arts, the glorification of one requires the degradation of the other. We are faced in our culture by the insurmountable, schizophrenic contradiction that sex, which is legal, in fact, is a crime on paper, while murder, a crime in fact, is on paper the best-seller of all time. Civilization is not yet ready to let love and death fight it out in the marketplace, with free speech and four-color printing on both sides. Censors refuse to see that a backwash of violence affects the victim. Any rotten thing you want to put on paper is O.K. with the district attorney, but if you put into a novel the description of the ordinary act of sexual intercourse between a man and wife, you will go to jail. At least sex is normal. Is murder?'"

Legman's message was coming through loud and clear to Holmes and me, but the other jurors were having trouble following his icy logic.

"He's crazy," Pat whispered to me, as we followed Legman to another room.

"Hysterical," Benjamin said, but was impressed with the overall concern with the psychological implications. The young penologist suspected Legman of Communist leanings. To me, Legman's ideas were music to my ears and I knew Holmes was digging the performance. His occasional "wows" after some piece of damning evidence was reassuring. My exuberant thigh slapping throughout Legman's diatribe encouraged Legman to greater heights. He took Holmes and me into his inner sanctum where there was a mountain of evidence overflowing the orange-crates and files it was stored in. He had catalogued every manifestation of man's deliberate inhumanity to man, but saved the best part of his act for last.

"You know I used to work for Kinsey?" he said, making a face that told us what he thought of him. Alfred Kinsey's book had just been published to wildly enthusiastic reviews. He pulled out a letter from Kinsey asking him to join his staff, full of praise for his work in the field of sexual enlightenment. "He's a closet queen, only interested in measuring the sizes of young men's penises. As if that has anything to do with the sex habits of the American male."

In a file on SEX, the index included such enlightening headings as INTERCOURSE: ORAL-HOMOSEXUAL-GENITAL-DIGITAL-ANAL, etc.

"I'm working on a book on oral genitalism that should open a few new avenues." He smiled one of his prize grins as he pulled out bizarre pieces of documentation from a century of writings to prove the world was mad.

It was clear to me why this man was so ignored. If for a second Holmes or I expressed an opinion contrary to his—after all, we had some doubts that Hemingway was a fag, and Henry Miller an anti-semite—he would stop in the middle of our doubt and launch a personal attack upon us.

"Why are you wearing those fag boots?" he asked, pointing to my Clark's.

To everyone but Holmes and me, he was clearly a nut-case,

a mad man, a Genghis Khan of the psycho-sexual world, anarchist, and champion non-stop talker of the decade.

"Well, Landesman," he said as the evening was drawing to a close, "what's it going to be? This is the kind of stuff you should be publishing. All that crap about 'look at me, I'm neurotic!' is over." He fastened me with one of his looks that made it obvious that he was worried about whether I was worthy of the opportunity he was handing me on a silver platter. He threw the manuscript, *Love and Death: A Study in Censorship*, in front of me.

"I've had this manuscript rejected by every publisher from Appleton-Century to Ziff-Davis; forty-two in all. I've had it stuffed down the toilet in front of me by irate editors. It's been misplaced by three big publishing houses. I've been abused, sworn at, and humiliated in front of secretaries. WHAT ARE YOU GOING TO DO ABOUT IT?" he screamed at me. Then he calmed down. "You know, Landesman, *Neurotica* could be something if you got rid of all that poetry and fake psychiatric prose. You've got a good idea there, the best that's come along in some time. It shouldn't be trusted to a dilettante like you." He tried hard to smile when he said that, but the grin froze half-way through.

I knew Legman was the man I needed to make something out of *Neurotica* without reading his manuscript. The only thing that was bothering me was how to work with him.

"I'll call you tomorrow after I've read the manuscript," I said, grabbing it. Legman put his hand over mine to stop me.

Looking me in the eye, his lips clenching until they were almost white, he said in a controlled hysteria:

"This is your big chance, Landesman. Don't blow it!" He let go of my hand. "If you don't publish it, I could always go back to painting walls. After all, that's what Hitler did for a living."

Everyone jumped on me on the walk back to the subway, except Holmes.

"He has no respect for you," Pat said.

"I was embarrassed for you," chimed in the penologist.

"A mad genius," concluded Benjamin.

I knew in my heart that Legman was for me; we needed each other. That *cause* that had been struggling to get out of me erupted in the Bronx that night, even before I read a word of his manuscript.

On the subway ride home, I started reading, passing the pages to Holmes as I finished them. We were cracking up with dismay and laughter at Legman's outrageous indictment of the Western world. Oswald Spengler in the Bronx? A Jeremiah crying in the wilderness with a howl that I had waited all my life to hear. Holmes, Pat, and I ended up at the Waldorf cafeteria, still reading over countless cups of coffee until Pat begged us to leave.

"What if Legman's right?" Holmes asked. We looked at each other, shaking our heads in disbelief at what we had experienced that night.

"My God, Johnny, do you realize we've found an honest man?"

"And not a minute too soon," Holmes added.

I had a restless night. When Pat and I got into bed, she was hurt because I took the manuscript with me. I couldn't put it down. Legman alone had a clear vision of the pitfalls that America was rapidly heading for:

> On to the pit: Well, we have been warned. Mene, mene tekal and murder was never written larger on any wall. We are travelling toward death. We love it, we want it, and we are going to get it. Sex, the opposite of death—may or may not save us. But we cannot hold back the flood with institutionalized amok.

I was convinced Legman was the prophet I was looking for. How was it that all the popular prophets of doom and despair—The H. L. Menckens, the George Jean Nathans, the Gilbert Seldes and Lewis Mumfords never tied up the connection between sex and violence in popular culture in the Thirties and Forties?

Legman, working alone, anonymously in the Bronx, had put his accusing finger on the problem. I couldn't wait to call him.

"Hello, Legman?"

"You hated it!"

"Only terrific," a frightening pause. "Are you still there?"

"Do I get published or not? Never mind the compliments. Save that crap for your entourage."

"I think we have some serious talk coming."

"Like what? Nobody edits me."

Don't you think we should meet again before I leave town?"

"Yeah, we can always arrange that. But what are you going to do about it now?"

"I'm going to publish you." Another long pause.

"O.K. now we can talk."

I was remarkably calm for having just made the biggest decision of my life.

That memorable weekend in July 1948 had other surprises. Holmes called. I told him of my decision to publish Legman.

"You've found your man, Jay," he assured me, "you two are going to be great together; you need each other." His support meant a lot to me, and his enthusiasm counteracted Pat's lack of it.

"He's nothing but trouble and you'll regret it someday," Pat had said. At the time, I thought she was being so petty, I didn't bother to explain why it was so important.

"How would you and Pat like to go to a party in Spanish Harlem and meet some new people? There might be some writers there you can use." We met at Holmes' apartment over the Dover delicatessen on Lexington Avenue at 55th St. I thought living over a delicatessen was practical as well as romantic. The Dover sold almost everything to sustain you in life except books, and I had no doubt that one day they would be selling *Neurotica*.

I met Alan Harrington, one of Holmes' friends, who knew the people giving the party. Harrington looked even straighter than Holmes, but since he had read both issues of *Neurotica,* he couldn't have been that straight. We all trooped uptown on a hot, muggy New York night. People were sitting on brownstone steps in their undershirts, drinking beer and fanning themselves—it was like a scene out of some low-budget gangster movie. Harrington recognized one of the guests, dressed appropriately in a T-shirt and jeans, coming out of the tenement. He was on his way to replenish the beer, but stopped long enough for introductions. His name was Kerouac, a name I didn't recognize, but he knew mine the minute Holmes mentioned *Neurotica.* It felt good not being anonymous in Spanish Harlem. After he left, Harrington mentioned that he was one of the writers he wanted Holmes to meet. He evidently thought a lot of him, having heard from friends that Kerouac was one of the few good writers around, although he'd never been published.

We followed the sound of bop to the top floor of the house and were met by two strange-looking young men dressed in bathrobes, which didn't surprise me as much as it did them, when Holmes introduced me as the editor of *Neurotica.* The skinny, toothy kid with the big horn rim glasses fell to his knees in a kind of mock-Japanese ceremony.

"I'm Myshkin," he said.

"I'm Rogozhin," the other guy said. When they got up off their knees they told me how much they loved *Neurotica* and what a privilege it was to meet its editor. I would have felt like a celebrity if only they hadn't been wearing their bathrobes over their street clothes.

Later I asked Holmes who the two nut cases were, but he didn't have much information on them at the time. Talking to them later during the party, the skinny kid said he was a poet and the other guy, slightly hysterical, identified himself as a certified ex-patient just out of Rockland State mental hospital. He immediately told us that he had sustained a series of insulin shock treatments administered by doctors who didn't know what they were doing while they were performing the operation.

"They constantly checked in the manual on shock

therapy while connecting me up." His laugh was even more hysterical than mine; we both saw the horror as well as the humor of the situation.

"Maybe you could write about it for the magazine. That's the kind of material I'm looking for. You know, straight out of the victim's mouth." He agreed and promised to send me something. "What's your name again?" I asked.

"Solomon, Carl Solomon. I'm a friend of Allen Ginsberg—you know, Myshkin." He added, as if he were passing an atomic secret: "You ought to get something from him—he's a great poet."

I didn't have the heart to tell him that I was up to my neck in poets already. It was writers just out of nut-houses that I was interested in. The bop music fitted in perfectly with the movements of the guests—slightly jerky, and speedy. They all seemed to be much younger than I, less well dressed, and much more fragmented. I couldn't drop into any of their conversations, yet people drifted up to me throughout the party, introducing themselves as writers, artists, poets, musicians, and promising failures.

"Look forward to reading some of your material," I told them all, in a voice I hoped didn't sound as condescending as it sounded to me. If I had met any of these people before Legman, I would have been all over them with requests—now they seemed superfluous to my new policy. I could imagine the scornful crucifixion of the people at the party if Legman had been there. Already I was worrying what to tell Rubenstein about the change: "Cool the poetry, Buddy," seemed almost too cruel.

Before I left, Kerouac came over to me to tell me what a great poet Ginsberg was, and Ginsberg told me how great Kerouac was, right after Solomon had already told me how great the two of them were. It was quite amusing to hear how everyone was more talented than themselves and none of them had broken into print. I was impressed by their enthusiasm, but I thought them rather childish when they started lighting fire crackers in ashtrays to put a little life into the party.

A reunion with my literary mole at a party at her bookshop was prefaced with another caution.

"It's not in your honor, so play it cool. A lot of big names will be there. Be careful how you come on." The window of the shop was full of Saul Bellow's *Dangling Man,* and most of the people at the party looked like literary executioners—arrogant, snobbish, waiting for a kill. *Neurotica* received some terrible reviews in *Partisan Review* and other little establishment mags which made me cautious about revealing my identify; they were not harboring any overwhelming desire to meet the editor of *Garbage,* as Legman would put it. When I had to introduce myself, I was definitely at a disadvantage. There was a minor disaster when I was introduced to Philip Rahv, the editor of *Partisan Review.* He was sitting while everyone else was standing, which put me at a further disadvantage. When I held out my hand to shake his, he pulled out his handkerchief to attend to his leaking nose. He had no comment to make.

"I know nothing about Henry James. Would you like to be disintroduced?" I asked. I was told that Rahv had a sensitive nose for spotting a phony, causing it to leak profusely; evidently I failed his test.

Moving right along, inspired by his creative rejection, I introduced myself to Delmore Schwartz who bolstered my spirits with a few, carefully-chosen words about the potential of *Neurotica,* but there was nothing I could use as a quote in an ad. I could have used Legman at the party— there were so many grown-ups that needed cutting down to size. I dropped his name around a few times without much reaction, except with the owner of the shop, who knew him and preferred that I didn't put in an emergency call to rescue me from this baptism of fire. The only thing that saved me from total rejection was the stack of *Neurotica's* next to the cash register. When I saw someone actually buy a copy, I had to resist throwing myself at her feet, like Ginsberg and Solomon had done, and saying "I'm Landesman, the editor of that magazine."

The most interesting-looking woman in the room

turned out to be a jazz singer I had long admired, Stella Brooks. Billie Holiday had once called her the only white woman who could sing the blues. She was pleasantly surprised to hear me rattle off the title of her one obscure record. Since our mutual recognition had established a bond, I felt I could be brutally frank.

"Whatever happened to your career—you should have been a star by now with your talent?"

"It's a long story," she assured me. "Everything was going to make me a star, baby. I've had club owners build special rooms for me to sing my songs in, and what did they do? The minute I didn't pack the room, they brought in Sarah Vaughan. They lie, baby. They're all the same— hungry. I suppose, I'm not hungry enough." She leafed through the copy of *Neurotica* she just bought. "Nice try, but I don't think you'll make it."

When I told Dorothy about the stunning amount of rejection I experienced at the party, she didn't try to cheer me up.

"New York's tough; get used to it."

But it wasn't a complete waste of time: I got an invitation from the owner of the shop to come around someday and share her orgone box, a sexy contraption you sat in with a vibrator or a good friend. It was popular among Village Reichians looking for the ultimate orgasm.

In spite of the rejection, there was no doubt that the New York trip was a huge success. I got a distributor to handle the magazine that ensured it being on prime news-stands throughout Manhattan. Flying visits to places that handled the magazine resulted in doubling most of their orders and a pat on the back for my anti-establishment views from the leading outlet in New York—the Gotham Book Mart.

The conference with Legman before leaving settled the future of *Neurotica.* He would be supervising the production and arranging for the printing of it in New York. His manuscript, *Love and Death,* would be serialized in four instalments beginning with "The Psychopathology Of The Comics," and when all four installments were published, the same type would be used to bring it out as a book published by the Neurotica Publishing Company. Legman would get a small amount of money for overseeing the production.

"No more poetry," he said with a shit-eating grin, "unless it makes a point. I'm going to get you writers who clearly see that America is on the brink of a nervous breakdown." I didn't have the nerve to ask if they would save America or push it over the edge.

Before I left, I had a chance to meet the eminent psychoanalyst Gregory Zilboorg. He certainly wasn't what I expected. Although it was during office hours, he was dressed in a black leotard, bedroom slippers, and a T-shirt. I told him of my meeting Legman and his profound influence on me. Incidentally, he looked like Legman, which made me feel even more uncomfortable. It was almost like a session on the couch as I unveiled my plans for *Neurotica*.

"Very interesting," he said, "you have a very good project. I wish I could do something for you, but time does not allow me to." Disappointed, I thanked him for giving me a free hour on the couch and promised to send him the next issue. As I left, I looked over my shoulder to catch him doing a little ballet step as he went back to his desk.

I took a chance on going to *Newsweek* to get some additional publicity. One of the editors took a fancy to *Neurotica*. I left him a copy after I told him about my background, which I thought would make a good story. A few weeks later, I was surprised to see a picture of *Neurotica*'s first issue in color and a write-up about the "Antique dealer turned publisher."

I declared a moratorium on playtime. All my energies were concentrated on the magazine; what little was left over was spent in the galleries. Cutie noticed the change. The playful scrimmages that were such a basic part of our relationship no longer interested me. I did my job at the galleries in such a perfunctory way, Cutie became suspicious. She never interfered in any of our personal lives, she always said, but kept a sharp eye out for any signs that things weren't going smoothly between her sons and daughters-in-law.

"You're spending too much time with your crazy magazine," she said when I began to show up late for work. "Are you having trouble at home?"

Cutie was right. My interest in Pat had diminished since the trip to New York. I was too full of enthusiasm to take Pat's warnings about Legman seriously, and her negativism had begun to annoy me.

"You wait and see, he'll be taking over the magazine before long," she warned.

Rubenstein agreed with her, protesting loudly that poetry was the basis of his interest in the magazine; my wanting to cut down on it didn't sit well with him, causing a rift between us.

To fill his place, I recruited a most unlikely assistant to help me handle the pile of poetry that was arriving daily, horrible examples of the armpit school. Since the job didn't pay anything, the title, Contributing Editor, was his compensation. Louis Triefenbach steadfastly refused to come to terms with the twentieth century. He adopted a style of dress and a set of values that came right out of Huysman's *Against The Grain*.

Huysman's description of a nineteenth century neurotic fitted him to perfection:

Physically ill, and feeble; morally arrogant; intellectually superior. Anthroped toward love and friendship; completely inadaptable so that every contact with the world and me caused him pain. Atavistic; in a constant state of irritation; an anti-social philistine, suffering from a mania for contradiction and unfit for the labors of common life.

On top of this list of attributes, he collected English blue and white china, smoked Turkish cigarettes, and was never seen in public without his yellow suede gloves. He wore wing-tipped two-toned shoes, a tattersall waistcoat, and a scarf, even in the summer. He lived with his mother and two immaculately-groomed afghan hounds. Certainly, he had all the qualifications for a poetry editor. I knew he was the kind of editor who could write a rejection slip that would either drive the poet to suicide or encourage him to take up a new trade, possibly plumbing.

Unfortunately, he took his job seriously. Instead of the ruthless, neurotic editor, he turned out to have a terrible flaw: he couldn't say no. Every minute away from his academic pursuits was spent in corresponding with the contributors, encouraging them with detailed analysis of their work in his efforts to bring it up to *Neurotica's* standards. Laudable as that might be, there was another flaw he developed on the job: he encouraged the more interesting cases of male poetic impotency to send him a photograph and a description of their physical attributes with future submissions, adding, "If you want your work taken seriously."

I warned him that such tactics might be misunderstood, to put it mildly, but to no avail. He began to use his home address for all future correspondence. In all fairness to Professor Triefenbach— he was an English teacher at Washington University—he did manage to get some very good verse that fitted in with the new image of the magazine. I lived in terror that Legman was going to hear about his highly-personalised style of editing and turn him in to the Post Office censors for soliciting through the mails.

In the autumn of 1949, *Neurotica* surprised all its subscribers by coming out on time in a new, improved format, that clearly showed Legman's influence. The whole issue was sixty four pages; his contribution took up thirty two of them, but it was dynamite: *The Psychopathology of the Comics* gave a tone to the magazine that was not only contemporary, but investigative journalism at its very best, something that was to be a model for the kind of reporting that became popular years later. Lawrence Durrell, Kenneth

Patchen, and Judith Malina of the newly-formed Living Theatre contributed pieces that faithfully recorded the crisis of the individual against a conforming society. Holmes wrote a very wry piece: *All The Good Roles Have Been Taken—The Plight of the Talented Untalented,* that provided a psychoanalytical hand-book to "making it in intellectual and literary life in New York." *Neurotica* now reflected the psychological implications of popular culture and its effect on the mainstream life of the community. It was an issue to be proud of, and evidently other people thought so too. Support came from the most unexpected places.

Russell Lynes, an editor of *Harpers Magazine,* stratified the American cultural scene into three classifications: Highbrow, Lowbrow and Middlebrow. I nearly fell over when I saw in *Life* that he included *Neurotica* in the Highbrow classification. I called Legman's attention to the accolade and congratulated him on a stunning debut. He wrote back that Lynes was typical of the kind of person that was out to "get us." "By giving the intellectuals the whip hand, they have taken the onus off the real villains—the rich who really rule the country—and given the public the intellectuals to hate." He concluded with a scathing indictment of both *Time* and *Life.* He mentioned that he was working with a new writer named Marshall McLuhan, who was preparing a piece that would "destroy the Luce empire." I thought he was being his usual, vindictive self. I had never heard of McLuhan—his name sounded like something from outer space, but so was Legman, I concluded.

5

There was no winter issue of *Neurotica*. Subscribers wrote indignant letters, my new distributor in New York was getting anxious, and Legman was furious.

"I'm all set to go. What's holding you up? Getting scared?" I didn't dare tell him the truth. When I returned from New York, the swift transition from antique dealer to literary contender created major problems. The antique business suddenly seemed so meaningless that I could hardly bring myself to show up everyday. The excitement of publishing America's first lay-psychiatric magazine was an enormous challenge, requiring full-time participation. The flow of manuscripts, the correspondence with writers, the planning of future issues, and Legman's editorial orthodoxy, were so all-consuming I had little energy left over for the mundane business of living.

My relationship with Pat deteriorated rapidly until one day I could no longer make it sexually with her. Although she was understanding, it only made it worse. My guilt was overwhelming. In a desperate attempt to overcome the temporary impotence, I charged into promiscuity. Where once an affair had a beneficial effect on my sex-life with Pat, it now destroyed it completely.

I thought of going into analysis, but how could it be that the editor of *Neurotica* needed the couch? It seemed like fouling my own nest. Legman would have probably declared me incompetent and perverted. And what would happen if I got the wrong psychiatrist? What if he hated

Neurotica and demanded that I get out of the business? I talked the problem over with Rubenstein, who knew all the psychiatrists in town. He preferred the European doctor who had his office in his home, where the rich aroma of Viennese cooking permeated the house, and an autographed picture of Freud enhanced the desk.

"Unfortunately, there aren't any of those left," he told me, "but my doctor is a very easy-going guy. He lets me do anything I want." It sounded promising; I decided to trust him.

At the first appointment, I couldn't resist throwing a copy of *Neurotica* on his desk: "Now that's my problem, Doctor." I pointed to the magazine. I knew I had picked the right man when he laughed and said,

"Yes, I understand. I've read the first two issues."

I went into therapy as though I was applying for an important job that I could only land if I was interesting to the interviewer. I sketched out my early life with enough amusing material about my relationship with Cutie to interest him. I was a little hurt when I didn't get my laughs from my paid audience of one. He did smile when I told him Cutie's graduation present to me was a jar of Mum deodorant. By the fifth session, I realised that something drastic was needed to keep his attention. I managed to interest him in my promiscuous behavior pattern.

"I see myself as some kind of charitable society, giving relief to the sexually needy. There are so many out there." I spent a whole session explaining how I operated as a lay therapist.

"I make the sexually deprived victim face up to the situation and do something about changing it. It's a cruel kind of therapy, but I demand that they rise up out of their bourgeois innocence, *get with it,* or die." I was constantly dwelling on my sexual success when I was in therapy to cure my impotency.

"What is it you want to do?" he asked.

I told him I wanted to get out of St. Louis. It was not a

flippant remark, I had been thinking about ways of escape ever since I returned from New York.

"I know, but what do you really want to do?" he repeated. Then it hit me what he was driving at.

"All right. I want to get out of my marriage."

When he said, "I think that can be arranged," I nearly emptied the Kleenex box. Through my tears I told him how much the family meant to me; how I loved Fred and Paula and Cutie.

"What would they do without me?" I asked. I told him how much *Neurotica* meant to me. "I have a chance to be something other than an antique dealer." I rushed on almost hysterically about meeting the new man in my life, Legman. "New York is my destiny," might have sounded a little dramatic, but it was the truth.

He thought my getting out of St. Louis was a good idea, the sooner the better. Talk about a permissive doctor; he was positively Machiavellian as he encouraged me to run out on my family and marriage. In a few more sessions, he urged me to be more honest with Pat about how I felt.

"You're a big boy now; act like one." He sounded exactly like Cutie. It was to her that I first broke the news.

"I want to move to New York. I think I can make something of my life there." She dismissed it as another of my silly whims, like taking a holiday at the height of the business season.

"Go to New York," she warned me. "You'll spend a lot of money and you won't have a good time."

Breaking the news to Pat required a little more subtlety. Instead of coming right out with it as the doctor prescribed, I encouraged her to be more independent, to find new friends.

"Have an affair," I jokingly suggested. "It might be fun." At first she was hurt, but let me know she had got the message. She would think about it. I made sure that she knew about my affairs by leaving little clues around the place. Although she was hurt, she put on a brave act in her attempt to be independent. She traded in her afghan for a cocker spaniel whose eyes were sadder than her own. She visited her mother more often. She went to modern dance classes, occasionally bringing home a friend to flirt with, to show me she was following orders. Her meals became infrequent and careless. Once, at a dinner party, she made a particularly unpleasant stew. When I complained, she said contemptuously:

"I put my heart into that stew." I told her it would have been more appetizing if she'd put some meat into it instead. When she began to write poetry and read it to me, I considered she was getting hostile, yet I encouraged her to continue with her attempts at self-expression. I was looking for an excuse to discuss my divorce plans.

I didn't have to wait long. Into her life came a walking, romantic cliché. There was an advertising campaign for Tabu perfume that featured a picture of a passionate violinist sweeping a beautiful girl into his arms in the middle of a sonata, unable to resist the essence of her Tabu. His real name was Morris, but as the romance heated up, we called him 'Tabu'. He was, like the model in the ad, a violinist, a very good one, playing regularly with the St. Louis symphony orchestra. They met at Little Bohemia, where he moonlighted in full gypsy regalia, strolling from table to table with his haunting melodies. Pat was attracted to his musical charms as well as his physical ones, and the two of them became inseperable.

It was a daring thing in 1949 to get a divorce, especially on career grounds, but the time was rapidly approaching to get it over with. She had someone who would give her the support she needed to face the situation. It was time to consult a lawyer. I wanted it to be a friendly divorce; the only thing we couldn't decide on were the grounds. What judge would accept *Neurotica* as a co-respondent? Neither of us liked adultery as a charge. The lawyer went through all the possible alternatives.

"Did Jay ever make you do things that were morally repugnant? Did he ever strike you? Did he sulk? Was he unreasonable? Ungenerous? Cross and irritable?" After going through the whole list of possibilities, he threw up his hands, "Why are you two getting a divorce? You sound like you have a perfect marriage."

Pat mentioned, as a joke, that she always had the feeling that sleeping in the Cardinal Richelieu bed was harrowing.

"Every time we made love, I thought the dwarfs holding up the canopy would fall and crush us during a climax." The lawyer and I looked at each other in a moment of mutual understanding.

"I can see the headlines in the papers: ANTIQUE DEALER FORCES WIFE TO SLEEP IN UNSAFE BED." The lawyer said he could put that complaint into legal language so horrific "you'd probably get five years in jail along with your divorce." Pat and I began to giggle.

"Why not," she said, "it's as good a reason as any."

I could hear Cutie saying, "I told you that bed was a bad buy."

There was a moment right before we were to appear in court that Pat got cold feet.

"I feel badly about letting you down, Jay." She was crying. "If only I'd had the baby, this wouldn't be happening now." I took her in my arms and tried to convince her it wasn't her fault.

"You're a beautiful girl with your whole life in front of you; you'll flourish without me."

"I still love you, Jay."

I reassured her that I still loved her. "Bad timing," I said.

"Take me with you. I'll help you. Legman is the cause of all this, isn't he? If you hadn't met him, we'd still be together. I hate him. You'd better find yourself a good psychiatrist in New York because you're going to need one by the time he's finished with you." I didn't bother to answer as it seemed so unlikely at the time.

After the divorce, I took Pat out to dinner. We tried to keep it light, but by the time the dessert came, she was in tears again.

"At least the divorce made the wire services," I said.

"It's not much to show for four years of marriage," she replied.

"Come on back to the place," I said, "and we'll have a real farewell."

It was the best fuck we ever had—even the dwarfs smiled down on us.

I wrote Holmes of my plans to move to New York. He wrote back that he had been seeing a lot of Legman. "Lung was on the menu the night I ate there. Uggh! He's running wild with projects I'm sure you'll want to avoid." When I wrote to Legman informing him of my plans, the tone of his letter was the first of many surprises. "Don't come to New York" was not exactly the kind of reaction I was looking forward to from the man for whom I had completely changed my life. Maybe Pat was right. When Cutie didn't do anything to stop me from going to New York, I took it as a bad sign.

In the spring of 1949, I was sleeping on a couch in my sister's home in outer suburbia: Stamford, Connecticut. It proved to be the perfect half-way house for my New York debut, providing me with the security of friendly faces to face the anonymity of the big town. I was nervous about my debut. On the first trip to Legman's lair, there was still the pungent odor of lung and cat shit that together with Legman's coolness didn't spell 'welcome home'. Legman made that clear to me with his opening greeting.

"If you think you've come to New York to play editor, forget it, Landesman. This is no laughing matter," he assured me in so many short pungent words, accompanied with a menacing forefinger with which I was to become so familiar.

"I never had any toys as a kid, and I don't see *Neurotica* as a toy, like you do. We've got a big job to do. They'll be watching us."

I couldn't imagine who he was talking about until I remembered the words he quoted from his favorite poet, Robert Burns:

Here, Land O'cakes and brither Scots,
Frae Maidenkirk to John O'Groats;
If there's a hole in your coats,
I rede you tent it;
A chiel's amang you, taking notes,
And, faith, he'll prent it.

I didn't understand its significance at the time, but it was
clear to me that he considered himself a Goliath in a den of
thieves and perverts. He had all the facts, and faith, he'd
print them. Just why he treated me as if I were one of the
enemy was a mystery. Was it my habit of giving a little
nervous laugh at those rude remarks and personal attacks
that infuriated him? Did he really think I had changed my
life on a whim? More likely he was jealous that *Neurotica*
was my baby and not his. Whatever motive Legman had in
constantly deprecating me, it didn't affect my enthusiasm
for the forthcoming battle. I was willing to be persecuted
as long as I felt there was a chance of winning and that I
could play a part in the victory.

The first thing that Legman did was to put me in touch
with every sexual conspiracy from Madison Avenue to
Bleeker Street. His years spent in running battles with the
sexual underground made him an expert in chronicling
the darker side of America's sexuality. "Man has become
extinct," he wrote in *Love and Death*. Walking down the
streets of New York, he pointed out that every building,
edifice, statue, sign, or garbage can was a phallic symbol—a
cenotaph to man's sexual demise.

"One slip, Landesman, and you'll be sucked in with the
rest of the victims," was his repeated warning. He reminded me of Captain Queeg in the *Caine Mutiny* who had
incontrovertible evidence that the forces of evil were con-
spiring against him. Legman had the kind of evidence that
would stand up in any court of human justice. Ironically,
his appearance in such a court would never take place—he
had no respect for institutionalized justice.

After working with Legman for a month, I could honestly say that he didn't have a good word for anyone. If the purpose of all this venom was to intimidate me, he was mistaken. He needed me to keep him from becoming a literary Gatling gun, spraying his paranoia indiscriminately in all directions, including the pages of *Neurotica*. If he was going to be difficult, so was I. Our editorial battles about which way *Neurotica* should go provided the fuel that kept us both on our toes.

Legman was Clark Kent and I was the poor man's Daddy Warbuck's. The editorial gesture planned for Neurotica 5 spelled out the problems we were wrestling with.

We define neurosis as the defensive activities of normal individuals against abnormal environments. We assume that human beings are born non-neurotic, and are neuroticized later. We do not agree that it is the measure of social intelligence and psychiatric health to adapt to and rationalize every evil. We do not subscribe to the psychosomatic fashion of throwing the gun on the corpse and the blame on the victim. We give space to the description of the neuroses with which human beings defend themselves from an intolerable reality. But it is with this reality that we are primarily concerned.

NEUROTICA is the first lay-psychiatric magazine. It is our purpose to implement the realization on the part of people that they live in a neurotic culture and that it is making neurotics out of them. The practitioners have their own journals. *NEUROTICA* is for the patients—present and future.

As we see it, the little literary magazine is dead. The "little mags that died to make verse free" have been replaced by subsidized vehicles for clique poetry, critical back-scratching, and professional piddle, served up with a certain transparent overlay of regional or radical futilitarianism. Having embraced the preciosity and academicism that the little mag was raised up to fight, the current types find themselves wholly without purpose and practically without audience.

The rich, living benefits of a definite audience and a definite purpose are reserved at present for the technical journals on the one hand, and the jungle of propaganda slicks and perverted pulps on the other. *NEUROTICA* would like to bridge the gap with a popular approach to a technical subject. The reader will be required to rise to the material. It will not be watered down. It will not be digested, expurgated, vulgarized, and suited to the hypothetical lowest possible mentalities that are not interested in it in the first place.

We want to describe a neurotic society from inside. It is difficult and we need help. We believe that the psychiatric perspective can best describe and most clearly interpret the impact of human society on the human individual. We wish to popularize and perhaps implement that perspective. The psychiatrist encourages the patient to speak. In *NEUROTICA* the culture will speak—and be analyzed.

After a working day with Legman, I dreaded the idea of taking a commuter's train back to Stamford and domesticity, so I would usually call up Holmes and see if anything was happening. He had changed considerably since I first met him; he looked more like the character in his story, *Tea for Two,* which won him the O. Henry Prize for the best short story of the year. He had been seeing Kerouac, Ginsberg, and Solomon and shared with me the gossip of their peculiar view of life, literature, music, and the secrets of the Benzedrine inhaler. They were all writing up their daily life on the streets of New York that involved entanglements with petty crooks, hipsters, and sexual partners. It was certainly different from anything I was familiar with, yet I was willing to learn more about it.

Holmes' pad was like Grand Central Station with characters dropping in at all hours of the day and night. On one of my visits, I found Kerouac sleeping on the floor and Holmes and his wife wondering what to do with the body.

"Let's go out and get a drink." I suggested. At the mention of the word "drink," Kerouac came to life. He had to meet someone in Times Square and asked us to join him. When we got there, he was like a kid in a circus, pointing out all the freaks hanging around the Pokorino hot dog stand, only he didn't see them as freaks.

"Dig how those cats operate," he pointed to a couple of

hipsters holding up a wall, "aren't they cool?" They looked like the usual transient trade hanging around Times Square but Kerouac gave them a special identity. His enthusiasm grew as we went from bar to bar where everybody took on special "angelic" qualities in his eyes. Holmes was able to keep up with his level of descriptive powers better than I. Soon tiring of it all, I slipped away to Grand Central to catch the late train back to Stamford.

Holmes introduced me to the Village bars, where I immediately felt at home. His sociological analysis of their patrons was helpful: the San Remo was for writers and talkers and girls who liked writers and talkers, artists at the Cedars, heavy drinkers at the White Horse, old Village characters at the Minetta Tavern. I had published an article, *The Unique Mores of The Bar and Tavern Social Milieu,* in *Neurotica* that claimed "bar life's popularity was based on the need for sexual adventure." I had no doubts that it held true in New York as it did in St. Louis.

Working with Legman should have drained me of any desire for any sexual encounters, and nearly would have if I hadn't met Bunny. She was appealing in a show business way: big dark eyes, a full set of dimples, and her heavy make-up gave her that Kewpie doll look I found cheap but attractive. She was the prize I was never able to win at the carnival. She was at the piano playing and singing some of her own songs from a little revue that just closed in the Village. Her deep-throated jazzy voice and clever lyrics "you only live once . . . or twice"—raised my flagging spirits; it was fun to be with people who were not analyzing the hell out of life.

Bunny and I were attracted to each other from the beginning. We hadn't exchanged more than a half dozen sentences when I asked her to accompany me to a more tranquil atmosphere, the Hotel Edison on Broadway. I didn't even have to promise I'd make her a star—she was the kind of girl whose life was one big audition. The Hotel Edison was hardly the place for a serious performance.

I began to look around New York for a more permanent

address. I found it on 53rd St. between the Museum of Modern Art and Birdland. Its main attraction was a neon sign advertising the Grecian Garden restaurant downstairs. Hanging just outside my window, its eerie light blinked on and off in the large, high-ceilinged living room which was almost the whole apartment. The toilet, shower, and kitchen made up the other room, with a spare space on the other side that would do nicely for storage. Bickford's coffee shop on the corner for breakfast, The Stage delicatessen for pastrami at high noon, and the Grecian Garden below for a late night kebab. My neighbors in the brownstone were the Puerto Rican superintendant and his very *West Side Story* wife, and an old man who lived in a broom closet whom I never saw dressed in anything but pee-stained underwear.

I was snug and content in my new environment, feeling for the first time a sense of belonging to Manhattan. When I walked out of my door onto the street I exchanged "hellos" with a half a dozen people before I hit the subway on the corner. The newspaper man even carried copies of my magazine, giving it a prominent place; I still got a thrill when I saw it displayed in shops and newstands. It was like seeing a piece of me everywhere I travelled.

I had my own version of Village life in midtown Manhattan. Directly across the street was a daily concert by Moondog, the blind bongo musician, dressed in old army blankets that gave him that monkish look. No one could pass him by without stopping to hear his weird and wonderful sounds and throw a few coins in his plate. I got to know him over pastrami sandwiches at my place. He turned out to be serious about his music; his bongos were his only possessions and he had no permanent address, preferring to live in the streets, sleeping in doorways at nights. All the jazz musicians on 52nd Street knew him from his nightly rounds outside their clubs; often Moondog would be invited inside to jam with them after their last set. Years later, Columbia released an album of his original compositions when he gave a concert at Carnegie

Hall. I often wondered if he ever missed the street life after his recognition.

I had my own cinema in the basement of the Museum of Modern Art, a convenient place to study the early films of the Weimar Republic and pick up girls. Erich von Stroheim represented the height of decadence and I would have worn a monocle if I could have gotten away with it, but all I had to show was the original recording of Lotte Lenya's *Drei Goschen Opera,* and a well worn copy of *The Third Man Theme.*

Birdland was right around the corner. Moe Levy who owned it at the time was a friend of a cousin of mine and he gave me a free pass. I used the place like my local club, always dropping in to see what was happening late at night. On one occasion I was there with Holmes and Kerouac enjoying a nite-cap, listening to Lester Young. Kerouac was too enthusiastic when listening to jazz; his finger snapping, head bopping, loud scat singing was too much for the sedate, cool afficionados of the new music. After several warnings to cool it, Pee Wee Marquatte, the black, midget maitre d' tore up my pass the next time I tried to get into the place.

The Stage Delicatessen was my favorite place to learn New Yorkese. The waiters and counter men spoke a strange type of language, half English, half Pastrami. They were masters of the friendly insult; if you were the target, it was a compliment. For a while, they thought I was Jerry Lewis and treated me with great respect. I had a bad habit of passing myself off as various celebrities. I did this once with a friend of Legman's, who was a literary groupie. I was passing myself off as the Southern novelist, Speed Lamkin, just because I liked the name Speed. When it got back to a curious Legman, he screamed,

"Did you have to assume the identity of a fag?" I heard later that Mr. Lamkin felt I was "cashing in" on his reputation and was more annoyed than Legman.

I don't remember who introduced me to Anatole

Broyard in the San Remo bar, but it was the beginning of my education in Greenwich Village life. Broyard seemed to know everybody who was 'superiorly aware', his definition of a hipster. He was already a legend by the time I met him. What a busy man! He taught a class at the New School that was very popular, he contributed articles to *Partisan Review* and *Commentary,* he took a fatherly interest in *Neurotica.* He was in analysis. His job as tutor to a millionaire businessman who wanted to write poetry left him little time to finish the novel he'd been writing for years.

A crowded social life included his obsession with the Mambo, a form of dancing that was popular among the Puerto Ricans. Every Thursday we would go with an entourage of new converts to the Palladium Ballroom, the home of this exotic dance, to study the natives in their natural habitat. It was very convenient for me—the Palladium was right around the corner from my new apartment. But more than convenient, it was a safari into unchartered territory that only Broyard and the natives understood. He was our guide, a teacher explaining to the assembled explorers the significance of the Mambo as a cultural phenomenon, an endangered species, corrupted by America.

"White dancers have appropriated the sexual energy of the Mambo and turned it into a ritualized, mechanical version of their own Anglo-Saxon attitudes." He pointed out to us how the American girls lifted their skirts, shook their breasts, wriggled on the floor while their white partners passed in convulsive movements above them. When the couple we were watching collided in this routine, there was a burst of spontaneous applause, proving Broyard's point.

"The Mambo is a sublimated image, a choreographic expression of sex. The Americans have turned it into a contest of pornography." Freud couldn't have put it any better.

"That's Cuban Pete; he used to be the best dancer here.

Now look at him!" Pete's partner was on the floor with a piece of Kleenex in her mouth. He was dancing over her, doing push-ups, and attempting to remove the Kleenex with his teeth.

"The American Kleenex has replaced the native hand-kerchief—a transference from the genital to the oral, and in Pete's mind, American sex is oral, requiring the use of Kleenex after the act."

Once I got over the psychological hazards connected with the Mambo, I was able to enjoy performing it in the approved Broyard fashion. He seldom joined us on the dance floor, but observed me from his table. Upon my return, he would give me helpful hints on Mambo etiquette. I lived in terror that my exuberance might be mistaken for cultural vulturing, but Broyard gave me a clean bill of health. I knew Legman would approve of Broyard's theories of American sexual imperialism as expressed in the Mambo, and suggested to Broyard that he write an article on it for *Neurotica*.

"It's an important area to explore. Just the kind of thing I'm looking for." Broyard agreed it was a significant contribution to understanding what was happening right under our feet. He promised to put something on paper as soon as he had some time. A few weeks later his article arrived, simply titled, MAMBO. The title was the only thing simple about the piece. I had no idea that the mambo was 'the Dance of Life's last step in the transition from instinct to alienation.' Broyard had a way of expressing himself in a formal manner that some people thought pretentious and over-analytical . . . but I was impressed.

Of all the writers that Broyard introduced me to, Chandler Brossard was the most interesting. Like Legman, he didn't have a good word for anyone, particularly other writers: "A moist crowd of humanity; reading them makes me feel as though I'm hacking my way through a luxuriant growth of mediocrity," was one of his kinder opinions on the state of literature in America. But what I liked about him was his healthy contempt for any of his fellow writers. Having turned his back on success that included being an editor at *Time* at 19, a Talk of the Town contributor at *The New Yorker* at 21, he was struggling to find his own voice in his current "work in progress."

"It took me years to get rid of *The New Yorker*'s dank influence. I mean, those people would have urged Ariel to get a pilot's license." He was writing his novel on the front seat of an abandoned car in front of his house; his domestic life was in turmoil, contributing to his jaundiced view of women and other obstacles to life. Why this extremely handsome and talented man was setting himself up as the bad boy of literature was a mystery to me. His refusal to participate in the literary and intellectual life reminded me of Legman. They were both aware of life's absurdities, but seemed to be victims of them, instead of victors.

In addition to all his other unsympathetic views of the current cultural scene, he hated the emerging Hipster. In fact, his novel was about the fallacy of Hipsterism.

"They measure their cool by the length of time they refuse to say anything to each other. I was at a party when they were so cool one froze to death in his silence and the other two turned to stone rather than risk a gesture."

I brought Brossard and Broyard to Legman's place on separate occasions. It was a disaster both times. Brossard was willing to listen, but concluded that he didn't need all the information that Legman poured out. He warned me to stay away from obsessive people like Legman. "They're too romantic," he concluded.

I had even worse luck with Broyard. I explained to Legman that Broyard and Brossard were going to write for *Neurotica* the kind of material our editorial policy demanded. "Not if I can help it they won't." It was his typical reaction to anyone who dared to invade his territory. Legman was locked in his own dogma which left little room for him to maneuver. But I knew I needed Broyard and Brossard to counteract his heavy-handed style and to give a semblance of sanity to the magazine. I knew if I got too dependent on Legman, the magazine would degenerate into a personal vendetta. It was the beginning of a serious rift, and I had been in New York less than two months.

Then out of the blue, I got a call from Beka Dougherty, my friend in *Time* magazine who had introduced me to Legman. Before she told me what the call was about, I had to get some of the problems Legman presented off my chest.

"That man is ruining my life, Beka." She laughed.

"But look what he's done for *Neurotica*. Are you seated?" She paused. "What I am going to tell you is highly confidential. The Boss is interested in buying *Neurotica*. "The idea that Henry Luce, founder and publisher of *Time*, *Life*, and *Fortune* was interested in acquiring my baby was too much to take in over the phone.

"You're kidding." I accused her of toying with my nerves.

"I kid you not," she flatly answered. "Henry has been thinking of starting a mass market psychology magazine for years. You can expect a call from Noel Busch any day. He'll be representing Luce. You know Busch don't you?" I had read his essays in *Life* for years and knew he had a brother, Niven, who wrote bestselling novels.

"Did you play any part in this, Beka?" Her answer was ambiguous.

"Let's just say I talked about *Neurotica* in the right ears. Didn't I tell you Legman was just right for you?" I didn't want to put down all that Legman had done to make *Neurotica* successful.

"There's no doubt he's the most remarkable writer on the American scene, but, my God, is he difficult to work with." I could see her smiling as she answered.

"Try having a love affair with him sometime. He's the most wonderful lover in the world." So there's the connection, I thought.

"Well, Beka, I divorced my wife, left my family, gave up my business, moved to New York, and if you don't call that a love affair, then what is it?" She laughed long and loud.

"Only the beginning," she warned me. "That man is devastating."

Her revelations didn't throw me into confusion—panic would be a better word. After it subsided, I decided the best course of action was to put a total blackout on the news to Legman. I had already discarded the idea of telling Cutie. I knew what she would say: "Never turn down money." What Legman would say staggered the imagination.

6

I didn't hold my breath waiting for that call from Busch. I suspected it was too good to be true. Legman and I were working together daily on the No. 5 issue and having big problems; the crunch came when Marshall McLuhan sent in his long awaited *The Psychopathology of Time and Life.*

In his first paragraph, McLuhan hinted at Luce's interest in starting a fourth magazine: ". . . aimed to be a monthly for the literary gourmet, the intellectually indulgent, the well read, the erudite, who sometimes preferred to smile superciliously than laugh outright." Did he know about Luce's interest in *Neurotica?* I certainly wasn't going to print it if there was a chance that Luce was serious about buying my mag. The article was a devastating attack that I would have published with unsuppressed joy under ordinary circumstances. But these were delicate negotiating times and I couldn't afford to take the chance. Legman became suspicious the moment I mentioned that maybe we ought to save it for a future issue, accusing me of "nervous Nellie" tactics. I had to tell him about Beka's call. He laughed, dismissing it as "wishful thinking on Luce's part."

Meantime, the issue was shaping up to be the strongest one we had ever put together. There was the theme of censorship and obscenity by Allen Walker Reed, the eminent professor of English at Columbia University and the editor of *American Speech.* He was also the author of *Lexical Evidence from Folk Epigraphy in Western North America: A Glossarial Study of the Low Element in the English Vocabulary.*

(Paris 1935). That was the kind of book that Legman had respect for. Professor Reed ended his article on a wry note that appealed to me: "Being normal in the world today consists in having the neuroses that most other people have. A saner, more realistic adjustment is worth trying for."

Instead of the third installment of *Love and Death*, Legman wanted to publish his works sheets on the chapter, *Avatars Of The Bitch*. These notes consisted of a breakdown of the themes of Ben Ames William's best seller, *The Strange Woman*. There were three columns: SADISM, SADISM AND SEX, and SEX. The first column was completely filled with examples of sadism. The Sadism and Sex column was seventy five per cent filled, while the third column Sex, was practically empty. It was certainly a masterpiece of anatomical research, proving Legman's theory that an author can get away with being as sadistic as he wants, but when it comes to describing the sexual act, forget it!

Our big argument was over some extraordinary letters written in reply to two ads in the classified section of *Neurotica*, while I was still in St. Louis. This was a feature I put in as a parody of *The Saturday Review of Literature*'s thinly disguised personal column for sexual contacts, the main reason that many people bought the magazine. *Neurotica*'s resident fetishist, John Goldston, wrote for *Neurotica*, *The World of the Borderline Fetishist* as well as the many fictitious ads that livened up the column. The letters were in answer to the two ads that read:

Youngster, California, seeks correspondence with domineering mature female. Box 119.

and

Strapping woman interested in works of Marquis de Sade would meet young man interested in Sacher-Masoch. State height and weight. Box 125.

Originally, I thought they were more of the Fetishist's wit and hunger for correspondence. Goldston denied he had written either one of them. I couldn't imagine how they got in the column. I opened a few of the letters and thought they were harmless answers from lonely subscribers, but as they continued to come into the office, they became quite specific in their attempts to interest the advertisers. In fact, I was overwhelmed with the intensity of their fantasy life.

I decided that Legman should have a look at them. Instead of being grateful, he turned on me with a fury I had never seen before. *He accused me of tampering with the US mails.* "A federal offense, Landesman, that you could get up to five years for. Send the letters forthwith," he telegraphed. I supposed he would drop the charges if I immediately complied. Of course, I sent the letters, but that wasn't the end of it. It turned out that the "strapping young woman" ad was written by him to counteract "the perverse California youngster" ad. Now, months later, I had the feeling that he was going to publish all the letters in *Neurotica 5* and I was right. He told me they were important documents of the extent of perversion among my subscribers and that "they must be exposed." Not only would it get me in trouble with the post office censors, Luce would probably have a fit as well. I was still counting on Busch to call to start negotiations. He did so in the nick of time.

"Could we get together and talk," he began. "I'm very much interested in meeting G. Legman." Would I set it up? There was no talk about buying the magazine or Luce. I assumed he was being cagey.

"I admire Legman's style," he added.

"You don't want to meet Legman," I explained. "He's a difficult character with a slight case of paranoia, and he's overprotective when it comes to *Neurotica*." With my experience of bringing Broyard and Brossard to meet him still fresh in my mind, I was sure introducing Busch would be fatal.

"I think I can handle it," he assured me. We agreed to meet at my place and ride up together to Legman's. How to break the news to Legman? Talking in terms of a take-over would get me nowhere; he'd starve to death and take his wife and cats along with him before he sold out. According to Legman, the real purpose of *Neurotica* was to influence the people who influenced public opinion. I decided my best ploy would be to persuade him that he had indeed converted Luce, the most powerful man in the media, to its message. Instead of Luce the enemy, why not Luce the Angel?

Legman turned pale as I told him Busch wanted to open negotiations; silently brooding over my "treachery," I could see his temperature rising. His fingers began to smooth the stray hairs of his walrus moustache. His mouth was in a locked position, like a dog with rabies.

"All right," Legman announced, "I'll meet Busch. Why not? Let's listen to what he says, but let me tell you, Land-esman," I braced myself for the attack. "It makes a lot of sense for Luce to have a mouthpiece like *Neurotica*. After all, his philosophy has always been to stop the spread of knowledge, neutralize the dangerous revolutionary. Read the McLuhan article a little more carefully." His eyes lit up. "Our timing is perfect for printing the McLuhan piece."

"Let's hold up on McLuhan until we discuss the deal with Busch, O.K.?" Legman didn't reply. He didn't have to; it was the first time since we met that he was able to complete what, in human terms, would be regarded as a smile. It sent a shudder through me.

Busch wasn't dressed right for the meeting. His casual St. Moritz slacks, stylishly a little too short, and his Brooks Brothers shirt would get an immediate rise out of Legman, but his Spanish espadrilles, laced half way up his leg was asking for trouble. He was too handsome, too tall, too gentile, and too *Time-type* for Legman ever to accept.

When Legman welcomed him with an unusual display of cordiality, I wondered if I could have been wrong. I became suspicious when I didn't see any of his cats around the kitchen. Did he send them to a relative or a neighbor like parents send the children away when there is talk about divorce or a death in the family? Busch began by complimenting Legman on his comic book article—his first mistake. Legman was unconstitutionally equipped to handle a compliment.

"Never mind the bullshit, just what do you have in mind, and where do I fit in?" Busch crossed and uncrossed his legs, a gesture that did not go unnoticed by Legman. He was staring at his boots while Busch tried to tell him how much Luce liked a well-documented approach to a subject, like his comic book piece, adding that he personally thought Legman was a master at getting to the truth, "the essence," of a very complex subject.

"That is what is called for in a magazine that will ultimately appeal to millions of readers." Mistake number two.

"You mean you're good at watering down the impact of my research so that any idiot like a *Time* or *Life* reader can understand it?" Busch displayed a firmness that surprised even me.

"That isn't what I said, nor is it what I meant." He tried to explain it all again, in what he thought was a more acceptable way. No matter how he tried, anything he said was immediately suspect and challenged. Addressing Legman, I mentioned that Luce would give us the perfect opportunity to get our message across to millions of people.

"Perhaps *Neurotica* is too highbrow, too technical at the moment. Luce could be invaluable in making our tough medicine palatable. Luce is not our enemy. You're the enemy! Flogging the reader with so much evidence he's unable to respond to the plain truth."

Legman snarled, but kept quiet. Busch tried again.

"The potential of a magazine with the ideas of *Neurotica* combined with the appeal of a Luce product couldn't fail to attract." Mistake number three.

"A sort of neuterized *Neurotica* you might say. But why

do you have to pay us money for something like that?" I noticed Legman moving closer to Busch. I laughed in my nervous way, as I had been doing all evening.

"Come on, Legman," I said, "the man hasn't been born who can neuterize you." Legman smiled again.

"You betcha life there ain't." I saw the golden opportunity slipping away. Busch was getting irritated. His position was untenable. He wasn't used to humiliation high up in Manhattan, so why should he put up with it in the Bronx? We were at an impasse, broken by Legman's suggestion we all retire to another room. Legman sat in a darkened corner, while he made Busch sit in the glare of the only light in the room. Busch was exchanging looks with me that clearly said, who's magazine is it anyhow?

As he sat uncomfortably in his chair, Busch's boots were swinging in time to the piece of music that Legman had put on for background tension; it sounded like the ride of the Valkyries. Then Legman struck.

"My wife has a pair of boots similar to yours," he began. "Beverly, would you bring out those shoes you got in Mexico?" He began an explanation of homosexuality in the arts that ended up straining logic to the limit. His inference was that Busch, by his boots, was part of a hideous cultural conspiracy, and I had brought up to the Bronx yet another "fag" to torture him. When he got through with Busch, he started on his brother Niven, "the perverted bitch heroine writer who hates women." Not content with that, he pulled out from his rich fruit-cake of memory, an anti-feminist article Noel Busch had once written for *Life*. Busch got up and I wouldn't have minded if he'd hung one on Legman. Instead, he thanked Legman for the "interesting" discussion.

On the way home, Busch still felt that Legman was brilliant, but agreed with me that he was a problem. How did I feel about going ahead with a deal without Legman? Much as I wanted to, I told him that would be like producing Faust without the Devil. His answer made my blood curdle.

"We have ways of making a magazine work," he said, confidently.

I didn't have to call Legman the next day. He was on the phone bright and early.

"Hey, Landesman, let's have lunch. I want to talk to you." His voice was reasonable. I agreed to meet him at a delicatessen on Union Square, opposite the printer where all the material for the No. 5 issue was heading. I wanted to make sure he didn't slip in the McLuhan piece while there was still a chance we could work out a deal with Luce. I was prepared to dump Legman if necessary. (The night before I smiled myself to sleep with fantasies of sitting with Clare and Henry Luce on their veranda in Fairfield County, munching little cucumber sandwiches, drinking tea out of Chinese export cups, discussing forthcoming projects, or occasionally establishing eye contact with his attractive wife.)

"That was a pretty lousy way to treat a customer," was my line of attack.

"You're right!" That was as far as he would go in apologizing.

"If they make me an offer, I'll give it very serious consideration." Legman nodded, approvingly. We ordered two pastrami sandwiches and root beer. Legman was ravenously hungry as if he hadn't eaten in days.

"Would you like something else?" I asked him.

"Yeah, the same thing again." For the first time I realized that Legman might actually be starving up there in the Bronx. He couldn't have been eating too well on the amount of money *Neurotica* gave him. By ordering again, he had scored a big psychological point.

"You don't want to work with those people, Irving." It was the first time he ever called me by my real name. Was he trying to remind me that we were just a couple of Jewish boys in the fight against the *goyim?*

"They are the scum of the earth. They will crush us into little pieces before we even get around to working on the first issue." I tried to hold my ground.

"What's new? You've been trying to do that to me ever since the moment I met you." He looked at me with his little-boy-hurt expression.

"Landesman, please—no wise cracks. I'm your friend, not your enemy. You're too smart to fall for the line of horseshit that lackey Busch brought us. What slime! *Neurotica* is just beginning to have impact. The proof? What other magazine is there so universally hated by the Establishment? Landesman, stick with me and I'll make you memorable."

Legman hit a nerve. It was very clever of him not to come out with my real reason for wanting to work with Luce, but he suspected that it had something to do with wanting to be a success in Cutie's estimation.

"Your mother wouldn't want you associating with all those gentiles," was his idea of a good joke. I gave a little laugh.

"Come on, Landesman, let's be serious. With me you're going to end up a footnote in history. I promise you that. There's no chance you could working with *them*."

McLuhan's article contained a thousand reasons why, but the one I remembered was this one:

"... and should Mr. Luce venture into the last sphere of human spontaneity and free intelligence, he would inevitably feel urged to reduce the world to the kind of subhuman order he does understand. In a word, he would attempt to annihilate it for its own good."

In one of those quick, dramatic decisions that I was addicted to, I told Legman to go ahead and print the McLuhan piece. Legman was right: better to go down fighting than sink without a mention in the history books.

The waiter came up with the check.

"Are you a union waiter?" Legman asked.

"Sure thing, Toots," the waiter replied.

"Good, then you don't need this." Legman picked up the fifty cents I left as a tip, and pocketed it. By the doorway, I looked back at the waiter still scratching his bald head in amazement.

"Landesman, when are you going to learn how to act in New York? Don't you know that tipping is undignified?"

At the printers, Legman showed me the proofs of the No. 5 issue with the McLuhan article already there and the Answers To An Ad piece. That sneaky bastard, I thought, but I let it go; there was no turning back now. I was committed to this walking disaster.

I mailed the subscribers' copies in Connecticut. I was afraid that the New York post office people might become curious about the contents. When the Connecticut clerk showed some interest, my heart sank.

"Hello," he said, taking one of the copies out of the envelope, "What do we have here?" I tried to allay his suspicion.

"Oh, it's just a medical journal." He weighed one of them to see if it had the correct postage. "Nothing of interest to the layman," I added, laughing nervously. He leafed through the issue, nodding his head, and I could swear I saw him smile once or twice.

"Wait here a minute," he said as he left his post with the copy, "be right back." He was still smiling so I didn't think anything was wrong. I knew it was too late to do anything about it, like grabbing the rest of the mailing and running. The clerk came back still smiling.

"The inspector would like to have a look into this. Don't worry, it's routine."

The minute I got back to New York, I phoned Legman.

"The jig's up. They're holding the issue for investigation." Legman couldn't have been more pleased.

"Meet you down at the printers, we've got to get another batch out to subscribers. Once they start an investigation, it will be months before they get a ruling. This time we'll mail them at Penn Station Post Office. They're always too busy to look into junk mail." He sounded overjoyed.

I called up Holmes to help us with the operation. The three of us began stuffing envelopes again, finishing in time to cart them across town in one push cart filled to overcapacity. It was a hot day in July when we started out the long trek, made unbearable by Legman's running commentary on the rosy future that was in store for me if the post office censors really did ban the issue. The idea of being prosecuted gave Legman that extra lift in his step. "This is what we've been waiting for, Landesman."

Holmes and I were exhausted from the struggle to avoid being killed by the rush hour traffic. Finally, we had to sit down on the curb, with Legman joining us, protesting. As he sat there, with his testicles hanging out through the split in his crotch, he looked up at the Penn Station Post Office and in that sonorous voice reserved for special occasions, he began to read the motto chisled above the entrances:

"Neither snow nor rain nor heat nor gloom of night stays these couriers from the swift completion of their appointed rounds."

It was the final touch of irony. I turned to Legman.

"What in God's name am I doing squatting on this curb, you, with your balls hanging out, a jail sentence hanging over my head when I could have been with Clare and Henry sipping mint juleps, surrounded by beautiful people who smell good?" He didn't crack a smile.

"You'll thank me someday, Landesman, for making an honest man of you." He signaled to us to get on with the job.

Of course, Legman made sure that Busch got his copy of *Neurotica*. In a subsequent letter to me, Busch expressed his disappointment at having to read of my decision in the magazine.

I heard no more from Busch, but I did hear from the District Attorney for the State of Connecticut requesting an early appointment. My brother-in-law gave me his opinion that there was nothing in the issue that could be proved obscene in a Court of Law. The Attorney General thought otherwise, and acting on instructions from the

Post Office censors, held a preliminary hearing. My brother-in-law, acting on my behalf, presented my case admirably. Patiently explaining that *Neurotica* was a serious literary magazine with no offensive language, he demanded to know what all the fuss was about. They would not tell us what the Post Office objected to, which meant to us that they were bluffing.

"If they decide to take it any further and prosecute, it would be an expensive case to defend. If you should lose, it would mean more than a fine—possibly a jail sentence. But I don't think they will," he concluded.

I went back with the news to Legman.

"Listen kid, they got nothing on you. I could crack any case they presented wide open. Let them bring you to court. I'll destroy them. This could be the most important case since the *Ulysses* trial. A grateful America will shower you with thank you notes for cracking the censorship laws. Writers throughout the world will wire their congrats on your courage in taking on the United States government. You're in a great position, Landesman, and you have me to thank."

Filled with Legman's rhetoric, I went back to my lawyer to tell him that I was prepared to fight the case to the Supreme Court if necessary. Legman, during the next four weeks, convinced me that he had been preparing for this all his life. Considering what it was going to cost, my lawyer suggested I consult with the American Civil Liberties Union, whose job it was to defend free speech and the First Amendment. Legman warned me against it.

"They hate free speech, and if they defend you, you'll positively get convicted." Having been brought up on the ACLU's defense of free speech, I thought it was another case of Legman's paranoia.

When I went to see Mr. Ernst of the ACLU, he might have been more sympathetic.

"Courts can be expensive," he repeated my lawyer's phrase. After looking over a copy of the magazine, he left no doubt in my mind that he considered this matter to be one not worth getting involved in. I was shocked when he advised me to try to settle out of court. I was sorry I didn't bring Legman along with me to hear this famous defender of free speech.

Legman fell in love with the idea of fighting the case. He saw himself as David in a battle to the death with our giant opponent, the U.S. Postal Services. To show me his faith in the righteousness of the cause, he made some changes in the text of *Love and Death* that I was going to reprint as a book.

"You'll love it," he told me, but when he showed me the changes I was not amused. He laughed uproariously at his little joke, and was surprised that I didn't share it with him.

"Yeah, your use of the phrase 'prick and balls' is funny to me and you, but do you think the boys in the post office are going to laugh? Why give them more ammunition to direct against us while we're defending *Neurotica?* Your timing's wrong. Play it cool until we win."

Legman was in no mood for compromising at this stage. He felt he had the censors on the run with victory assured. I pleaded with him; then I tried bribery.

"*Love and Death* is just the first of your books to see the light of day. What about all the others? What chance do you think the cunnilingus book will have it we don't win this fight? What about your anthology of dirty jokes? Your limericks? I could publish them all if we win. We're a good team, but we've got a hard fight ahead of us. I'm backing you one hundred per cent. God knows what its going to cost me, but I believe in you and the cause, but let's win with *Neurotica* before we take on another fight."

It made sense to everyone but Legman. He was beginning to get that conspiracy look about him—his voice became almost inaudible in his attempt to contain his rage. It didn't take long for him to turn the whole affair into a personal attack.

"Landesman, you're a pimple on the moon of progress. I've met your castrating editors before. You'd still be playing at publishing if it weren't for me."

I couldn't understand how he could fight me on this so soon after I proved to him with the Luce rejection how deeply I was committed to him.

"It's me that has to face the music, not you. It's me that is threatened with a jail sentence if we lose, not you. It's going to cost me everything I have to fight this case, so why are you deliberately sabotaging our whole relationship?"

"I'm telling you Landesman, don't mess with me."

"Thanks for the warning." There was nothing more I could say to convince him he was wrong. I had to dump him; he was too crazy to work with anymore. Without him, I had no defense. I instructed my lawyer to make a deal. It cost me five hundred dollars to hire a new attorney who knew how to handle the problem—in short, a bribe. There was no further action, but the No. 5 issue was banned from the mails. All the dreams of cracking the censorship laws were over. Goliath had won yet again and little David was licking his pride in the Bronx. Knowing Legman, winning to him was not as beautiful as losing.

In the short time of my close association with him, I learned to distrust experts, do-gooders, power, the Establishment, my heroes, all liberal tendencies, celebrities, and success. I was going to need something very powerful to believe in if I were to survive.

7

Without Legman breathing down my neck, New York began to look like a better place. I realized I was actually enjoying myself. On one of my excursions, observing the people hurrying past me, someone tapped me on my shoulder. Ah, somebody's lonely and wants to talk! Turning around I was confronted by Mr. Peanut, a familiar figure around Times Square, dressed in an oversized peanut costume with a top hat, handing out samples of Planter's peanuts.

"It's me, Jay, don't you recognize me?" I looked in the window where his mouth should have been without recognizing the face or the muffled voice.

"It's Carl. Carl Solomon. Remember me?" I patted him on his shell around where his shoulder should have been.

"Nice one, Carl," I said, offering him a cigarette. The two of us stood there, conversing quite naturally with Mr. Peanut letting out a jerk of smoke occasionally.

"What about that piece you were going to do about your sojourn in the asylum? Have you had any luck in getting it down on paper?"

"Yeah, man," Solomon said, getting excited. "I'll do that. This is only temporary, you know. Good seeing you, Jay. I've got to move on now. I never know who they may have following me." Before he left, I wanted to give him a goodbye embrace, but feared someone might get the wrong idea.

"By the way, Carl, *Neurotica* is paying five dollars a page now." I saw his head bob up and down, and wondered how Mr. Peanut's top hat managed to stay on at such a jaunty angle. Solomon was certainly doing well since he had his lobotomy.

His friend, Ginsberg, must have heard about our meeting. The next time I saw him in Washington Square park, he asked me if I would like to look at his journals. I had heard from Holmes that he kept a meticulous account of everything he did since his circumcision.

"If you have a shorter version, I'll look at it." He seemed disappointed, but a few days later mailed me a little poem that I liked very much. It had a nice rhythm and rhyme and a play on words that was very interesting. He called it *Pull my Daisy*. I learned much later that he and Kerouac collaborated on the piece. When I told this to Legman, his only comment was, "did it take two of them to write that piece of shit?"

Sometimes after talking to the various writers around New York, I felt I was the only one left who wasn't writing a novel or keeping a journal of my day-to-day life. Somehow I didn't see the people as characters for a future work of art, which probably enabled me to relate to them as human beings. Brossard described this syndrome in a piece *Parties, Pathological and Otherwise* that he did for *Neurotica*. "Writers go to a party loaded down with all the paraphernalia of their trade . . . each disguise and costume fitting tightly over the other making them feel like a huge artichoke." I knew what he meant. That's exactly how I felt in New York that first six months, peeling leaves off myself as the various situations arose. With Legman, I revealed a stubborn streak by refusing to become a complete masochist. With Broyard, I exposed my willingness to make a fool of myself on the dance floor doing the Mambo. My sympathies for Brossard's colorful arrogance and support for his ideas that fiction should make that "wild leap into the abyss" gave him a picture of me as a fellow conspirator.

With Bunny, I exposed my addiction to B-Movie dialogue. I took her to corny places like Ed Winston's Village night club where you could dine and dance on a dime, do Bogart lines out of *Casablanca* and not feel you were out of place or time. I used to sit at the bar where she played cocktail piano and sang in that deep, boozy voice of hers, the lyrics of the great ballads that told you all the ways love could go wrong. Each lyric was a comment on our affair as it sadly drew to a close. Her show biz style didn't play well in the San Remo, the Bronx cottage, or my place. In her living room, she was on a constant try-out for the big Broadway show. But I was no angel.

I was having a few auditions of my own that required some serious foreplay. I took up the offer to join my Reichian friend in her twin orgone box. It was quite a ceremony even before entering its thick, ozone walls. I had to drink two bottles of Budweiser to get the blood level up, take a shower, practice some deep breathing—I was almost exhausted before I entered the box. Access to the big, wide, wonderful world of orgasm was not easy. My instructor shoved a manipulator into my hand that looked like the nozzle of a sprinkling can attached to a hose, and instructed me to run it along my body for maximum pleasure (it was the forerunner of the modern vibrator). Being in such a confined place with another naked body seemed to fill me with those mysterious elements that are necessary to orgasm, but it didn't particularly make a believer out of me. Yet I had a lot of orgone energy left over for Stephanie, the refined literary groupie who was auditioning me for a minor role in her life of conquests. I don't know how she performed for writers with bigger name value, but for me, she had a remarkable act. She would pretend to be asleep as I made my descent and the sexual act was devoid of all conversation. I thought it was very cool of her to fake snoring, like other girls faked orgasm.

I wasn't always so successful with women. Miss Social Anthropologist, who I picked up at the Museum of Modern Art, came back with me to share the experiences of her first encounter with abstract art. Evidently, being seduced by the editor of a lay-psychiatric magazine appealed to her sense of the improvisational. She excused herself to attend to what she called "precautionary measures." Taking her bag, which looked like a surgeon's kit, she went to the toilet. The sounds that emerged in the beginning were only slightly disturbing, but as time passed, I couldn't tell if she was attending to the plumbing or building an erector set: the clanking of metal, the mashing of gears, and squeaking of pliers—what was it? I become so engrossed in surviving that all interest in going to bed with a chastity belt disappeared. When she finally emerged—rather pleased with herself—her explanation that she had some trouble with her "Dutch Cap" was an anti-climax. I reminded myself to call Legman and ask him if this meant I had a Vagina Dentata complex. It was one of the few things he hadn't accused me of.

By the end of winter, 1950, I had used up most of my disguises, forcing me to get down to the business of putting *Neurotica 6* together without Legman.

I needed something very Legman-esque to give the issue the punch that readers expected. He had taught me the value of the conspiracy theory, and an idea sparked off by an article in *Life* gave me the basis for a conspiracy piece that even Legman would be proud of. *Life* canonized the homosexual actor Clifton Webb's phenomenal success in two films, *Sitting Pretty* and *Mr. Belvedere Goes to College;* "A piece of pure Americana." If true, that America has taken this effete characterization to its breast, the effeminization of the American hero was complete: Belvedere was up there with Paul Bunyan, Jesse James, and Daniel Boone.

I wanted to know why. When the homosexual image becomes big box office, it's time to look at what's behind it. Was there a Gentleman's Agreement to propagandize the homosexual hero in America? How much exposure would it take before the rot set in? Was the critical acclaim for "sensitive" novelists, whose themes were disguised propaganda for homosexuality, becoming a cultural force in America? The reprint of Ronald Firbanks' five novels (by

New Directions)—reviewed so favorably by homosexual critics without once discussing Firbanks' homosexuality, or that his novels were homosexual fantasies—was the literary event of the year. How much more was to come? The fact that Truman Capote, Gore Vidal, Speed Lamkin, and a dozen more homosexual writers were establishing their literary reputations without any of the critics mentioning the underlying nature of their work amounted to a conspiracy of silence.

If propaganda can bring whole nations to war, why should the sexes be immune? If Belvedere represented a fifth column in the attempt to make homosexual images palatable in the box office, we could expect more in other areas. How soon will the minority seek to impose its views of life and love upon the majority of non-homosexuals? By not coming out of the closet, we are stuck with the effeminization of artistic and sexual values.

My research proved that by putting myself in Legman's shoes, I was capable of his kind of hysteria, paranoia, and bigotry in proving a conspiracy existed where no one else would see one. I called Legman with the news of my discovery. "It's too big for you, Landesman," he told me. "Leave that kind of thing to people who know how to handle it." I took his advice. I brought Holmes into the project. His research and style of writing was so much more legitimate than mine. He was able to put my theories into a coherent pattern that would make the piece a valid contribution to understanding what was behind the Gentleman's Sexual Agreement. We both had the feeling we'd hit upon something that other writers ignored. It was great to poke fun at all the high falutin' nonsense that was being passed off as serious cultural analysis by the critical fraternity of the day. Our "mile high hints" of who were homosexual and what part they played at "log rolling" their way into notoriety stayed this side of being libelous, but we used the name of Alfred Towne on the article and claimed he was a "mid-westerner who's left the country." While it might have seemed far-fetched back in the 1950's, there have been many articles since then using the same line of attack, and these they called "fearless." I had a Spring issue that even Legman would approve of.

I hadn't seen anything of him for months, but I heard in the Village that he had gotten the financial backing to publish *Love and Death* on his own. I called to congratulate him on his debut as a publisher. "The book got a mixed review," he said. "It only shows how schizophrenic the critics are. The reviewer loved and hated it in the same review." Unknown to readers and critics, Legman told me he had put a special dye in the ink for the cover that came off on the reader's hands "when they start sweating with guilt." Evidently, I was one of the few people who read it without getting my hands stained. I still thought it was a brilliant book and I wanted to help him get it around. I offered him the back cover of *Neurotica 6* to print up all his schizophrenic reviews of the book in return for doing the production. My readership, which was now around 7,000, was the perfect outlet for him. He agreed to the offer, so we were back in business again without his editorial assistance to give me problems. I'd missed Legman—I needed someone to give me a hard time.

When my old friend, Geraldine, gave a party in New York to celebrate the anniversary of the death of Artaud, I looked forward to meeting the weird collection of Artaud cultists, so naturally I wore a suit and tie to throw them off the scent that I was a secret admirer of the 'mad' writer. I had been introduced to him through Carl Solomon's piece that he wrote for *Neurotica, Report from the Asylum—Afterthoughts of a Shock Patient,* comparing his experiences in the Asylum with Artaud's. "A lunatic is a man who has preferred to become what is socially understood as mad, rather than forfeit a certain superior idea of human honor," wrote Artaud in an essay on Van Gogh. "A vicious society has invented psychiatry to defend itself from the investigations of certain superior and lucid minds whose intuitive powers were disturbing to it," concluding that, "every psychiatrist is a low-down son-of-a-bitch." Solomon reminded readers that Artaud was honored with the Prix Sainte-Beuve for his essay.

Several people looked at me as if I had dropped in from Mars, and I must confess I did look out of place in that collection of beards, turtle-neck sweaters, and dark glasses. I noticed a young girl, dressed differently from all the others, having quite a good time talking to a group of her friends sitting on the floor. She looked expensively square: the kind of girl who was so pretty she could get away with anything. It took only a couple of minutes to discover that she was also the bitchy type. Geraldine walked by the girl with a tray of paper cups, and the girl looked at Geraldine and all she could see was her enormous breasts, protruding over the tray.

"If you ever got caught in the rain with that dame, you'd never need an umbrella." Her girlfriend thought that was the funniest thing said all evening.

She knew I had overheard it.

"That's not a very nice thing to say about your hostess," I said, moving closer to her.

"Well, it's true, isn't it?" she replied, moving her large felt skirt with applique flowers out of the way so I could sit next to her.

"Don't be so square," she said to me as I settled down.

I looked around the room to see who she might be talking to—surely it wasn't me.

"You look like you've just come from the office," she added, pointing to me.

I played along with the role. "Yeah, would you like a job?"

It was a mistake. She lost all interest in continuing the conversation, turning her back on me and returning to her circle of friends. She saw me staring in disbelief.

"I don't type," she said, and turned away again, satisfied that she had gotten rid of another pest.

I walked away without saying another word to her. When I caught up with Geraldine I asked her if she knew the girl.

"No, but she's your type."

And she was right.

"Terrible girl," I said to Geraldine. "I'd like to meet her sometime, but tonight is not my night."

A week later, New York rushed the season with a sunny spell of weather that had everyone gravitating toward the Washington Square fountain to get their first taste of the sun. I was there with Broyard, taking in the scene of Morris dancers, throbbing bongos, and 12-string guitars entertaining the assorted audience in an impromptu amateur night variety.

The bitchy girl who had given me a hard time at the party was sunning herself in the empty fountain not a yard away. I hadn't noticed her until Broyard said hello. I didn't know if she had recognised me when Broyard introduced us, and I was hoping she hadn't.

"This is my friend, Jay Irving Landesman, the editor of *Neurotica* and a very good mambo dancer."

She was wearing the uniform of the day—peasant blouse, a wide belt around another flaired skirt, and a pair of Capēzio flats. I thought of all the good lines I could have used to make her uncomfortable, but she looked so vulnerable I just said a square "hello." Broyard called her Peaches, which I thought was improvised on the spot, but her complexion in the bright light was as soft and juicy as the name implied. Evidently the Broyard connection made the difference, because this time she flashed a smile that told me that she might have been waiting to meet me all her adolescent life. It was careless of me, I know, but I returned the smile that said the same thing. We were already playing tennis and the score was LOVE ALL.

"I have a friend, Shepard Rifkin, who took me back to his place to show me his *Neurotica*'s. Wait till he hears I've met the editor." She looked up at the sun that had quietly settled behind a cloud, and I decided that God had recognized, if not blessed, our meeting.

Broyard was getting restless. "How about a game of hand tennis, old sport?"—eager for a little action—"Why don't you get a ball over on 4th Street, and I'll keep Peaches amused until you return. I need some exercise," he added. I told him I would go if Peaches would walk me over to the store. She got up and, without waiting for Broyard's approval, started to walk alongside of me.

"See you later, Anatole," I said triumphantly.

It was only a five minute walk to the store that sold little rubber balls, but I knew that it was going to take hours, probably a lifetime. "I thought you were a businessman," was her way of letting me know she remembered me from the party.

"And I thought you were a bitch," I replied.

She had short blonde hair, natural as gold. I couldn't determine what color her eyes were, but in spite of her smiling so much, I knew they were coloured *hungry*. She had beautiful teeth, a perfect gum line; she was up to my nose in height and probably weighed more than I did, but it was distributed better. Her finger nails were dirty.

Together we walked past groping couples and gandy dancers and checked out a chess game between two old men that had been going on for thirty years. Mothers in the park looked as young as their babies and some were prettier. The baby I decided to talk to was an ugly little tike with a snotty nose and eyes in a natural squint against life. I picked up the baby and put it in Peaches' arms. She rejected it without thinking twice. Her protest sounded like Butterfly McQueen: "I don't know nothin' about birthin' babies", and made me feel sorry for the mother.

"The kid's going to be great when it grows up," I told the mother.

Too bad Pat didn't have that child, I thought; I would have been a good father.

Crossing the busy intersection at West 4th Street, I could see she didn't know how to cross a street.

"Didn't anybody tell you to stop at the curb and look both ways?"

I put my arm around her as we narrowly escaped being run over by a taxi that appeared from nowhere. She laughed at our near escape. There was a lesson to be learned from her reaction to death, but I was so pleased I had gotten my arm around her waist so soon, I didn't have the time to take it in. I knew I sounded like her parents, but I couldn't help feeling protective towards my new charge.

In the store, she noticed the new issue of *Neurotica* displayed so prominently. "You may be square, but you're an editor," was her idea of a compliment. I turned, as shy as Jimmy Stewart kicking a load of horseshit.

"It ain't nothing, Miss, shucks."

I suddenly decided I didn't want to go back and play silly hand tennis; Broyard would only beat me anyhow. I asked her to join me for a drink at the San Remo. She didn't question the morality of deserting Broyard; she was probably as irresponsible as I was in those matters.

She went straight to the ladies' room when we arrived in San Remo's. In spite of the crowded bar, I found an empty booth and twiddled my anxiety buttons until she returned. I noticed she hadn't washed her hands. She ordered a beer; I suggested she have something more interesting. "You're with an editor." I felt more in control when she ordered a Manhattan. This was a special occasion, I reminded her. I explained that I looked upon our meeting again as a reconciliation.

"At that party I liked you because you looked so different from the usual Village character; but my looking different turned you off." I wanted the answers to a hundred more questions without seeming to be the District Attorney of the State of New York. What I found out about her was enough to get her a scholarship to the New York School for Social Misfits.

Her odyssey from a promising Jewish Princess to a fully-fledged, middle-class rebel began at a progressive school in New York with an extended course at a fashionable boarding school in Virginia, where she learned to sing hymns in the choir of the Methodist Church. She soon discovered peanut butter as a cure for loneliness. She returned to New York a fat, intelligent Jewish girl who found that

Greenwich Village was hospitable to lonely little misfits. She worked her way through a few artists, a longshoreman, a cab driver, several black musicians, and a homosexual; that left her with a feeling that there was a romantic quality about the loser. They had the time for a little fat girl. When it ended in an expensive abortion in a New York hospital, she settled down in a friendly art school in Philadelphia where they were impressed with her talent as a sculptress. "Malvina Hoffman was not as good as you when she was a girl," her teacher said. The compliment only encouraged her basic slovenliness—the thought that she might be good at something, or that someone expected her to be good, only contributed to her rebellious nature. "When I was five years old, I asked my mother "When am I going to get my freedom?" She liked talking about herself almost as much as I did, trying to make it sound as shocking as possible. By the time she finished her second Manhattan, I discovered that her father was a successful suit and cloaker who never had time for her, and a mother who claimed she got ill everytime she looked at her daughter's poor, swollen body. The only school she ever graduated from was the Dubarry Success School, where she shed an impressive number of pounds and felt for the first time a part of the human race. She was going to the Fashion Institute of Technology at the time, a school started by her father and his friends in the industry, taking a course in textile design. I couldn't visualize the beautiful, fast-talking, wise-cracking girl sitting opposite me as having been a hundred-and-eighty-nine-pound loser. I didn't try and compete with her in rejection stories, sensing she didn't particularly see me as a serious contender in that field. If she was looking for sympathy, she certainly won the day. The way I expressed it may not have been the most subtle, but it worked. It was getting on to cocktail time; I suggested we have another at my place.

We took a bus uptown and as we passed 42nd Street, I thought what a good idea it would be to show off my new prize to Bunny, who was playing the cocktail hour in a basement club opposite the Library. Bunny and I were at the good friends stage of the relationship, so bringing another girl around wasn't a problem. I really wanted to hear what Bunny thought of her. Was she as terrific as I thought she was?

Bunny was at the piano, singing my favorite song, *It Never Entered My Mind,* when we entered. The place was rather empty, giving me the feeling that we were both auditioning for Bunny. I didn't mention that I knew Bunny until Peaches—whose real name was Fran—came back from the toilet. I noticed that she still hadn't washed her grimy hands.

Bunny gave me a big wink as she began to sing another Rodgers and Hart song, *There's a Small Hotel,* in memory of our night at the Edison. Fran confessed she knew all the lyrics to the popular songs of the 30's and 40's, admiring the way Bunny was interpreting them: "I like the sad songs the best." The place was filling up with what was called the Desk Set—secretaries with their bosses; the "I'll-call-home-and-be-a-little-late" syndrome. Already there was a queue at the phone.

At the break Bunny joined us. I got the feeling they would have liked each other if they ever got together again. Walking her back to the piano, I asked her what she thought of Fran. She looked at me rather sadly: "She's just right for you." It sounded like a put down. Fran's opinion of Bunny was more generous: "She's quite glamorous, in spite of her cross eyes." I told her that's what attracted me: "She reminds me of my mother."

It was only a short walk to my place on 53rd Street, but it seemed longer when the compulsive talker suddenly went quiet, suggesting she might be having second thoughts about going to my apartment, which smelled of roast lamb from the cooking of the Grecian Gardens. She looked around the place, a little disappointed. She commented on the linoleum I had dripped with Jackson Pollack finesse: "Very clever." But she wasn't impressed with last year's Eames chair or my ad hoc orange crates for end tables. A cocktail table and couch completed the inventory.

"I wish you'd known me when I was in the antique

business; the place would have looked like a set out of Ben Hur." I pointed to my satin eye-mask lying on the unmade couch, "That's the only thing left over from those days."

That seemed to cheer her up. Well, if she got bored, there were a lot of magazines she could read. While she went to the toilet again, I put *The Third Man Theme* on the record player and mixed a martini, hoping that she'd forgotten she was drinking Manhattans. The record didn't encourage her to be foolish and the martini only made her go to the toilet again. Fran was either very nervous or had a kidney complaint; I had never known anyone to piss so often. She recognised Lotte Lenya's recording of the songs from *The Threepenny Opera* and leafed through a copy of Angus Wilson's *The Wrong Set* that I had lying on the table with obvious delight. I held out my hands for a dance, but she insisted she didn't dance. After the record was over, she made another trip to the toilet. This time, when she came out, she was looking troubled.

"Don't think I'm crazy, but could we go to my place? My folks are away in the country for the weekend. We can have it to ourselves."

The classic line, "I never laid a hand on her, your honor," popped into my head at the suggestion that she was being hustled.

"Could I borrow this?" she asked, holding up the copy of *The Wrong Set*. Great, I thought. That book would tell her more about me than my sparse apartment. I thought Angus Wilson was the most decadent English writer on the scene, and I associated myself with a dozen of his characters.

On the way over to catch the Eighth Avenue bus, we passed a photo machine in a sleazy arcade. She liked the idea of us taking a picture together. Smiling broadly at the camera, pushing each other off the stool to get a position to show off our best profile, the camera lied as usual: she had sucked in her cheeks so much she looked like she was giving me a blow job, and my smile lacked an upper lip. At least I now had a record of what a Dubarry Success School graduate looked like.

She lived in the Kenilworth on Central Park West and 75th Street. Five seconds after we entered her apartment, she excused herself again to go to the toilet, leaving me in a very large living room that looked like a small wing of the Metropolitan museum. The smell of bees-wax hovered in the air, reminding me of days at the Landesman Galleries. The paintings, all beneath glass, were of New York, circa 1919. I recognized the Flat Iron building in the autumn and Fifth Avenue crowded with open deck buses in the winter. I sat down in a Chippendale wing chair facing windows that looked over the park. The lights were just beginning to glow in the windows of Fifth Avenue. It looked so unreal, like Hollywood's version of a Manhattan skyline.

When Fran returned, she heaved a huge sigh of relief. I was mystified.

"You're not going to believe this, but I haven't been able to piss since I met you. I was so nervous. It was misery."

She put her arms around my neck, kissing me lightly to let me know it wasn't my fault. It was a relief to me, too. I welcomed her kisses with a mere slip of the tongue in her mouth. We did the room together. It could have been frozen around Good Taste, 1928. She pointed out portraits of her parents that looked like they were done by a fashionable artist of the time. She mentioned a brother. "You might have seen him around the Village—a little sharpie with glasses." It was a description that could have fitted a hundred guys in the Village. I don't know why she mentioned him except to let me know she wasn't a spoiled brat only child. We sat together in the window seat, watching New York turn dark, sipping a nice, cold martini that I made.

"When I was a kid I used to sit on the ledge of this window with my feet over the side and look down at all the little figures below me. Sometimes I wanted to join them with the big jump. I often think about death, do you?"

The very thought of looking down from such a height

made me dizzy. For a second, I thought she was going to show me what I was missing. She looked so lonely and lost that I took her in my arms and hugged her like I never hugged anyone in my life. Neither of us said a word. We kissed again, and I followed her into a room that was almost as bare as my place. The time between foreplay and the post-coital cigarette had been well spent. I asked why she was smirking. The smirk changed to a Cheshire grin.

"I was just thinking what the editor of *Neurotica* would say if he knew he had made it on my father's bed."

I didn't say a word, but picked up the phone and started dialing Broyard's number. He would be able to explain a crazy statement like that.

"What in the world are you doing?" She grabbed the phone out of my hand.

"I'm just calling up for a second opinion."

She hung up the phone as we both laughed at the ridiculous scene. We slept together that night as if we'd been doing it for years. In the morning I had a hang-over. At breakfast, the sound of her cracking the soft-boiled eggs made me wince. We were joined by her brother, Sammy, who acknowledged her introduction to me with a smart ass line.

"Hey, Franny, if you're going to let this guy meet the folks, better get him into the sun. He looks terrible."

She told me she had lots of things to do that weekend, so I split. When I got home, I wrote a letter in my head to Cutie:

Dear Cutie,

Yesterday I saw New York's fabulous skyline from a penthouse on Central Park West. A pretty girl lives there who is as crazy as I am. I think I'm going to marry her. I miss you.

Love and kisses,
    Jay

P.S. What you wouldn't give to get your hands on some of the antiques that are in her house.

Falling in Love

Any ideas I had of a spring romance were scuttled when I called Fran around dinner-time the following Monday. Her "hello" was extremely off-putting.

"My, that's an aggressive hello."

I could have said something less friendly, but she beat me to it.

"Aw, fuck off," she said in a voice that sand-papered my ear-drum.

I simply hung up the phone. I expected her to call right back with some kind of explanation, like she was being tortured by her parents and her "fuck off" was a code of some kind. When she didn't call right back I felt so lousy I called up Legman—he couldn't depress me half as much as she had.

He was in a good mood.

"Hey, Landesman, I'm a funny writer. I've just done a hatchet job on L. Ron Hubbard's *Dianetics* that has me in hysterics."

The fact that his *Love and Death* was selling so well was obviously putting him in a good mood. I mentioned I was seeing copies of it all over town.

"Would that piece on Dianetics be right for *Neurotica?*"

There was one of his significant pauses.

"Why not," he said. "That last issue of yours was a piece of garbage. Who is Alfred Towne?"

I didn't want to tell him it was Holmes and me; he would only have crucified us. I asked him if he liked it.

"Amateurish, third-rate Legman."

I took it as a compliment. We made a date to meet and discuss issue No. 7. I mentioned that I had another piece by Solomon and Alfred Towne.

"Now, Solomon on the asylum was good, but my article on Hubbard will really be sensational. I call it *Epizootics*. It's hysterically funny."

Dianetics was on the best-seller list at the time, making it a timely piece.

"I'll publish it without even seeing it—how's that for a vote of confidence?"

Instead of him being pleased, he used it as another example of what an irresponsible editor I was. I laughed it off with the explanation that I had learned to edit from him. He didn't laugh, but there was still a friendly tone to the conversation. Legman couldn't afford to like me—it would have been against all his principles. To him I was still a playboy, playing editor. He might have been close to the truth at that moment because I had fallen in love with Fran and could think of nothing else but her strange behavior.

By Wednesday, I got a letter apologizing for her rudeness. She explained she was on the way out of the door with friends who were late for dinner and panicked at the sound of my voice. The "fuck off," she explained, was meant for her friends who were telling her to hurry up. "How can I get that book back to you?" I wrote her to drop it off at my place at an appropriate time. She arrived the next day at dinner time with the book and a new personality. That tough, bitchy Fran disappeared as she tried to make up for her telephone manners.

"I loved *The Wrong Set*. I can see why you liked it—they're all so decadent. The characters fit in with your satin sleeping mask."

I mentioned that if she stuck around long enough, she'd probably discover I had other attractive habits.

I asked her to stay for dinner; I'd get something from the Grecian Garden and bring it back with a bottle of cheap Greek wine. The light show of the Grecian Garden's sign playing against the wall above the couch was the perfect touch to go with the script I intended to write for her that night. I realized that she knew nothing about me. I filled in my background in the antique business, my former marriage, my dominating mother, the identity problems leading to *Neurotica*, Legman, and the missed opportunity with Henry Luce. Fran gave me a sympathetic smile.

"That crowd wouldn't have suited you. There's nobody hipper than the editor of *Neurotica*. I told my girlfriend about you and she was jealous. Her boyfriend edits a magazine called *Blood*, which nobody ever heard of."

Her vote of confidence encouraged me to be serious for a moment.

"When I first came to New York, I was going to set the town on its ass. I really thought *Neurotica* was the only voice around screaming for an end to censorship and sexual repression in a savage society.

"Have you ever been in analysis?" I asked her.

"Not right now, but I did spend some time on the couch last year. Have you?"

"Only superficially". I didn't want to go into the impotency phase that originally drove me to the couch. Right now I was only interested in getting her on my couch. I knew she had a bedroom full of problems, but she was a classy uptown broad in full rebellion. Anybody in rebellion was attractive to me, and her style was one that I was familiar with and was sure I could handle. She was looking for someone to go down the dissenting path with her. Being editor of *Neurotica* was as anti-establishment as you could get. Along with her acid quips, there was a vulnerability about her that I liked; it was an up to date poor-little-rich-girl syndrome.

"I think we ought to see each other more often," she said, dropping her guard.

"Like every night," I answered.

On only a bottle of cheap wine, I didn't have enough nerve to take it any further. But she did.

"Why don't we go to the country next weekend?"

It came as a surprise, but a pleasant one.

"I think I could stand it for two nights," she added.

I asked if we would have to sleep in separate rooms. She took great delight in telling me how her parents were very broad-minded when it came to that kind of thing, but were basically very square.

"Don't be put off if they don't talk to you. They usually ignore my friends."

She told me I didn't have to talk to them either. I accepted.

"I'm looking forward to doing an inventory of your father's house."

She squinted her eyes and, in an old maid's voice, she asked me:

"You don't, by any chance, love me for my father's Windsor chairs, do you?"

We spent a beautiful evening together, slipping into each other's lives, and finding it fairly comfortable.

Driving up to her parents' home in Connecticut with a chauffeur and a cook in the front seat, her mother and father seated behind them, and Fran and me acting like kids, holding hands in the rear, wasn't a bad way to travel. I had forgotten there were people around with such style. But style was their business. Her father, gazing out of the window in abstract thoughts, completely uninterested in who I was, was the perfect picture of the self made millionaire—total concentration on self. Her mother's distinguishing characteristic was her chain smoking, much to the annoyance of her husband. They didn't exchange one word during the two-hour drive to Sandy Hook. There was enough time for me to tell them the story of my life— the *Readers Digest* version—but I sensed a remarkable lack of interest. Any hint of how smitten I was with their daughter would have suffered the same fate. I understood then why Fran was a promising neurotic; her parents were also rebelling. She thought it was against her, but the editor of *Neurotica* guessed that her parents were rebelling against each other; Fran was just incidental.

Once we got off the Merrit Parkway, the family came to

life and started to argue. It was about where to do the shopping. For the first time her father became aware of my presence, wondering, no doubt, what I was doing there. By the time our wheels hit their driveway, I knew the only way I was going to get their attention was to become the new houseboy. I helped Clarence, the chauffeur, bring in the groceries and other supplies. I made a fire in the large, stone fire-place and prepared a cold pitcher of martinis. The house had a more contemporary look than the apartment in the city, although it was over a hundred years older. I tried to draw the old man out by asking the usual tourist questions about how old the ceiling beams were, how much of the house was original, and what was it before it became such a showplace. He gave me the house tour, and when I asked Fran if she wanted to join us, she said she'd heard it all before. The old man wasn't too bad as a guide; when I told him my parents were in the antique business, he pointed out the rarer items he knew would be appreciated. I felt like giving him a tip at the end of the tour: "Don't worry about your daughter, I'll take care of that from now on."

Fran took me out on the terrace where I could see the view of the forest of pine trees at the edge of the rolling lawn and the lake that ended in a noisy waterfall. It wasn't the setting of the *Philadelphia Story*, but it was as close as I ever got to it. I couldn't understand why she was so blasé about the place.

"It's his real love; it's all he cares about. We're just part of the landscape."

Turning an old farm house into an estate of that magnitude was a remarkable achievement. Wasn't she being hard on the old boy?

"It's his creation. He didn't do it for us. He did it for himself."

I couldn't believe I was taking her parents' side. I thought she was ungrateful. But there was time to work on that problem.

At the moment I was trying to breathe some life into the living room by making another pitcher of martinis and turning on some loud music, getting into my Gene Kelly imitations that had me dancing all over the furniture.

"Don't you love the way he moves?" Fran wanted her mother to appreciate my little show. Her mother, after her second martini, was easy to win over. It was her father who was unimpressed. "Watch the furniture, kid," was his only comment on the performance.

At dinner, the conversation flowed easily whenever the subject was food. Samuel Deitsch was a cordon-bleu graduate, and he had the protruding belly to accommodate all the rich sauces he'd learned how to make. It was all a little too fancy for me. I tried to get a laugh with Legman's story of boiled lung:

"It's good for high blood pressure, I'm told."

When it came to food, her father didn't have a sense of humor. He was a short, fat, volatile man with a great shock of wavy grey hair promoting a very masculine image except for the ring on his pinkie finger. There was no communication between the family on any subject except food.

"Now you can see why I was such a fattie," Fran said, refusing to eat the rich desert.

Fran's mother retired right after dinner, a little the worse from the booze. Sam slipped off to his library to listen to his music alone. There was nothing for us to do but go to bed.

We had the top floor of the house to ourselves. It was still a hot night for Spring; sleep didn't come easily. Feeling adventuresome, we climbed out, naked, through the window, exploring the roof top like a couple of tom cats. We found a place to sit down and study the moon's behaviour. The sound of the waterfall behind the cricket's song was sexy. The barn cast a long shadow across the expanse of lawn that made me wonder if someday I'd fulfill a dream of converting a barn into a home. My mentioning this brought forth a flood of childhood memories from Fran. She'd wilted in the country with nobody to play with and her parents coming out for the weekend with all their guests and their monumental indifference to her.

"I really hate the place," she told me.

"That's because you've never been here with me."

She wouldn't accept that.

"Maybe I could stand it if they weren't around. They always make me feel as if I should be grateful for what they're providing, but I'm not."

I wished I could have been more sympathetic, but it irritated me that she didn't appreciate such an ideal setting. I told her she had Paradise right under her nose.

"Not my nose," she corrected. "Under their noses."

Some suspicious wasps moved in, driving us back into the house. In bed, holding her close as if the wasps were still chasing us, I decided I was going to teach her to dance if it took a lifetime.

The next morning before anyone was awake, we went for a walk. She took me along the lake to where the Indians took their baths on Saturday night, and then we cut across a forest of sweet-smelling pine trees. At the top of the hill, we looked down at the house, the lake, and the trees just coming into full leaf.

"Calendar pretty, isn't it," I said.

She told me it was prettier before they put the tarmac road through.

"There were no neighbors for miles around."

She stopped every so often to pick the wild flowers that lined the road.

"Don't you think mother would like these?"

"With a garden full of flowers," I said, "why bother?"

"But these are *my* flowers. Those in the garden are *his*."

I was put in my place. We must have walked for miles, yet we were still eager to go on, testing our lungs with deep breaths of country air; there was a spring in her walk that was out of character with the anxiety-ridden, urban, self-indulgent girl I knew. For the first time since we were together, she felt free enough to let me see that happiness was not out of the question with me.

When we got to the waterfall, we stripped and screamed with childish delight, invigorated by the coldness of the water, and clung to each other in a record-breaking embrace. We dashed into the lake, swimming great lengths I would have thought impossible; she even beat me in a race. I was impressed.

Everyone was still sound asleep when we returned to the house for an intimate breakfast on the terrace. She may have hated the country, but I never saw anyone bloom as radiantly as she did over that last cup of coffee before the parents came down to take their place as the real grown-ups of the world.

There were chores to do. While the chauffeur did the house-cleaning, I took his place behind the wheel for a drive to town to pick up more provisions. The large general store in the nearby town of Sandy Hook had managed to survive in a world of encroaching supermarkets by handling everything a country squire and his family could need from birth to death. The store was still run by the same family Fran remembered from her childhood, and they greeted her like a member of their own. I bought two denim work shirts and some bubble gum. Fran filled her prescription for Dexedrine at the friendly druggist who remembered her as the fat little Deitsch girl who used to have a double chocolate sundae with her four-eyed baby brother.

We moved on to the next big town where shopping centers were still a novelty. I wheeled the big cart around as her mother filled it up with professional pride. I complimented her on her decisive purchasing techniques. "I should know by now; I've spent my life shopping for two houses." Although it was not meant to be bitter, she managed to show uneasiness with her role as housekeeper for a very particular man. Once the shopping was done, including the stop-over for more liquor, there was a friendly atmosphere between her mother and us; she wanted to be on our side, but years of masking her feelings made it difficult. It was simpler to retreat into alcohol.

Fran pointed out the house where Elia Kazan lived. I brought the car to a screaming halt.

"What are you doing, you crazy thing?" Fran shouted.

"Let's stop off and say hello! I'm sure he'd like to get to know his new neighbors."

She looked at me as if I were crazy.

"Don't embarrass us, please."

Her mother watched us with amusement.

"I could do an interview with him for *Neurotica*. It's my big chance."

I started to get out of the car. Fran panicked.

"Where's your sense of adventure, kid?"

I got back into the car before she had a chance to get hysterical. I thought I was with a crazy girl who delighted in shocking people, but that incident put the lie to my assumption.

"Who's square now?" I asked the girl who was hiding her head in her hands.

On Sunday, the house was full of guests. It was at those times that her father came to life. If it was a guest's first time, he would conduct a house tour much like the one he gave me, but in more detail, and to a much more appreciative audience. He basked in the warmth of their praise, treating them to a lunch of smoked salmon from Scotland, and steaks cooked in the outdoor pit. He delighted in making his special dish of home-grown eggplant charcoaled over a low fire, much like a chef on TV would have done. In the afternoon, he organized walking tours around the grounds, giving a gardner's advice on how to get the best out of a bulb. There was no limit to his charm during such moments. I could see why Fran was so resentful—if only he paid her one tenth of the attention he lavished on strangers, she might not have been such an unhappy girl; I began to see what she was going on about.

The ride home after the weekend was timed to hear Jack Benny on the radio. It was the only time I heard her parents laughing. The minute the program was over they sat in silence. I had no idea what they thought of their daughter's new boyfriend, if indeed, he was her boyfriend. I suspected Fran had made this trip with many new friends they never saw again. They would have really been nervous if they had known how happy their daughter had been on that early morning walk and how serious I was about keeping her that way.

They dropped me off in front of my place. I stood on the sidewalk with a huge bunch of freshly cut flowers in my hands, waving goodbye. The flowers looked out of place in my apartment, introducing a foreign element it wasn't used to. In the morning I wrote a letter to Cutie—a real one—that told her I was feeling guilty about taking that monthly draw from the Galleries with them getting nothing in return. I was ready to do some buying like she had been nagging me to do. I wanted to re-establish my connections with the business world. I didn't mention meeting Fran, or that I wanted to furnish my apartment with things I could pick up at the auctions. If Fran was going to spend time at my place, I wanted to be sure she would be comfortable. I decided I didn't like the sparse look anymore.

As my pad began to take on a new look, so did our romance. We saw each other nightly and frequently, after a late night in the Village, she would stay over, although we wouldn't get much sleep. I courted her with intimate dinners at little French restaurants, afternoon screenings of old films at the Museum of Modern Art, and the new films at Radio City Music Hall. She took me to plays at Broadway theatres that we didn't have to pay for because her parents knew the managers. We met at art gallery openings and discovered that we didn't share opinions in art: she hated the new abstract paintings. At a De Kooning exhibition where everyone was enthralled with the new look, she took her stand: "You like that kind of painting? I'll do you one. You won't be able to tell the difference." It irritated me that she could be so square about art when she was so rebellious about life. Introducing her to Clement Greenberg didn't help; she thought he talked a lot of nonsense. Her taste in literature wasn't much better. Her father's library of James Branch Cabel and her admiration for *Winnie The Pooh* hadn't prepared her to appreciate

Celine and Artaud. Fran needed a complete course in romance and literature—and I was prepared to be the tutor.

She had been going around with losers so long that the feeling of inadequacy when she was in the company of Broyard, Brossard, and company was obvious; she was scared to death. And she hadn't even met Legman. I thought I would introduce her to him as an engagement present. Yet she was always welcomed at the Broyard table at the San Remo. One day she met him in the street and he said, "I have given my friend Jay Irving Landesman permission to woo you." Fran was an easy laugher, a great asset to a table full of men. They valued the presence of a beautiful girl who always gave the impression that she was game for anything. When Broyard organized one of his field trips to the Palladium, she was eager to go, but once she got there, she prayed that no one would ask her to dance. She never seemed to want to go home, another point in her favour. After the San Remo closed, there was always someone's pad we'd go to to finish the conversation. Talk was the main activity; dead air was a hanging offense.

When it came to action, Fran was careful. Back at my place, after one of those long nights when Fran, Milton Klonsky, and I were pretending to be asleep on the couch, the steady movement of my hands around Fran's breasts were skillfully misdirected by her. I found myself playing a finger dance with Klonsky, who told me later he rather enjoyed it. She wasn't the dare-devil I thought she'd be when it came to advanced foolin' around.

When the opportunity came up again, it wasn't Fran who backed away—it was me. My ex-wife, Pat, made a spectacular entrance in New York. I was with Fran on the way to a Spanish Harlem dance hall to score some pot when she appeared. Before the introduction, Pat's line, "Chloroform, anyone?" certainly made a strong impression, and it didn't fit the picture I had given Fran that Pat was a square who was holding me back in my wild pursuit of enlightenment. If Fran was awed with the chloroform

line, Pat's disclosure that she'd been in the Village for only
two days and had already scored with Dylan Thomas was a
bombshell. In the taxi she gave us a run down on the San
Francisco poets reading their poems in bars and coffee
houses that made the Village look almost provincial. I
could see Fran was so impressed with Pat's style she was
wondering why I ever let her out of my clutches. I don't
know what she was thinking as she watched Pat and I fling
our arms and hips around the dance floor, but it couldn't
have been all bad if she appreciated inventive dancing. It
was the first time we had been alone for a long time; it gave
me the opportunity to find out what the hell was going on
with this ex-Arthur Murray dancer.

"You were wrong, Jay," she told me. "Always pick a wild
flower, but the next time give it room to grow. Could I stay
at your place tonight?"

When I didn't answer quickly enough, she added,
"Don't be so old-fashioned."

Back at the table, Fran and she hit it off with no signs of
jealousy. As much as I thought it would be amusing to have
a fling with Pat for old time's sake, I declined the offer.
Evidently I wasn't a daredevil either.

I scored some grass from my contact and left her on the
dance floor with some strangers who looked like they
wouldn't be strangers for long. Fran couldn't get over how
hip my ex-wife was, and teased me about ditching her "just
when she was becoming interesting," a remark I didn't
understand at the time. Pat showed up at my place the next
afternoon when I was having a meeting with Broyard. She
casually added Broyard to her list of literary conquests,
and, not wanting me to feel left out, she put me on it also,
probably as an afterthought.

"Lovely woman. You should have held on to that,"
Broyard said as she left to continue her mission. She disappeared in the Village where I heard reports of her continued successes. I can't say I was sorry to see her out of my
life again, although I was secretly proud that she turned
out to be so hip, if a little indiscreet.

When I mentioned to Fran how would she like to meet my sister, she said, "not much." It stung a little, but I was getting used to her barbs. On the way up to Stamford on the train, Fran was reading her copy of *Vogue*, commenting on how lovely the models were. Remarks like that annoyed me. My suggestion that only dykes talked like that put her in a bad mood. I dropped the subject.

"Once you get past my sister, I've got a brother you'd fall in love with. Cheer up."

She reached into her purse and opened her pill box. I complimented her on its variety.

"I'm covered for any emergency: sugar substitute, aspirin, Contact, sleeping pill, pain killer, appetite depressant, Miltown—the usual equipment for a modern girl."

I suggested she take something appropriate for the occasion.

"I don't know if I have anything strong enough for that, but a couple of pain killers might help."

I thought the meeting went well. She stayed awake through all our reminiscences of our early family life, occasionally nodding approvingly at some of our sure-fire material. Fran was grilled about her family and passed the examination, although Gert gave her a low grade when we were alone in the kitchen. Fran was taking a nap.

"Her family sounds nice. Is this romance something serious?"

Gert was getting quite nervous. Not to disappoint her I said I'd probably pop the question any day.

"Lots of luck, man," she said, imitating my constant use of that word. "You've got another Aunt Bessie on your hands."

The reference made me laugh. Aunt Bessie was a family joke whose main mission in life was to stay in bed.

The trip was successful from another point of view. Gert gave me a Landesman Galleries chandelier and a beautiful, large, Venetian mirror she wasn't using. I took the liberty of inviting her and her husband to Fran's house in the country: "I'd like to show you how well I've adjusted to country life."

I'd made myself quite at home on the weekends we spent at her parents' estate, elevating my houseboy status into chief flower arranger and indispensible jester, although we had different definitions of just what a jester's role was in the country. Would a jester read all the public notices in the town hall about road widening and right of ways? I did. Should a jester be criticized for talking to strangers and asking them to give details of their personal lives? I was. Does a jester take chances? I did. Do jesters die young? There was something about the country that brought out all the childish qualities in my personality. Fran was adapting to the jester's ways. It wasn't only because the jester paid her a lot of attention, but the thought of his withdrawing the attention was one of the reasons she didn't laugh when the jester asked her to marry him.

"Why don't I move in with you?" she said, instead of "yes."

"None of your old-fashioned immorality," insisted the jester. "If you don't marry me you'll be sorry for the rest of your life."

That gave her something to think about.

Holmes took it for granted that we were an inseparable couple, destined to be the new Zelda and Scott. At a party on Long Island, I pointed out to Fran the area where Fitzgerald set *The Great Gatsby*. We saw the lights across the bay beckoning us to join 'his' party on the other shore. Surely we were as romantic as his characters—cool, good looking, and deeply shallow.

"I'd make you a damn good husband."

She had to admit I was right. She told me it was going to be difficult to break it to her folks.

"They'll be dead set against my marrying so young. My mother always wanted me to go to Europe before I got married."

Before we left Long Island, I told her she was born to break the rules.

"Your parents expect you to defy them. Why disappoint them?"

At dinner that night, asking for her hand struck me as

delightfully old-fashioned. I liked the role, determined to play it straight. Fran took great pleasure in seeing me squirm at my futile attempt to be one of the grown ups. She giggled throughout the meal, creating a tension that made my job even more difficult. All my dirty looks only made her try harder to make me uncomfortable. Her father didn't have any idea what was going on, but Fran told me she had let her mother in on it. After dinner, Fran took her into another room, leaving me to face the old man alone. When he turned on the TV to watch Arthur Godfrey's talent show, I assumed it was out of habit rather than deliberate rudeness. During the commercial for indigestion pills I broke the ice.

"Fran and I want to get married."

I had to wait until the commercial was over before the conversation continued.

"How are you going to support her?"

He didn't think being the editor of *Neurotica* was a profession. Not only did he look like Legman, he thought like him.

"If she told me she wanted to get married, I could have gotten her a union cutter at my factory who makes $4.50 an hour." He had a sly sense of humor.

"Don't worry about that angle. The Harvard University computer has gone beserk and sends me checks for subscription renewals every month."

He knew I was a respectable Jewish boy. Fran told me he had made inquiries about the Landesmans, including looking them up in Dun & Bradstreet. Arthur Godfrey was coming back after the commercial break. He didn't have much more time to waste on me.

"I can't tell her what to do with her life. If you're what she wants, what can I say?"

He turned off the set when Fran and her mother returned. The grown ups looked at each other like lost children.

"It's all settled," I announced.

Fran seemed a little disappointed that they didn't put up

more of a fight. I mentioned that July 15 was my 30th birthday and I'd never forget our anniversary if we got married that day.

Once they got used to the idea, they were quite looking forward to making all the arrangements. It was their suggestion that we have a big ceremony on the terrace in Connecticut and be married by the same Justice of the Peace who'd married them. A nice touch. Fran got nervous at the idea of wearing a fancy white dress, settling for something more stylish, less fancy. While they didn't show any signs of either losing a daughter or gaining a son, they did show a lot of concern about what was to be served at the reception. I wrote Cutie a letter telling her the news. "She's got good teeth, she's Jewish, and her folks are pillars of the community. You can count on some good food at the reception." I added that the whole family should come.

After I bought a dark blue suit there was nothing for me to do, but I longed to get in on the act. I told them I would take care of the wedding announcements. Fran and I met at Tiffany's. We waltzed by all the china, glass, and silver displayed for newlyweds, chuckling that if we had to have a big wedding we had, at least, escaped the horror of recording patterns for friends who wanted to give us a present. I asked her what she thought her folks would give us. I thought of my father's gold watch episode, wondering if times have changed. "Why don't we put on the announcement, *please send cash?*" For the first time she asked me how *were* we going to support ourselves. "We'll sell the wedding presents." She almost believed me. She was graduating from her textile course in June and could go right into a job.

Holmes, Broyard, and Klonsky were impressed at how quickly I wrapped up the romance. Holmes was particularly delighted; he had a soft spot for Fran and was the only one of my friends who treated her like an equal. Broyard called me to meet him for drinks a couple of days before the wedding. I thought he might be arranging some kind of bachelor party. Instead, he introduced me to

William Barrett, who had a piece of fiction he wanted to place in *Neurotica*. Barrett's reputation among the intellectuals was high; his articles on existentialism in *Partisan Review* were hot stuff. He turned out to be less stuffy than I imagined, and his piece of fiction was a brilliant parable of existential thought. Flattered that *Neurotica* had won over another serious writer, I promised him it would appear in the next issue without changing a word. When Broyard told him I was getting married, I was surprised to hear his reaction: "Another good man gone down the drain." Somehow it didn't seem like the right reaction from the father of American existentialism.

Cutie arrived the day before the wedding in time to meet Legman, who was at my place, haranguing me about the best method of birth control.

"Take her temperature every day, Landesman," he warned me. "In the rectum," he added.

I could just see me having Fran do that little exercise.

I would have given anything to prevent my two most favorite people from meeting, but once they did, there was no stopping them from comparing notes on my inadequacies. Legman had no trouble convincing Cutie that I was nothing more than a playboy.

"He belongs in the antique business. He has a businessman's mentality—he doesn't want to pay for a thing."

That was the only good news Cutie heard that afternoon. When he started talking about the Post Office threatening to take away his mailing privileges—which I never heard before—Cutie sensed he was a trouble-maker.

"Don't get my Irving into trouble," she warned him. "He's marrying a nice girl."

She asked him if he was Jewish.

"Of course, isn't everybody? Do you want further proof?"

He reached for his fly. Cutie laughed. When he left, she surprised me by saying she liked him.

"He's very sensible."

He had promised her he wouldn't get me into any more trouble than I was already in.

I made Cutie a glass of iced coffee to lower the temperature that Legman's visit left in the room. It was mid-July and already in the 90's. She hadn't taken two sips before she launched into a lecture, but it sounded like an ultimatum to me. She wanted me to come back to the business. All was forgiven now that I was about to settle down. I knew Fran was due at any minute.

"You'll love her, Cutie; she's just like you."

I jumped up to let Fran in. They gave each other a little hug and Fran immediately excused herself to go to the toilet. The next thing I heard was the sound of the shower running. Cutie looked puzzled. I covered up by saying that Fran had just come from shopping for last minute things for the wedding and was probably freshening up a little.

"She's very unconventional isn't she," Cutie said, trying not to sound too old-fashioned. Once I realized that Fran was actually taking a shower, I was secretly pleased she had such *chutzpah;* I knew the shower story would go instantly into Landesman folklore. Fran came out, fresh and beautiful, full of smiles. I was sure Cutie would forgive her, if only Fran hadn't flopped down on the couch and picked up a copy of *Flair.* Cutie gave me a look that I remembered from my bad childhood days when I defied those teachers. I passed on that look to Fran when I caught her eye. She put down the magazine and sat up smartly, like a well-trained airedale. Of course, the damage had been recorded, but Cutie had a forgiving nature. "I hope I'll see you at the wedding" sounded like the tag line of a Jewish joke. Was it possible that Cutie had developed a sense of humor in my absence? Fran must have thought so. She immediately got up to give her another hug. Cutie responded with a peck on her cheek and gave me a look that said, "God help you." What she actually said was "I'm very happy for the both of you. You are perfectly matched." She exited with all the dignity she had left.

"So that's Cutie," Fran said. "You don't look like her at all," she laughed, adding, "Why didn't you tell me she was cross-eyed?"

I knew I should have been furious with her for putting on such a terrible act with Cutie, but I wasn't. I liked her spirit and she looked so pretty in my large shirt.

"How did you like her two gold incisors?"

We both laughed so much that by the time I finished making us a couple of martinis, no drink ever tasted so cool and refreshing.

"She's come a long way to see her Irving married," I said. "Give us a break, kid, and be nice at the wedding—at least say 'hello' to her."

9

On the day of the wedding, I rose without disturbing Fran. The longer she remained asleep, the less trouble she'd get into before the ceremony. As I sat in the kitchen having a cup of coffee, I looked around at the perfectly designed room with all its major appliances mixing so well with the shelves of early American pewter and glass. I had a twinge of guilt that I could be so happy among that display of good taste and materialism. I thought of poor Legman, sitting in his miserable kitchen, wondering where his next meal was coming from and realized that Legman and I were the most mismatched pair of conspirators in the world. Fighting the good fight with Legman didn't seem as rewarding as living the good life with Fran.

The caterers were the first to arrive. By the time they had everything set up, I found Fran and her brother Sammy drinking vodka and orange juice for breakfast. They teased me about taking the wedding so seriously when I wouldn't join them for a drink. I told them that if I didn't take it seriously, who would? I warned Fran to take it easy on the booze. "You don't want to fluff your lines."

Once I had changed into my wedding suit, I began to relax. Standing on the terrace, greeting the guests, directing them to various areas to freshen up or meet their hosts, I wondered why I ever bothered with publishing a magazine when I was born to be a great maitre d'. In spite of all the vodka and God knows what pills she needed to face the ceremony, it was I who fluffed my lines. How does one say "plight my troth" when the heart is already in the mouth? Following the traditional kisses from everyone, we drifted out to the terrace for the reception that starred the Lobster Thermidor. The house, as usual, got most of the congratulations with the floral arrangements a close second.

Cutie came to tell me how delicious the food was and how lucky I was to find such a nice girl, in that order. Fran's folks liked Cutie from the first time they met, appreciating, no doubt, her no-nonsense approach to life. Of course, when Cutie said to them how lucky Fran and I were to find each other—"they're two of a kind"—they were less enthusiastic. "I think she's too young to get married," Fran's mother told Cutie with a knowing smile that surprised Cutie. "Maybe he'll settle down now and come back to the family business," surprised Fran's mother even more. I came up and put my arm around Cutie and said, "It's not such a bad life here."

"You could have done worse," was her way of approving of me for the first time in years.

The old man hadn't hired a photographer to take any pictures at the wedding, nor did he, an amateur photographer, take any. Whether it was an oversight or a deliberate act, there was no record of how beautiful Fran looked in her white summer wedding dress or what a nice figure she had when she slipped into her bikini and led all the younger guests down to the lake for a dip. It was quite a sight to see Holmes and his wife running across the lawn with bottles of champagne in their arms and big smiles on their faces. Even Broyard and Ernest Van Den Haag had to admit the trip wasn't a waste of time.

The only thing I forgot to arrange for was the honeymoon. It never occurred to either of us that we wouldn't spend the night and following days enjoying the pleasures of the countryside. It was my sister Gert who decided we had to make an exit. It was the traditional thing to do, she assured us. The word "tradition" should have told us it was a mistake, but since we had accepted the tradition of a big wedding, it seemed like folly to rebel now.

"But it's so nice here, why do we have to drive back to the stifling city?" Fran pleaded.

I told her I was only following orders. After I loaded the car with all the weird wedding presents, we were given the traditional send off with rice and shouts of approval. It was difficult trying to look like I was enjoying the departure from what looked like Paradise, no matter how much smiling and waving goodbye I did. The guests couldn't help noticing how quiet Fran had become, refusing to smile or even wave one little farewell.

Instead of starting out our married life with an argument, like most couples do on their wedding night, we said nothing to each other. Had she known how easily she could have convinced me to stay by insisting that it was a foolish idea to leave, she would have kicked herself for not trying harder. On the drive back there were times when I wanted to reach out to touch her, to let her know that I had made a dumb decision by listening to Gert. I couldn't. The distance between us had become too great. It was only when we pulled up to the apartment that I realized we drove the whole way without touching once. I tried to get a laugh by carrying her over the threshold; it fell flat as we entered the stale air and mess that welcomed us home. For the first time, the neon sign of the restaurant didn't cast its magic spell.

I was a little hurt when she mentioned not feeling well and played it cool when she asked me if I would mind if she slept in the other room. We agreed we shouldn't make another mistake by doing the expected thing. We kissed, quickly going to our separate beds as if we'd been married for years. It wasn't easy falling asleep listening for signs of life in the other room. I was really angry with Gert for making me leave a good party.

In the morning I tried to sleep as late as possible to avoid any incriminating exchanges. I had the strangest feeling

137

that I had taken on something that I wasn't sure I was going to be a success at in spite of being highly qualified for the job. I certainly didn't feel I had made a mistake; rather, it was like making a good buy in the antique business or, as Cutie would say to a customer to clinch a sale, "It's a good investment and you'll get a lot of pleasure from owning such an objet d'art." Fran, who was really not eager to get married, must have seen me as something on sale she couldn't resist, perhaps a beautiful stole that she didn't really need, but it would look so good on her, she had to have one.

There were indications all along, I suppose, that Fran and I were the perfect mismatch, but I was in love with the picture she presented: rebelliousness combined with fragility, her incompleteness and inconsistent character. The challenge it offered was right up my alley. I failed to see that the criticism and rejection she subjected me to was being passed, like a baton, in a direct line from Cutie, to Legman, to Fran. I lacked the perspective to realize that there was some secret part of me that demanded that I have someone in my life who could be relied upon to give me a hard time.

We spent the next afternoon with Holmes, Broyard, and Klonsky at a Brooklyn movie house that was showing the long suppressed Tod Browning masterpiece, *Freaks*. Like me, they had been waiting years to see that film. We were not disappointed, but Fran didn't see the beauty or the point of the film. All those armless, legless bodies, hydrocephalic heads, the bearded lady and alligator-skinned man caught up in a love story betwen a rich midget and a scheming bitch, didn't impress her. Nor did she think it was amusing that we all came out of the movie singing the show's theme, *We Will Make You One of Us*. The only laugh she had was Klonsky's belated wedding present—a visit to a soft drink parlor for an egg cream. It was the perfect Jewish joke: an egg cream that doesn't have an egg or cream in it.

Broyard's present was an invitation to spend the next

few days at his place in Fire Island. It never occurred to her, she remarked, that we would take our honeymoon with the inseparable duo, Broyard and Klonsky, but the opportunity to get out of the city proved too tempting to resist. We both thought we would have a chance to spend some time alone on a beach that stretched for miles, but we didn't realize how much our company was needed. I was drafted into playing volley ball, while Fran sulked and sunned some distance away. The players were disappointed she didn't sun by the sidelines so she could admire their stunning athletic powers. By the end of the day, both of us were burnt to a crisp. We went to bed that night a good three inches away from touching with the wild idea that there was a conspiracy to keep us apart.

We went back to the city, but still the closest we got to each other was rubbing lashings of Noxzema into our burning skins. At least, it put us in touch. We rang some laughs out of the wedding presents. There was little to salvage. I liked an hors d'oeuvres tray with little compartments I thought ideal for my collection of pickled herring, olives and gherkins that, along with pastrami sandwiches, made up my basic diet. The rest we threw away. Fran thought it was just a lot of stuff to dust. I reminded her of her mother's gift of six Golden Fleece scouring pads with a wry grin that hid a disappointed heart.

Fran got a job immediately as a textile designer for Bianchini, a position that suited her perfectly; there was something so satisfying about repeating the patterns of her designs and seeing them end up on scarves and men's ties in the windows of Bergdorf-Goodman. For a girl who had never lifted a finger, she adapted rapidly to the domestic routine after I gave her a few helpful hints and told her where to get good, cheap cuts of meat. She'd be able to do the shopping in her lunch hours and clean the flat in the evening. I had to break her of the habit of arranging the magazines on the cocktail table like a dentist's reception room and remind her that the Venetian mirror needed polishing.

Fran's father had always been in charge of interior deco-
ration in both their homes, so it was natural for her to let
me give the apartment style by choosing everything that
went into it. Her father's preference was early American,
mine was Early Decadent—everything was black. The
wicker chairs were painted shiny black to match the black
formica table that I picked up from the trash outside the
restaurant downstairs. On the mantelpiece, Fran's sculp-
tured horse looked dramatic and never failed to win approval from visitors. But what gave the room its emotional
impact was the hull of a wrecked ship that had been transformed into a piece of sculpture that hung on the wall. It
was an allegory, with figures attached to the hull representing life at the bottom of the sea in Davy Jones's locker.
There was a figure on the ship in the style of Giacometti,
peering through a telescope that I identified with completely, seeing him as the captain of the voyage, looking
out for dangers that might lie ahead.

Legman and Fran liked each other from the start. He
came on as if he were the only man in New York who
enjoyed women. "If women only knew how wonderful
they were and how delicious they tasted they wouldn't have
anything to do with men." I had hoped that Legman
would try to explain to her the importance of *Neurotica,*
but he couldn't have cared less. He was hell bent on leaving
Fran with the impression that he knew how to treat women
with the dignity they deserved. "I love women," he shouted
and then rushed off to our laundry hamper, digging into
the mess of soiled clothing and coming up with a pair of
Fran's panties. Holding them up to the light, he got quite
serious. "Landesman, this girl is too virtuous for you.
Didn't your mother ever warn you against wearing holey
underwear in case of an accident?" Before he put them
back in the hamper, he sneaked a sniff. Fran found him
amusing as well as fascinating the first hour, but as he
started his birth-control routine her eyes glazed over and
she seemed to be falling in love with the sugar bowl by the
time he split.

In those first few months, Fran was dazzled by the flow of traffic in and out of our apartment. The place was becoming a showcase for the wide assortment of talent that *Neurotica* attracted. Fran was spared the occasional subscriber who showed up during office hours to see what the editor of their favorite magazine was really like. They usually started out by asking for back issues, and by the time they left, I knew all the details of their sex life. I liked to talk about sex anywhere and with anyone. It was a subject that never failed to bring out the best and the worst in people. I had an almost pathological fascination with how people really acted out their fantasy life. I always wanted to know why people got tattooed or why they took such jobs as morticians or lavatory attendants.

Anything that was unusual or anyone with an unconventional point of view found our place hospitable. Marshall McLuhan and Legman in the same room improvising their wild ideas could have filled several issues of *Neurotica*. In fact, McLuhan had just finished a book, *The Mechanical Bride,* and I wanted to publish a long excerpt from it. Legman and I took him out to dinner at a Chinese restaurant after one of those long cocktail hours and made a deal. When McLuhan pulled out a tin of sardines and asked the Chinese waiter for a pair of chopsticks, I got a little nervous as he patiently tried to explain to the waiter that he didn't eat meat on Friday because he was a Catholic. He was having a problem in communicating his message.

Kerouac, whom I had gotten to know through Holmes, brought around Neal Cassady one afternoon as the place filled up. Cassady found a sympathetic audience for his frantic imitations of a parking lot jockey while Kerouac was off in a corner confessing to Fran how lonely he was. The two of them came back another time at two in the morning, climbed on to the balcony outside our window and knocked on the glass, scaring me out of my wits. "Jay, Jay, come out and play," they chanted. They wouldn't take 'no' for an answer. Letting them in through the window, Jack went to the kitchen and brought out a couple of saucepans they converted into bongos and treated us to a private concert of rhapsodic noises that included some of the best scat singing in Christendom. Kerouac's idea of devoting a whole issue of *Neurotica*—written by him—to Bop didn't sound so crazy at three o'clock in the morning. It was interesting enough to encourage him to come back and talk it over in the morning when he wasn't so "out of it." It was difficult trying to sleep with a vision of what Legman would think of that brain storm.

Fran thought it was a better idea than my articles on the effeminization of the culture. She thought it was in poor taste, but I had been accused of that so often I considered it a compliment.

But the Bad Taste Award went to her father the night they came to dinner at our place. Fran had been trying to avoid such an eventuality ever since the marriage; she didn't share my sense of social obligation. Fran tried to warn me that it would be a disaster. "You know what a perfectionist he is. He won't like anything here, much less anything I might cook up. Why don't we meet them at Chan's Chinese? You can pick up the check for once." There was something a little perverse about seeing them squirm, but it appealed to me. I insisted we extend the invitation so I could have him on my home ground, using my rules instead of his. I was proud of our little enclave, eager to show it off to them. How could they not admire the ship's hull sculpture? Would they recognize last year's Eames chair? I knew they hated the color black.

They arrived not five minutes before Fran came in from work loaded with provisions for the evening, looking like a Polish refugee. The big problem: where could they sit? The Eames chair was too low for her father to descend to gracefully and the couch was too high for her mother to sit on comfortably. My suggestion that they sit on the window sills was rejected. They kind of swayed there, trying to find a restful place for their eyes, making no comment whatsoever on the decor. I made them a martini in my favorite herring jar, explaining in a serious tone how it was much better than the Stueben pitcher we got from one of their friends as a wedding present. "Contains the cold better," I added.

Fran had to wash the dishes from the previous night. Her plight did not go unnoticed. His eyes shot skyward. When her mother finally mentioned how interesting the room was, his eyes stayed there. I filled the silence with a steady monologue of semi-autobiographical material which only brought forth a request for another martini from her mother and a pained expression from her father. Their discomfort was impressive. A knock on the door interrupted my monologue. It was the old pensioner from next door, standing in his pee-stained underwear, asking me to fix the toilet. When I returned, I was confronted by a very high-strung hostess. Fran was putting the meal on the table with all the style of a scullery maid—gracious serving was not one of her accomplishments. She served a stew that she had made during her lunch hour. The minute her father tasted it he dumped the plate and its contents on the floor.

"This isn't fit for human consumption."

I wondered if Fran had called up Legman for his lung recipe. She burst into tears. Her mother went to comfort her.

"That meat was bought under a guarantee, sir, and at an attractive price."

The laugh I hoped would release the tension was witheld out of sheer malice. By the time I mopped up the floor, the chances of our surviving the evening as a foursome had greatly diminished.

Her father's bad manners worked like a tonic on me; I felt I had finally captured his attention. Her mother called him an animal.

"I'll drink to that," I added cheerfully.

The old man remained unrepentant, feeling, no doubt, justified in his original theory that his daughter would have done much better to have married a cutter. After they left, Fran stopped crying long enough to remind me that she'd warned me what would happen. I explained to her that her father's act was based on deep psychological resentment at losing her. That cheered her up considerably.

"Don't worry, he'll hate himself in the morning. The advantage is all on your side. They'll be as docile as lambs next time we're together."

"If there is a next time," Fran added.

As I forecast, the evening had a therapeutic effect on them. Realizing that there was no chance of either of us ever conforming to *their* idea of the good life, our bridge games in the country turned into miniature therapy sessions that allowed all the hostility and distrust to come out into the open in between the bidding.

"One no-trump," I would bid. "What does it all mean?"

"Two spades," her father would shoot back. "Why don't you get a decent job and find out?"

Fran would be too intimidated by now to do anything but pass. Her mother had trouble focusing, but didn't want to let her partner down, so she'd throw in a bid that didn't make any sense at all. When I bid four no-trump, he smiled. I counter attacked:

"I don't want to end up like you—rich, respected, and a slave to materialism."

By this time Fran found it easier to wet her pants than make a bid. Mother would be on the verge of passing out, but managed to tell her husband that she wanted a divorce.

"Double," shouted the old man. "Just wait a few years; when you've outgrown this childish rebellion, you'll begin to enjoy life as a grown-up."

"Redouble," I screamed.

I assured him I would never conform. Then he would lead with some foxy card that completely sent me down on the first trick. Later in the evening, Fran suggested that Torquemada was a Prince of Pleasure compared to me, and if I ever suggested she play bridge again with her father as a partner she would flip. I was beginning to enjoy the game, going so far as to buy an auto-bridge set to help me plan my strategy for the next encounter. I was able to function with my in-laws because I never took them seriously. I often deliberately created situations that gave them the opportunity to criticize us just to keep up their morale. I had learned from Cutie that grown-ups were never so happy as when they had something to correct.

I was more successful teaching Fran, who had no sense of rhythm, to dance. She knew only one step that I called The Frankenstein Hesitation, but by the time we were ready to make our public debut on the terrace to an invited audience of one—her mother—she danced as gracefully as Shirley Temple.

We were beginning to have good times in the country. If the city afforded me the opportunity to play the editor, the country provided me with the perfect chance to play the Country Gentleman. I was the self-appointed flower arranger, sending up the Japanese art with massive displays that would have caused a sensitive Jap to commit Hara-kiri. Fran was impressed with my chopping of firewood. Taking over the outdoor barbecue concession, complete with a 'what's cooking?' apron, revealed another of my hidden talents. On shopping expeditions at the supermarket, I held up traffic in the aisles as I engaged strangers in a discussion on the merits of S & W canned asparagus. Fran and her mother would desperately try to disassociate themselves from my scene.

There were so many things about the country life that I liked it began to worry me. Fran was no longer sure that I was only playing at being a Country Gentleman. She wanted to have less to do with her parents than I did. Maybe it was because I was missing my own family so much that I tried to become a part of hers.

Coming back from the country, nerves rested, I always felt a touch of sadness the moment the key entered my door. The first thing that hit me was the stale odor of the last party. The place was decorated with empty bottles and over-spilled ashtrays; it was too depressing compared to the well-groomed environment we'd just vacated. I began to nag Fran about taking better care of the place. I would unwrap the flowers, arrange them in one of the wedding present vases, regretting that I had thrown away so many of the other wedding gifts. Fran would rush off to her job with my words, "this place is a mess" ringing in her ears. "And don't forget we have people coming to dinner tonight." I tidied up the place the best I could, opened the windows to let the fresh air in, and on the way to my makeshift desk, looked at my reflection in the Venetian mirror above the mantel, noticing that my tan seemed to be fading and that I was looking as tired as the mirror— uncleaned since we got it. What does Fran do with all her time, I thought.

Opening the day's mail no longer had the old excitement. If it didn't contain a check for a subscription, it was put aside. Manuscripts continued to pour in. I seldom read them past the first line, and if they didn't have a self-addressed and stamped envelope, I'd throw them in the waste basket. After making up the bank deposit and taking care of subscribers' complaints, the whole routine of running the magazine's day to day activities took less than an hour, leaving me the rest of the time to spend searching out creative ways to fill the days.

My first telephone call would be to Holmes to see if we were meeting that day to do any writing. We were always planning articles to sell to other magazines. We had interest from *The New Yorker* in our expose of Walter Winchell, whom Holmes and I loathed. Gossip had become a fine art in America. Robert Harrison, publisher of *Confidential*, with the largest circulation in America, was stripping away the mask from America's idols and heroes, revealing a sordidness that the public relished. It had become so powerful that movie stars' publicity agents fed them unsavory information about their clients just to get the publicity. It set the pace for a dozen imitators, *Spy, Peep, Secrets, Inside,* etc. marking the beginning of the break down of privacy in America. It was something that I totally agreed with and wanted to take a step further by exposing the exposers.

We had some inside information on Winchell; his daughter was running wild, getting into troubles that Winchell tried to cover up. Hot stuff. Our prospects for success as a writing team were enhanced by an offer from Chandler Brossard. He was set to become the managing editor of the revived *American Mercury*, famous in the 20's as a crusading magazine under the editorship of H. L. Mencken. Brossard admired our *Neurotica* articles and thought a series exposing the vulgarization of movies, TV, and mass entertainment was the kind of material he could make a splash with in his new job. We decided to firm it up over lunch.

Holmes was struggling with his novel in the middle of our planned collaboration, yet he always had time to contribute a few hours a day. We usually ended up drinking through a dozen ideas for articles at Glennon's or P. J. Clarke's. Glennon's was almost a second office to me; I was always leaving messages that I could be reached there. The place reeked of such failure that even owner Jimmy Glennon wouldn't drink there anymore. When I walked into the bar with the line, "Whatever happened to Anna Mae Wong?" the ex-child star, the ex-subscription editor, the ex-art director, or the ex-movie queen would always nod approvingly. They knew it was only fair comment on the fall from grace that so many of them had experienced. When the cocktail hour approached, we'd have collected a half dozen people to join us on the pilgrimage across the street to P. J. Clarke's, where they had blocks of ice in the men's urinals and the best hamburger in town. Clarke's at that hour began to fill up with the successes of Madison Avenue, always a target for our scorn. These 'sell outs' were shining examples of why success was a danger to your health. We drank to get high, they drank to alleviate the pressure of the job. Sometimes their aggression would overflow into a fight that ended out on the street. "Don't stop it," a Gin and Tonic implored, "this has been brewing at CBS for months." We would always find someone at Clarke's whose guilt about being successful called for him to pay for round after round of drinks. Such generosity only increased our contempt for his plight. Off we would go, bidding him a pleasant journey on his flight to nowhere. We couldn't afford to be seen with successful people. Kerouac was about to be published by Harcourt Brace, but nobody believed the book was going to make him a success, which meant he was still acceptable company. We were all in the same groove, seeing ourselves as romantic losers who wouldn't sell out. We weren't looking for answers so much as looking for the next party.

So it was with great pleasure that Fran and I accepted her folks' invitation to the Metropolitan Museum's party of the year. That her father was on the board of trustees for the Museum's Costume Institute lent an extra touch of danger to my being among those present. All the most fashion conscious people from the industry and media were gathered together to reassure each other that there was still life in the old labels. I had to rent a tux for the occasion, which I didn't mind, except it didn't have a decent label to flash should I be challenged. Fran's brother Sammy joined us, and what a pretty picture the five of us made as we entered the glittering arena. We were greeted by the stars of the rag trade, who didn't look as impressive as their labels, and I looked much more impressive than mine. I had several brilliant exchanges with these people on the psychoanalytical significance of the popularity of the trouser suit for women, declaring to my slightly bewildered audience that it heralded the forthcoming emasculation of men. Of course, I needed another drink after that, but it didn't stop me from cornering various strangers to discuss other sexual-psycho aspects of fashion. Before the evening was over, I felt like the ancient mariner who stoppeth one in three to tell his version of a world he never made and had always loathed. In memory of that evening, we posed for a photograph looking like the family of the year. Needless to say, Fran and I were the only ones smiling.

Our only other foray into the world of the rich untalented was the evening spent with a millionaire pupil of Broyard's, Hy Sobiloff. Something of a legend in financial circles, Sobiloff was trying to create one in the literary world as well. Discovering that he had a natural gift for poetry, he once engaged Delmore Schwartz to tutor him in the art of poetry for fifty dollars a session, the going price for a top psychiatrist. Schwartz, tiring of the job, turned him over to Broyard, who rather liked the fringe benefits that went with the job: weekend yachting parties with starlets, fancy restaurants, and champagne.

Broyard regaled us with amusing stories of Sobiloff's gift for high living and the perils of being a sensitive millionaire. When his girlfriend painted her left breast with a portrait of a piglet that resembled him, he was unable to write for weeks.

Broyard suggested that I have a look at some of his poems for *Neurotica*. The fabulous picture that Broyard painted of his life-style was much more interesting to me than his poetry, but I was curious to meet the man. If he was so generous, there was always the possibility that he might become a silent patron of *Neurotica*. I had visions of Legman and Sobiloff meeting at some fancy restaurant with Legman demanding lung stew and Sobiloff asking the head waiter for a muzzle for Legman. When the invitation finally came from Sobiloff, Fran thought it was a dumb idea. "You meet one millionaire, you've met 'em all."

We got together at his Fifth Avenue apartment, decorated in early 'French potential.' He kept us waiting while he completed a deal for a piece of property in Massachussets. He looked like an undistinguished Jewish businessman with high blood pressure. When the butler served us sparkling wine instead of champagne, I didn't get the feeling I was in the company of a poet with an open pocket book. He let drop that Conrad Aitken was going to write the introduction to his collected poems. It depressed me no end. I was afraid he was going to read them all to us, but Fran saved the day by asking, "When do we eat?" He had the nerve to suggest that he send out for some sandwiches and we could listen to a few of his poems while we waited. "Are you kidding?" Fran asked in that bitter style of hers.

His choice of restaurant was the kind he'd take his accountant to. His girl friend showed her displeasure by a steady barrage of abuse aimed at his physical powers. She had a mean line that would have won her a nomination for an award had it been in a play. Broyard was a little embarassed, Fran was annoyed, but I found him quite poignant as he talked about his miserable childhood and his secret life as a would-be poet. The evening was devoid of any material that would bear retelling, ending rather abruptly with the demands of his actress friend to hit the nightclub circuit, plans that we were obviously not included in.

Broyard came by with a selection of Sobiloff's writing. As a favor, I selected something I knew Legman would go for. It had a line about his father being a coward that would remind him of his own father, who bent Legman's airgun over his knee in what he called "a symbolic act of castration." When the poem appeared in *Neurotica*, Sobiloff complained bitterly to Broyard that we had humiliated him by printing it on the page opposite an ad for Legman's pamphlet on the *Cause of Homosexuality*. In the contributors' column I wrote that Sobiloff was "an American poet," but "*schmuck*" would have been more accurate.

Fran and I tried out a lot of different scenes that autumn in an attempt to find a niche, but discovered we didn't fit into any of them. Our bridge-playing frontier was extended to far away Queens, where a straight cousin of mine offered bridge evenings and snacks and if Fran would like to drop by their hat shop in the Empire State Building and pick out a nice hat at wholesale . . . Then there was Brooklyn Heights evenings with Fran's former friends from art school who were smugly pursuing success in the world of fine arts. Attractive and stylish, smart and hungry, they would probably make it without any help from us. They were the kind of people who still believed in the Museum of Modern Art.

When I got Fred and Paula's invitation to spend Christmas with them in St. Louis, I was delighted to escape our vigorous pursuit of people for a while. I longed to see Cutie and the family, but most of all I wanted Fran to see the Galleries and share my past with me. I knew she thought St. Louis was nearer to Siberia than New York, but I couldn't think of a better Christmas present to give her than Fred and Paula.

10

From the moment they met us at the airport, the going was rough. The picture I had painted of my sophisticated brother and his wild, red-haired wife was not the one Fran saw. Fred was dressed in his normal way, about ten years behind the fashion, with his longish hair glistening with Dixie Peach Pomade, and his fly not quite closed.

Anybody in a matching suit was a business man in Fran's books, even though the unzipped fly should have been a clue that he wasn't all that serious. Paula's high-pitched nasal voice, that I have always considered one that Emma Goldman might have used at rallies, was an additional irritant: Fran's ears were already ringing from the flight. Paula's natural red hair that Fred claimed made her look like a Titian hadn't changed, but I could see that Fran was surprised to see so much of it on such a small body. Paula was only five feet tall, but she took great pride in keeping in perfect condition what God had given her. Fred never acknowledged any greeting as being proper without a limp handshake; it was not his habit to show affection in public. I should have thought that would have gone down well with Fran because *never* in all the time I spent with her family did I see anyone embrace.

But once we got to their house, little pieces of the puzzle began to fit together. Their houseman, Joseph, a black man of indeterminate age, wearing a pair of knee pads made up of pieces of an old tire, was a nice touch that Fran appreciated. Once relaxed before an open fire with a generous drink and the initial questions that could be answered with a "yes" or a "no" out of the way, Paula's skill at getting to the heart of the matter began to weave its old magic.

"All right, now let's get serious," Paula began. "Do you ever think of coming back to St. Louis, Jay?"

When I told her "I'll take the fifth amendment on that one," she understood what I meant. Of course, I thought of going back to St. Louis someday, but to say it in front of Fran would not be marriage-building. Paula's sensitivity to my predicament was acknowledged with a discreet wink.

She wanted to know all about our life in New York: what kind of friends did we have? What did we do for kicks? Were we missing anything? Did we ever think of living in the country? Did anybody ever get laid at parties? Were there any laughs? An impartial judge sitting in on the answers to those questions would have thought that Fran and I were living in cities separated by an ocean. He would have recommended a trial divorce. I was the optimist and Fran the pessimist.

Freud would have made a note that Fran had a harsh and punitive super ego, and I had a sense of humor that was destructive. Had Freud known more of the facts, he would have realized that I was a very serious guy who had to cover it up with laughs; but then Freud didn't know anything about game-playing. Fred, who was wiser than Freud, put our differences down to "real love based on mutual misunderstanding."

Fran was immediately charmed by Paula's inquiring mind; she realized that all her searching questions were only an attempt to share some of her own doubts with Fran. Paula was always a partisan, and she encouraged others to make a definite stand. That was something Fran found difficult to do and I was grateful. We seldom argued either in private or public. Our rare differences were only flaws in her character, easily corrected by a few hours of my concentrated sulking, or a note left on the table: "Forget about dinner tonight—meet me at P. J. Clarke's. Kisses. J."

I gave her a wide berth during our time in St. Louis; I didn't want to give anyone the impression we were newlyweds. I spent most of the time at the Galleries with Cutie, going over the books and trying to straighten out the mess Cutie had made there. She was under the misapprehension that I had come to my senses, treating me as if I had never been away. I accused Cutie of blatant commercialism, appealing to the low grade hobbyists and off-the-sidewalk merchants: "The windows are a disgrace; I can't tell whether this is a serious antique shop or a pawnbroker's establishment. What image are you striving for?"

"Profit," she spat out, looking at me as though I were an idiot.

Guests who had heard that the Landesmans were unconventional would have been shocked to see the glittering array of matching silver, crystal, and chinaware at the dinner preceding the party Fred and Paula threw for us. But after cocktails, when filing into the dining room and seeing frosty stinger drinks awaiting them as the first course, they would have been reassured that their original impression was correct. This collection of people might have been misjudged at first sight; most of the men looked like successes in their expensive suits, but there was always a subtle flaw that gave them away. Either their hair was too long or too short, their finger nails too dirty or bitten down to the quick, and nobody wore a Van Heusen shirt or an old school tie. Their women were either overdressed or underdressed, depending on their husband's status. Fran, though more fashionable-looking than anyone at the party, saw herself as a pot-smoking, jean-clad rebel in a den of squares, or even worse, at a party for grown-ups where she had to behave herself or be sent to bed. She reacted accordingly. I wasn't surprised when she deliberately smashed one of Fred's records on the floor during a lull in the attention. She felt it to be her due. She was further disappointed when nobody seemed to mind or even care. To a group of people who saw nothing sinister about sneaking off to a broom closet for a quick blow job, the breaking of a record was a pathetic gesture. Yet it didn't go unnoticed. Fred later told me he thought it was a good sign, "a step in the right direction," as he put it.

In an attempt to instill a sense of history into Fran, I took her on a grand tour of my childhood. I went back to the old neighborhood to recapture some of the moments of triumph and failure I'd experienced there. The corner confectioners was run by a man called Hornberger. It was very special to the neighborhood, providing it with all the necessities of life, and very important to me. It was the oasis that my father sent me to for his Muriel cigars and Cutie to fetch Pet Evaporated Cream and a loaf of Wonder bread, and "don't forget to bring back some black thread." It had a lending library of Tiffany Thayer, Baseball Joe books, and my mother's favorite author, Edna Ferber. I could read a dozen magazines for free: *Photoplay, Popular Mechanics, Doc Savage, Amazing Stories,* and *Weird Tales.* It was where I bought Christmas presents for my pals and halloween masks for enemies; also my athletic equipment and school supplies. Spring was always identified with the coming of the Phillipino yo-yo demonstrators to Hornberger's.

The shop tour over, I pointed out the houses where the local bully, Abe Cooperman, lived. Being his friend was not easy. He once threatened to destroy all the Landesman boys for using "big words," but when his friend, Tony LaPippero, the local bad-boy, explained to him that he wouldn't get any points for beating up such helpless weak-lings as the Landesmans, he settled for a double ice cream cone. I showed her the alleys and ashpits, still overflowing with goodies, and the garage in back of our house that I once turned into an art gallery to give my pal, Joe Salina, an exhibition of his watercolors. My dad thought Joe was very talented and bought one of the paintings, much against Cutie's advice.

The family house, once the pride of the block, was now a run-down, shabby building that still had one of the flats for rent. St. Ann's Orphan home was gone, and the traffic light had been replaced by modern boulevard stop signs that left no time for communication. Nobody was around from the old days to verify my travelogue, yet I left the old neighborhood with a warm feeling that it was the best of all possible worlds to grow up in.

Knowing that Fran was a dedicated movie-goer—she once told me that she usually attended two double-features in a single day—I took her to see our downtown movie palaces, still operating with all the class and style of my youthful days. They no longer had the wonderful stage shows with chorus lines and comedians direct from New York or Dick Powell as Master of Ceremonies at the Ambassador Theatre and Ginger Rogers as one of the Ambassadorables. I finally scored by showing her how we used to sneak in through the side doors, pointing with pride to the one I had used. That little display of rebellion appealed to her. We proceeded downtown.

She liked the names of the department stores we visited: Stix, Baer and Fuller, Scruggs, Vandervort and Barney, and Famous Barr. I showed her my favorite neon signs: Splinker, Dorfmont, Bradshaw & Kravitz, Rice-Stix, Dick X-ray Company, Swizers Licorice Candy Company, and Win-U-Preserves. I introduced her to Mr. Krell who ran the out-of-town newspaper stand on the corner and greeted me like a five-star final. We had an ice cream in Theodore's Tea Room, where my father's murals now clashed with the neon decor. "His cherubs look Jewish," she said. I explained that all his cherubs looked like Tannhauser's off-spring until Hitler came to power. I was dying to tell her more about Benjamin C.'s odyssey from artist to antique dealer, but she was up to her neck in Landesmania already; by the time we left she knew enough about me and the family to last her a lifetime.

I considered the trip a success when she confessed that the only thing she really enjoyed was meeting Fred and

Paula. "I wouldn't mind seeing them again," was the way she put it.

"And Cutie's Christmas dinner with the chicken liver dressing meant nothing to you?"

Cutie hovered around everyone to see that they ate up, paying particular attention to Fran's eating habits. When she had seconds of everything, Cutie told me later that I had made a smart marriage: "She's a good eater". With Cutie's approval ringing in my ears, we departed for N.Y.

Upon our return, the place looked shabby in comparison to the rich decor of Fred's house. Along with a pile of manuscripts forecasting a bleak future for civilization awaiting me, were a couple of invitations to New Year's Eve parties. I felt that we had been entertained enough to ignore them. The excuse I used, however, was that I didn't want to go to any parties where I would have to drink out of paper cups. Instead, we spent New Year's Eve at a neighborhood movie house that was showing Orson Welles' *Macbeth*. We both hated it. It was not a good beginning for 1951.

A phone call from a cautious Legman with the news that the galleys of McLuhan's book had arrived rekindled my interest in *Neurotica*. Reading McLuhan was like reading a sanitized Legman. Legman and McLuhan saw the writing on the wall. McLuhan's style was cool, his content hot, and he mixed the two with a pinch of pepper that made it palatable even to the people he was attacking. (When, years later, McLuhan's ideas were given unreserved support from *Time Magazine* and the establishment in general, Legman's reappraisal was vicious). We had quite a lot of material on the folklore of industrial man, as Legman called it. We agreed that it would be a good idea to devote the complete issue of *Neurotica* No. 8 to the "role played by the machine in winning the battle *against* man, instead of *for* him." It was to be entitled *Notes for a Martian historian*.

Between my worries about the "influencing machine" and writing with Holmes of homosexual conspiracies, I began to feel as though I were operating under siege. Was it worth it? The writing sessions with Holmes were always productive and often fun, but if any excuse for not working came along, I seized upon it to vent my frustrations. It was a bleak winter, made bleaker by Legman's determination to devote the ninth issue of *Neurotica* to the castration complex.

"This castration thing is so big," he told me on the phone, "I can't even lay my wife anymore."

"I know, Legman," I said. "It's bigger than both of us. But I think the Machine issue will cover that nicely."

There was a long silence on the phone. I could feel his lip curling up, ready to strike.

"Are you there?" I asked. "Hello?"

"You're trying to do it to me again, aren't you?"

"Do what? Put out a good issue on the machine?"

"Don't do it to me, Landesman." It wasn't a snarl; it wasn't a request: it was spoken so softly, it couldn't have been anything but a threat. "Why are you doing it to me?" he repeated, this time even softer.

"Doing what?" I was beginning to lose patience. There was another long silence. "What's the trouble, Legman?" I thought I sounded reasonable.

"I WON'T LET YOU DO IT!"

Now that he was screaming again, I felt safer. "Take it easy. What are you on about?" I had lost the thread of the conversation. He began to speak very slowly.

"I know what you're on about, Landesman. I heard about those articles you're doing for that fake editor, Brossard. It's all over town."

"For Christ's sake, Legman, you don't have any monopoly on conspiracies. I've got to put out a magazine. I'm broke and *Neurotica 8* is going to cost three times that of an ordinary issue." It was a mistake: whenever I mentioned money, he got furious.

"You're more than broke," he started to shout again: "you're morally bankrupt! You've sold out. I'm disappointed in you, kid. AND IT'S MY IDEAS YOU'RE CASHING IN ON and I get nothing but a kick up the

bum." He paused, lowering his voice again. "Congratulations—you've invented a new form of castration." He
laughed, which was always a bad sign. "You're going to try
to silence me like all the other shitty editors I've worked
with before. But I'll publish the castration issue without
you, Landesman."

I was so relieved to hear this and so furious at the same
time, that I refused to tell him, "you'd be doing me a
favor." Instead, I told him he had a very short memory: "I
published you when nobody would touch you. I couldn't
have been all that shitty. Think it over, Legman. Once you
publish the castration issue, what do you do for an en-
core?" He didn't laugh, neither did he explode. It made
some slight sense even to one with his peculiar outlook.
"Besides, Legman, what are we fighting about? Castration
is a long way off; let's don't bite off more than we can
chew." I left the conversation on that high note and hoped
that he could take the joke, even though he couldn't take
me.

The confrontation with Legman forced me to accept the
fact that I was running out of enthusiasm. I couldn't go on
with *Neurotica* without his invaluable work; it was his contribution as production man and chief writer that was
giving the magazine its punch. His insights were so original and far ahead of what was going down in those days
that I put up with his furies because I knew he was right.
The real problem was that I was losing interest in attacking
the enemy his way. I had some other ideas of how to win.

I spent a month playing with the idea of turning the
barn in Connecticut into a place for us to live in during our
weekend visits. It would be a half-way house to indepen-
dence without breaking contact with the folks. I still enjoyed dancing on their terrace and entertaining their
guests, but I wanted guests of my own to entertain and a
ballroom in a barn with a three-piece band. No matter how
hard we tried to please, we were only a part of the landscape. I wanted to create a place for them to stretch out in
and be our guests, so I could spray them in to fit in our

painting. I began to read the local paper, *The Newtown Bee*, with great relish; I even imagined I could be writing for it once I settled down as a country journalist. I went so far as to buy a pair of blue jeans, something I had never done before. There was something ludicrous about seeing all the city folks in the local supermarket in their pristine blue jeans and white sneakers. Now I was thinking of joining them.

For a test run, I invited Broyard, Holmes, and a few other friends to taste a little country life as we experienced it, complete with sizzling steaks on the outdoor barbecue, perfect martinis, and a little Bach for background music. Even though it was winter, the grounds were still attractive, with swans resting on the lake. The contrast between our life in the city and what it was that night was so obvious it wasn't worth commenting on. Broyard and Holmes agreed: "It's all here, Jay. What more is there to strive for?"

The dream was short lived. Fran would have none of it. "Yeah, while you're in the city, I'm stuck out here with the crickets and my folks. Even if we did do the barn up, the folks would be watching over our shoulder like wardens. They'd complain about the noise of the cars coming and going, the loud music, and the quality of our friends. It would never work. Besides, I hate the country. Everytime I see a tree I want to kick it." So much for country life. Another escape route closed.

All of us were planning ways to escape. By Spring, everybody I knew was reassessing their life. Holmes and his wife were separated. Brossard was making good at the *American Mercury*, but he was still writing in an abandoned Pontiac parked outside his house. He wasn't actually living in it, but he claimed it was the only place where it was quiet enough to write. Even Carl Solomon, married only a few months, was living apart from his wife. Paul Mazursky broke up with his beautiful Sino-Jewish girlfriend. We couldn't find a couple who were still together. Even Kerouac was having trouble. It occurred to me that you couldn't stay married and make it in New York.

Our marriage was riddled with contradictions and abortive attempts at clarifying each other's expectations, yet they remained as muddled as ever. Fran had a peculiar attitude toward her job. Never feeling that it was important enough for a career, she never missed a day, nor was she ever late. She would always leave any party early to get her sleep. I resented it, kidding her about being so conscientious about something that was, after all, only a job. I was hoping that she'd share my unorganized life, contributing her own special brand of privileged hi-jinx to make it work better for the two of us.

To be fair, we were both incapable of accepting any rules that weren't ours. But when I tried to lay down a few rules about housekeeping, Fran wouldn't accept them. "I married you to get away from all that crap. I thought you wanted to hang out with people who would tell us what's bad for us, not what's good for us. You should have been a rabbi." She added, "You're always telling people how to live." I couldn't convince her I was trying to do the opposite—tell people how not to live. "Don't take it seriously" was the best piece of advice I had for anyone.

The only mistake I ever made, I began to realize, was taking *Neurotica* so seriously. Was there really any purpose in continuing publishing? Starting out as a magazine hospitable to the neurotic personality, it was turning into a periodical that preached against it. What did my readers really think? I had the brilliant idea of sending out a reply card questionnaire:

As editor of *Neurotica,* I would like your help in determining the future of the magazine. After two years of publication, we have received so much ambiguous criticism both favorable and hostile that we are confused as to how you, our subscribers, really feel about *Neurotica.* Would you take five minutes to fill out the questionnaire and mail it back to us?

Do you want *Neurotica* to continue?

Do you feel that *Neurotica* fills a definite need?

Would you renew your subscription?

What articles or contributors have you liked in the past?

What type of material would you like to see more of in the future?

Additional comments⎯⎯⎯⎯⎯⎯⎯⎯⎯⎯⎯⎯⎯⎯⎯⎯

The percentage of response was shockingly small and very mixed:

> "Your shit stinks" . . . "Don't try and be an arty Police Gazette" . . . "more analysis and attacks on thought conformity" . . . "Continue probing of society for cultural dishonesty especially at high-brow level" . . . "I don't know how I feel, particularly whether your writers are more neurotic than your readers or the opposite but in any event it's original and uses the axe instead of the scalpel" . . . "I wish you would give the homos a better break" . . . "no, no, no" . . . "yes, yes, yes" . . .

Legman came in for some abuse:

> "Let Legman either rest or write about Chaucer" . . .

> "Legman's neurotic trash—reveals merely his desperate need for psychoanalytic treatment" . . . "No nut-cracking by G. Legman or his type of pseudo-sensationalism."

I was very disappointed. Where was my audience? Was I getting through to anyone out there? Perhaps *Neurotica* had said all it had to say and the time had come to close up shop. I discussed this with Legman who turned down the idea with his usual scorn. He was still convinced we were breaking through.

There was one reply that gave me a twinge: "What I think would make an interesting study is how it happened that a personable young lad like yourself ever gave birth to such a brainstorm in the first place. Go straight, boy. We're all behind you." The writer had obviously observed me somewhere and was unable to connect me with the image of *Neurotica*. Certainly watching me flinging arms and legs in the air at the Palladium would never convince him it was the same person. Go straight? I was straight! I was already wearing Bianchini ties, seconds that Fran brought home from work. I had a score of ways of throwing people off the track. The one rule I had: avoid the obvious and always do the unexpected.

The purchase of a sensational car had a profound effect on future events. We kept it in the country for use on weekends. How thrilled we were to be on our own, driving anywhere we wanted to without having to ask anyone's permission. Had it been an ordinary car, it would have been the best fifty-dollar investment ever made, but this was a car with built-in therapeutic properties that no amount of money could buy. A rare model Ford V-8, four-door convertible with a LaBaron body would mean nothing to the ordinary person, but to the auto-erotic personality, it was the big O., painted canary yellow, black, with wire wheels; its white leather interior smelled of good times past. I felt like a champion behind the wheel, whizzing up the country lanes in search of new sparring partners, my able second Fran next to me, encouraging me to run more with the crazies and less with the squares.

There were only a handful of crazies in Connecticut, but we managed to find them. In Robert Lowrey, a successful writer who had forsaken Manhattan for the country, I found a sympathetic ally. His past was similar to mine, making me curious about his future. Back in Columbus, Ohio, he was publishing little books that were prized by a handful of people for their originality. Encouraged to go to New York, like me, to try for the big time, he became a successful writer and keen observer of the changing scene. Like me, he was married, but he moved to Connecticut to escape the pressure of the city, unlike me. From the first pitcher of martinis we polished off, I could see his master plan of escape was not working. He took us on a ride around the countryside at ninety miles an hour, extolling its beauty and the advantages of being a Country Gentleman writer. At that speed, I suspected he was kidding himself. I wanted it to work for him, because I wanted the same things. He talked of the past as if it were yesterday, remembering it all with the enthusiasm of a child, his small eyes compulsively working overtime as his life whizzed by. He noticed, for instance, that Fran was digging his amazing act as the crazy writer in exile. She had a way of coming alive when danger lurked, giving the impression that any excess, no matter how destructive, was better than no excess at all.

We were sad when we heard, a few months after meeting him, that he had cracked up and was doing time in a sedation center, where we visited him. How depressing it was to see the wild man so subdued, drinking vitamin-enriched orange juice. Any dreams I had of escaping to the country melted away, much to Fran's relief.

My dreams of making it as a free-lance writer faded as most of our ideas for articles were rejected. Holmes and I finished the pieces for Brossard, who paid us a handsome six hundred dollars, but they weren't scheduled to be printed for months. With *Neurotica* now almost a sideline, my main business was finding a way to live in New York without a cause. I must have had that in mind when I went to the toy store F. O. A. Schwartz and bought a red-tipped pogo stick! It seemed to be the perfect instrument to celebrate the rudderless life we were drifting into. I hung it on the wall opposite the hull of the lost ship.

Birds were singing somewhere that spring, but we didn't hear them. Fran and I tried to talk about what was happening to us, but we couldn't communicate. The differences that made our early days together so interesting, now seemed like serious problems. Filling up the house with people, no matter how stimulating they were, seemed like a Chinese dinner, leaving me hungry for something more substantial. Fran found the parties and the drinking too much and began to beg off after a few hours, using her job as the excuse. It worried me that Fran took her job so seriously until I realized the real problem was simply that she didn't feel comfortable in the movie I was directing.

Although I never saw it at the time, she had a lousy role. She was type-cast as 'the little woman'. All that talent for the appropriate quip, the acid remark, her brittle style seemed to desert her in front of the crowd who might have appreciated a creative put down or two. She seemed terrified to join in any of the conversation, and, since conversations in those days were mostly between men, a woman had to say something really provocative to get any attention. As a woman, she was ignored by almost everyone, except Holmes and Kerouac, the only two friends of mine that she liked.

Holmes's affection for her as well as his understanding of her plight was a strong bond that helped her get through many a night. Kerouac, even more sentimental than Holmes, had much more in common with Fran than me. When I would see them in a corner of the room talking very earnestly while all around them nothing but madness prevailed, I flashed on Fran's capability for sadness. There was a look on her face that I had never seen before.

The next day, I asked her what she and Jack were talking about, mentioning the fact that she looked sad. For the first time in months she smiled that Cheshire cat look of hers that I always found so attractive. "He said he was sorry for me because I seemed to spend my life in rooms filled with yelling men. He said he was lonely and asked me to be his girl." I asked her why she had such a sad look on her face. She said she was scared. I didn't take her seriously at the time, but as my days became pointless for weeks on end, I began to get scared myself. I would wander through the city with fellow conspirators whose luck was worse than mine.

My old buddy, Stanley Radulovich from Little Bohemia, was living on Sixth Avenue above a Gypsy tea room, so depressed about the failure of his marriage and his career as an artist that he checked out the size of the gas oven door and, finding that it fitted his head, gave it a couple of tries without any luck. He claimed he was too depressed to turn on the gas the last time he tried it. I liked Radulovich; he could be gloomy Sunday one minute and Bugs Bunny the next. We used to watch cats copulating on smart midtown fire escapes with a boredom that was frightening. We saw the same giant Hieronymous Bosch murals of untouchable transients everywhere on our pub crawls. We saw the unconquerable Dagmar hurrying down 45th Street alone and proud of the most publicised tits in the nation till she ducked into a beauty salon and was lost to us.

A wave of anti-intellectualism hit the serious people that Spring. Vitality was reserved for exhausting bouts of hand-wrestling, and insights were lavished on up-and-coming boxers. The New York Giants received more airplay in the Cedar Bar than Art. The sports pages were devoured the way 'little magazines' used to be. Sheila Graham, Cholly Knickenbocker and Hedda Hopper loomed bigger than the Triple Thinkers. Searching questions were asked of old-time movie bit-players. Evenings were devoted to re-enacting favorite scenes from film classics. Ex-cocksmen bragged about not being able to get it up for weeks. In the twilight of anxiety it all looked sick, but there were laughs mixed with the jitters. The predominant pose was contemptuous and you couldn't get more contemporary than that. If you weren't contemporary in New York, you were *nothing*. It seemed that Fran and I were seeing too many nervous people lately and I was beginning to twitch a little, but only in one eye.

One weekend we decided not to go to the country, so we invited all the names we knew to a party to celebrate my recently acquired pogo stick. Even Legman showed up, but when I took the stick down from the wall and claimed it was the most fiercely contemporary weapon invented, he gave me a quick goodbye and wished me luck with the "flotsam and jetsam people that you've become famous for collecting." I introduced my new friend, the pogo stick, to the assembled guests ("all the beauty and brains of New York," Broyard declared, cynically), very seriously explaining my theory and demonstrating my skill with the weapon. As people arrived, I'd hop over to open the door. Everyone was delighted with my new toy, waiting for the opportunity to sample its delights.

The stick became the focus of attention, more popular than any guest. Its significance was being seriously discussed. The existentialists wondered if it would catch on in Sartre's circle. Freudians saw it as a liberation of the repressed psyche. The Blake expert, Klonsky, who had fallen off one in childhood, declared it "dangerous," Ginsberg saw it as an extension of Celine; Solomon pulled for Artaud. "It's the real journey to the end of the night," declared a wit. Kerouac, the ex-footballer, took possession, sure that he'd make a touch-down, but he was thrown for a loss a few seconds later. "It cuts Zen," someone shrieked when he fell off. The guests were getting into the game.

Kerouac rushed to the kitchen to collect the old saucepans for an improvised rhythm section while others fought for possession of the big stick. A circle began to form around Carl Solomon, who had snatched it away from Broyard, making brilliant, insulin-shocked leaps that looked like he was heading for the big coma. His confidence was exhilerating to the guests—they began to clap, edging him on to jump faster and higher. The whole thing began to take on the sinister overtones of a *totentanze*. No one wanted to be left out of the season's best futility rite. A chorus of "go man, go" encouraged Solomon to even greater efforts. Paul Mazursky moved in to stop Solomon. "Back, you fools," Solomon hollered. "This is the first time I've had it up in years." Holmes shot me a look of incredible bewilderment. I hollered across the crowd: "Germany, year Zero. The Weimar Republic lives." Just as everyone was on the way to a collective orgasm, Solomon leaped so high that the weight on landing was too much for the floor, spilling him over the split linoleum like a piece of human wreckage. Someone in the back of the room broke the

silence with the line, "no one ever beats a pogo stick."
Mazursky picked Solomon up—"Great audition piece,
baby, you're hired." The remaining guests in the circle
extended Solomon polite applause, and the party went
back to being nervous.

The Crystal Palace

With the publication of the machine issue of *Neurotica 8* in the Spring of 1951, the dream was over. Everything I had to say was on record now and with copies of the magazine in all the great libraries of the world, there was a chance that Legman's promise of a footnote in history would be kept. Future historians would discover that *Neurotica* had chronicled America's illness long before others recognized it. Violence was going to become a part of the everyday life in this country and there was nothing that *Neurotica* could do about stemming the tide. I was completely disillusioned and wanted a way out. I decided to give Legman the magazine, lock, stock and barrel.

But it wasn't easy giving him something for nothing. He was immediately suspicious, questioning my motives as though I was bent on committing a crime. He wasn't satisfied with my explanation that I had nothing more to say. He became abusive when I told him I had lost interest in changing the world and wanted now to change myself. He accused me of being selfish. I told him I was turning over all the proceeds of the current issues, all the files, back issues, and records of the operation to him. He thought about it for a few seconds.

"Yeah, yeah, but who's going to pay for my coal bill this winter?"

The real reason for the dramatic decision was that Fran and I weren't having any fun anymore. All that running around to bars and parties, putting everyone and everything down, had ceased to be exciting. Who cared who had

169

a writer's block, who couldn't get it up any more, who wasn't having orgasms, who was selling out, who knew who and what they could do for me.

Fred and Paula had rented a house in Connecticut for the summer. Seeing them sitting around their fireplace, laughing easily, entertaining friends with no need of impressing anyone, doing things with their two children, reminded me what marriage was all about. It seemed that I had forgotten almost from the wedding day that I had a partner, not a maid. It was like buying an insurance policy and forgetting about it. Now I was anxious to cash it in. I wanted what Fred and Paula had. I decided the only way to get it was to return to St Louis and go back into the business world. How could I break it to Fran? I knew she loved New York, but what was more important—making some kind of life together in the sticks or drifting apart in the Big Apple.

When I put it to her, she looked like someone who had just been handed a life sentence, with no appeal. I told her if she didn't like it in S. Louis she could always return to her mother and father. The thought of that knocked all the fight out of her and she accepted the inevitable. I knew what was good for us. I read her a quote I had come across a few days before in Ed Sullivan's column. It was Elsa Maxwell's farewell to New York. "I'm so sad to leave my favorite jungle, New York. Lawless, careless, casual, terrible, electric, thrilling, murderous, heartbreaking, gay, fascinating, divine New York." If Elsa Maxwell, New York's greatest party-giver saw no future for the town, was I not right in moving too? Fran agreed to give it a try. I promised her she'd never regret it. She was relieved when I told her to leave everything to do with moving to me.

The plan was to take the records and the record player and ship the piece of sculpture. We would drive the beloved touring car through a scenic route, spending the night wherever we found ourselves. It would be the honeymoon we never had. All that was left was to tell her folks. They didn't like it, but were powerless to do anything about it. For the first time, I had the upper hand: "When you visit us in St Louis, you won't be disappointed in the quality of the meat."

A few days before we left town, I called Holmes over for a farewell drink. He was sad at the news but totally supportive. Holmes was the only friend I was going to miss, yet I was curious about what would happen to my other pals. I was going to miss Broyard's conversation and his beautiful, speechless girls. But even Broyard was giving up—he took a job writing publicity copy for Columbia Records Classical Record Club, a far cry from his trenchant analysis of the cultural scene for *Neurotica*. Radulovich was separated from his wife, working as a window display artist. Mazursky was heartbroken over his busted romance, but at last he'd gotten a break with a role in Stanley Kubrick's film, *Fear and Desire*. Kerouac's marriage was in deep trouble. He came by one day while I was still publishing and told me how desperate he was to get out of town. I gave him fifty dollars for a short story that I never printed. I was sorry that I hadn't really gotten to know him; Holmes spoke so highly of his talent, something I was out of touch with. Ginsberg, whom I had as little to do with as possible, was still running around town connecting his friends with each other, a kind of literary go-fer. I remember thinking at the time that none of them were going to make it.

On the day we vacated the apartment, I left the key with the lodger in the pee-stained underwear. He surprised me by telling me how much he enjoyed having me as a neighbor. "It was always lively around the place with the comings and going of all your crazy-looking friends; it gave me something to look forward to."

"Come on, Jay, let's get moving," yelled Fran, waiting at the door—of which one of my cynical friends once said: "Through these doors pass the most beautiful and neurotic people in the world."

It was late afternoon as we drove down the West Side highway, trying to think of a way to say goodbye to New York that wouldn't be too corny. I settled for a little hand-holding through the landscape of New Jersey. Fran stared out of the window, straining not to look back on what was once the center of her life. From the sad look on her face, I knew what it felt like to be kidnapped.

The car hummed, top down, toward Atlantic City, where we planned to spend the night. I only knew the town by the Monopoly board and instinctively avoided the Boardwalk. When I asked the taxi driver the way to a cheap hotel, Fran exploded.

"Aren't you even going to take me to a decent hotel?"

A sulking passenger near to hysteria didn't make the search for a night's lodging any easier. "Wait until we hit the open road," I told her, "we'll stay at the best motels."

By the time we reached the Blue Mountains, the feeling that she was a prisoner was no longer possible—the scenery was too breathtaking to complain about, even from someone with a bad case of Urban Blues.

Deciding to spend the night in a log cabin in the National Park provided a chance for us to be alone with nature, not the best companion for Fran. To my surprise, she liked it well enough to stay an extra day, but we shouldn't have. I met a couple in the adjoining cabin who played bridge. He was an insurance salesman, his wife was stout, and the evening was a disaster. To Fran, it meant that these people were the kind of friends she'd have to put up with from then on. I didn't make the mistake of talking to strangers again on the trip for fear of running into another insurance salesman. The marriage would have been in serious trouble.

Arriving in St Louis at dawn, the city looked like it had died, with a skyline that no Chamber of Commerce would dare put on a picture postcard. On the way to our new home, I took perverse pleasure in driving through the worst parts of the town, pointing out to her areas that politicians refused to acknowledge existed. I became a one man optimist with a hi-neighbor spiel on the advantages of living in a decaying city. "There's no place to go but up, kid. Where do you find street car tracks anymore? Dig the gas lights." Avoiding the scenic route was a clever bit of strategy—Fran had a lot of cement in her blood and it flowed when she saw a promising ghetto. "That's the good side of town . . . wait until you see the seamy underbelly, the rich side."

Gene and Ellie had bought a house in the suburbs to accommodate their growing family, making the top floor of Fred's house available for us. Once again we could choose anything we wanted from the Galleries; this time I went for the more conservative look, with occasional minor deviations. Fran picked out a fire engine red wall paper for the bedroom that was considered quite daring. The bed that I had bought in New York at an auction of Robert L.— Believe It Or Not—Ripley's collection was not as old as the infamous Cardinal Richelieu bed, but a lot safer. I scrupulously avoided anything that had a decadent label. In my study there hung a large portrait of an 18th century English gentleman in the style of George Romney. The only capricious touch was the kitchen that we used as the living room, and decorated like one.

A Christmas card that we especially made up for our friends back East to let them see how we were progressing in our new environment was a photograph of Fran and me in the kitchen, in front of a weird painting by Arthur Voelker. Around the photo was a hand drawn frame of the Venetian mirror that was a source of such irritation in our New York place. There wasn't a sign of any Christmas cheer expressed anywhere in the photo. A note on the back of it to my sister Gert summed up what our life was becoming:

> We're caught in the vicious circle of bridge, drapery talk, houshold hints, and Xmas cards. Please forgive. Better keep up with your bridge; we're becoming experts. Whom to play with? Miss you all very much and counting the months till July. Everything going fine.

Fran, seated on a soda fountain chair, looked as foreign as the E.T. figure in the painting. I was standing behind her in an open neck shirt, with an untied bow tie, looking stern and pleased with myself. And why not? I had made the transition to businessman so smoothly it even surprised me. Cutie couldn't believe I had ever been away.

When nothing opened up for Fran in the textile design line, I brought her, kicking and screaming, into the Galleries. It was a tradition with Landesman boys to bring their wives into the Galleries, always with disastrous results, according to Cutie. "Who needs all those fancy gift boxes and tissue paper Paula ordered when I've been using the *Jewish Daily Forward* to wrap china for years? Customers are going to get the impression we're too high-priced with all that fancy stuff."

I put Fran in charge of decorating the windows, hoping to benefit from some of that talent she had for design. Her windows, according to Cutie, kept people from coming into the Galleries. "Whoever heard of putting only three pieces of bric-a-brac in a whole window," she asked. "People will think we've gone out of business," she added. The minute Fran left after fixing the windows, Cutie would fill them with the gaudiest samples of the Landesman Galleries collection. "Now people can see what we've got," she would say proudly.

Although Fran was annoyed with Cutie for messing up her windows, she was happy to be able to bow out of the job. But I wouldn't let her get off so easily. I had plans to train her in sales techniques, but she turned out to be customer shy. If a customer came in, she hid behind a large piece of furniture, praying she wouldn't be found. "I don't know what's the matter with the girl, but a sales person she'll never be. Keep her out of the Galleries—she's losing us business," was Cutie's final word on the subject. But again I wouldn't give up. I decided to set up a project that involved Fran's skill as a watercolorist. The chandeliers that we sold to distinguished St. Louis families would be painted in the rooms where they hung, creating a permanent record of our contribution to gracious living.

Cutie gave me such a disapproving reception that I almost gave up, but Fran liked the idea and did a series of ten paintings that were knockouts. We made a special exhibition of them that delighted the owners and impressed future customers.

Mrs. William Rhinelander Stewart Bush was one of the people that Fran met through the project. They discovered that they had many complaints about St. Louis in common, and I was one of them. Fran complained that I was going too straight, and she complained that I wasn't straight enough. When Mrs. Bush told me a few months later that "her life was in ruins"—she was getting a divorce, I once again took up the challenge of keeping her amused.

On one of her visits, we spent the afternoon antique hunting and the evening slumming in the dives of downtown St Louis. Dancing together to the music of a country and western band at the Dublin Village Bar, we were quite a sight for the local inhabitants. It didn't bother either of us, nor did anybody notice as we danced our way out of the place into a cheap hotel across the street where I signed the register for a room, Mr and Mrs Christopher Isherwood.

The room was right out of an Isherwood Berlin short story—three different patterns of wallpaper on the walls, a light bulb on the end of a shadeless socket, and an iron bed that may have seen better days, but it still looked romantic. Both of us were aware of the ridiculousness of the situation, there was nothing to stop us from living out our separate fantasies.

Somewhere deeply buried between her hunt for carved wooden Victorian Easter eggs and the need to rebuild her life, there was a curiosity about questionable places and people. I suspected that was why she was attracted to me. I was the token *baddie* in her life. For me, she was the dream girl of all time.

Watching her take off her white gloves, her veil, unhook her string of pearls, let loose that tightly wound head of well bred blonde hair over her white shoulders, and step out of that classic black dress, I thought I was in some early German movie.

"This is an historic occasion" she said, lighting a cigarette in her holder.

"Why?" I answered. "Ain't you ever been to a cheap hotel before?" She gave me one of her special deep throated laughs.

"I mean, it's first time I've made love with a Jew."

At last, I thought, I've fulfilled my destiny—she is finally amused.

She returned to New York some time later to take a job with a theatrical lawyer-producer who handled a glamorous collection of actors and directors known as the Little Mafia. It included Ben Gazzara, Harry Guardino, Frank Corsaro, and Michael Gazzo. Their reputation for brawling, boozing, and balling was as firmly established as their talent in the theatre. They were the hottest properties around, as they were the first to admit.

In their attempt to keep Janet amused, they took her for rides around the Eighth Avenue bar and motorcycle set, raising the maximum amount of speculation that Janet Rhinelander Stewart was taking a walk on the Wild Side. On a return visit to St. Louis around this time, we were making the rounds of the low-life and found ourselves in a bar where the waitresses had more tattoos than the customers. Aware of the attention we were getting, I suggested we make an early exit. Fran and Janet were enjoying the general excitement the wild, rocking music was having on the bar's regulars. All I could see were the bouncer's lower finger joints that spelled out "love" and "hate."

"What's the matter, boys?" Janet asked. "Getting chicken?" Martin Quigley, a master at public relations looked around the room, shaking his head.

"It's not that I'm chicken, Sweetheart, it's that I hate to lose to the losers."

It was a satisfying feeling to learn she eventually went

into therapy. She used to see people who indulged in psychoanalysis as self-indulgent. Her analyst proved to be a wise man, recommending that she spend some time at a quiet institution in Connecticut that specialized in preparing people for re-entry into the real world. There she found a few old friends in residence; they gave her confinement the atmosphere of a society party.

There was also a young, handsome, jazz musician kicking a very big habit. When the time came to leave, she moved with him into her Park Avenue apartment. The therapeutic jam sessions that followed became legendary in jazz circles as much for the music they produced as for the eccentric housekeeping habits of the hostess: Janet always spread newspapers over the Oriental rugs to catch the spit from the musicians' horns.

She was proud of being able to enlighten us on origins of certain jazz terminology. She loved to tell the story of why black musicians called a car a "short." She quoted Oscar Pettiford's classic explanation: "It's shorter than a bus, ain't it?"

Now that I had finally given Janet the ultimate amusement, I could relax with her and enjoy the game we fell into—her trying to build my character and my trying to destroy hers. The game that Fran and I fell into was another story. I tried to control every movement of her life while she had no idea of what game I was playing. All she did know was the terrible feeling of being trapped. She became an expert at hiding her real feelings. She was only twenty three and miserable. I was thirty two and enjoying every minute of it. After a few quiet months of pregnancy, nature handled the problem with a miscarriage. It was her first, but my second. I was terribly disappointed and, in a strange way, so was she. Once she accepted her pregnancy, she looked forward to having the baby, for she needed a friend. Now she'd lost it. Her sense of inadequacy brought on an increasing depression that no amount of classes in ceramics could cure.

Fred, ever sensitive to the shifting moods of young married women, saw trouble coming: "We don't want you to get bored and go back to New York. What would amuse you?" he asked Fran. After nixing the idea of buying Devil's Island—it had come on the open market—and having Fran run it as a brothel, or mass producing copies of old masters, he talked of opening a night club.

"Look," he said to us in all seriousness, "we could use a place to hang out in. Attract some new faces. Have a party. If Marion Davies can spend fifty thousand dollars to give a party for Johnny Ray, we can treat ourselves to a bar. Even if it closes in a month, it won't cost much." It was always easy to spot when Fred was being serious—his upper lip twisted in an evil smile. "There's nowhere decent to have a drink in this town. What do you think?"

I was nodding along with him as he outlined the project, but I had some serious doubts about it being marriage-building.

Fred was always thinking up projects for me to carry out, so I naturally resisted the offer. "It would be something for Fran to do," he insisted. "She could decorate the place; she has a good eye for that kind of thing." I was still reluctant; the idea of Fran spending her time in a bar didn't fit in with my plans for grooming her for motherhood. I might have been influenced at the time by my reading *The Decline and Fall of the Roman Empire*. Visions of saturnalias, orgies, and excesses involving drink which had brought down the Empire were fresh in my mind.

I didn't hear any more about the bar until a few months after the New Year, when Fred asked me to look at a place that had just come on the market.

"It's the old queer bar, Dante's Inferno, on Olive Street, that's been closed since New Year's Eve. It's got such a reputation that it's going for a song."

Fred could never resist a bargain. All the decorations from New Year's Eve were still up; a little piano sprinkled with twinkle dust stood at the edge of a tiny stage with half-filled glasses on its top. The whole place was frozen the night it closed, looking like a painting by one of the Albright brothers—all that was missing was Dorian Gray. The owner was eager to unload his liability.

"The rent is eighty dollars a month, and two hundred for lock, stock, and some old dresses in the ladies room," he laughed.

Fred bought the place that afternoon. At dinner that night he asked Fran if she would like to have her own bar. It was the kind of line a girl seldom hears outside the movies.

"Of course, you'll have to design it yourself," he added. "There's just one thing. Don't count on me to do any work, but I'll give you anything you need to make it into the kind of place you want."

I knew that meant he would supervise every detail of the project. The light that shone in Fran's eyes made any further sales pitch superfluous.

For the next month, Fred worked twenty-four hours a day. The crew of workmen that gutted the place were all friends, some of whom just dropped by to see what was happening and were immediately caught up in the excitement. Fred gave them a pair of overalls and a paint brush or a hammer and nails and put them to work. He consulted with Fran every step of the way, guiding her through the project like a child, but Fran wasn't ever fooled that she was making any of the decisions. She just adored being his girl Friday, checking out a hundred problems.

Out went all the formica, in went the marble. Out went the neon lighting, in went the chandeliers. The walls were stripped down to the brick and then painted a flat black. The bar top was stripped of a thousand rings and brought to life with a natural shine that you could see your reflection in. Fred used many of his favorite things, marvellous bits that he had saved for years, waiting for just such an occasion. He used drug store chairs, doors of etched glass, elevator grills, marble busts, gold leaf pier mirrors, marble top tables from an old soda fountain, a pair of life size brass monkeys, and to top it all, behind the bar went a mirror so seductive, it made ugly people look handsome.

They used so many Landesman Galleries chandeliers that the bar looked like a shower of crystal and was promptly christened The Crystal Palace. Fred designed a sign with the Bal Masque theme—couples dancing under the chandeliers of a bygone palace. Fran worked on the sign for weeks, cutting hundreds of tiny holes in the print to give the impression that the chandeliers were actually lighted.

Gibbon had become an obsession with me, but I could never read more than a couple of pages at a time without going off into a reverie about how similar it might be to the decline of the Landesmans under my brothers' extravagant notions. I couldn't completely ignore the project either. There had been other projects I hadn't been enthusiastic about that turned out to be profitable.

As usual, I handled all the practical details of setting up the operation. We wanted a manager who could double as a bartender, accountant, bouncer, and sociologist. Fran suggested her friend from New York, the cab driver and *Neurotica* collector, Shepard Rifkin. Fred wanted to hire him the second he heard his name. After a preliminary phone interview, we brought Rifkin down to handle the job, in spite of his warning to us he didn't like people who drank!

Hiring a bartender was a snap. The first person I interviewed, I hired. His qualifications were too good to ignore. He was Irish, big, and looked like a young Charles Laughton. His background was impressive, but not necessarily helpful to a bartender. He had been an underground agent for the Anti-Defamation League, a part-time instructor of sociology at Washington University, a member of the local Fascist party, and before that a Trotskyite political activist. The fact that he knew how to make cocktails was incidental.

"What kind of place is it going to be?" Jack O'Neil asked, after we settled on the salary and working conditions. "Queer, straight, posh, or neurotic? Upper class, upper middle, or lower upper?"

O'Neil came down unexpectedly to view the progress of the Palace before he actually started working. Mistaking Fred, covered in plaster on a ladder for a workman, he snapped his fingers and yelled out,

"Boy! Is Jay around?"

Later, when I introduced Fred as his real boss, O'Neil didn't bat an eye at his obvious faux pas. Instead of shaking Fred's plaster-encrusted hand, he kissed his ring finger.

"Please forgive me, Baron," clicking his high-heeled shoes like a Nazi S.S. Commander. "At your service, mein Führer."

He didn't want to leave any doubt where his future loyalty lay.

Shepard Rifkin arrived with pamphlets from the Yale Institute of Alcoholic Studies and an extra pair of horn rim glasses. He was taking no chances, he said. Confessing that he was an "anal compulsive," he showed a deft hand at controlling the details of the business, but he couldn't control O'Neil's extravagant tastes in brand-name liquors. He was driving the liquor salesmen mad with delight as he ordered the rarest of bourbons and scotches—twenty-five different brands of scotch alone were displayed proudly on the back bar.

Anyone dropping into the Crystal Palace a half an hour earlier than official opening time would not have believed it was going to open at all. Fred was still on a ladder adjusting the lights, workers were still painting, the chairs were being dried under sun lamps. It magically all came together a few minutes before opening time. Fred, Fran, and I were still looking out for last-minute mistakes, but it was perfect. O'Neil and Rifkin were smartly attired in red Eisenhower jackets, black bow ties, white buttondown shirts, standing at attention for a final inspection. O'Neil held his hands under his chin like a puppy dog, hoping that one of us would compliment him on his brilliant manicure.

"Well, fellows," Fred said to the crew, "you've done a splendid job. Let the party begin."

At the end of the evening, after all the congratulations, the people that had contributed to its success sat around the big family table enjoying the post-mortem on the first night's operation. We all agreed that the audience had lived up to our expectations.

In spite of its success, I remained aloof. I had been brooding in my lair, getting very critical of Fran for having such a good time at the C.P. while I was struggling through Gibbon having no fun at all. I was stalled, left at the post in a race that I knew I could win. What was stopping me from entering? *Decline and Fall* began to pale as Fran came home night after night, filled with brandy and enthusiasm, daring me to come out and play.

"You missed a great time" was beginning to get to me. When Rifkin was off sick, O'Neil asked me to help behind the bar.

"Didn't you used to make a wicked martini in New York?" he asked. Like an old fire horse, the bell rang and I shot right behind the wood to become the assistant bartender. I confessed to Fran that it felt good to be where the action was. I was getting the same kind of charge behind the bar as I used to get in the early days of publishing *Neurotica*. Working with O'Neil inspired me in the same way Legman had, with this difference: O'Neil was on my side 100 per cent as soon as it became obvious that I was running things. His loyalty to Fred, however, never wavered. One night Fred knocked over a drink, soaking himself. Without stopping to think, O'Neil automatically doused himself with a drink so as to share his Führer's predicament.

There was no question that O'Neil, from the beginning, was the real star of the show. I couldn't wait to close down the Galleries and get down to the Crystal Palace cocktail hour, an important ritual in those days, which began at five o'clock and under O'Neil sometimes lasted a lifetime. It was a ceremony, a therapy session, a time for assignations; there were lectures in class stratification, Geopolitics, and always a great deal of discussion about sex. Coming into the C.P., as it was called by the regulars, after a hard day at the office, you found yourself in a self-contained crystal womb; before the first tinkle of frosted martini hit your lips, you began to feel a little bit better about your chances of surviving the night.

As the band of thirsty ad men, investment brokers, engineers, doctors, and sportsmen arrived, O'Neil stood at attention to greet them, executing their drinks orders with all the ceremony of a Japanese Tea House. His florid gesture of laying down the napkin in front of the customer and then presenting the drink as though it was a masterpiece created especially for them did not go unappreciated.

There were some who said he refused service to more people than he served. While we had a rule that male customers must wear a tie and jacket, O'Neil was faced with a dilemma when two very butch dykes asked to be served:

"I'm sorry, madame, ties are required." Nothing pleased him more than to exercise his authority. He was able to size up anyone's background by what they ordered to drink and how much they tipped. Pity for the poor chap who ordered the wrong brand name or tipped too little or too much. O'Neil had a pet theory that overtippers were middle class aspirants to upward mobility, unworthy of a "thank you." Yet he had nothing but contempt for the upper class who were notorious cheapies. He would acknowledge them with mock servility; people who didn't tip were never acknowledged.

You could sit next to anyone at the cocktail hour and never be bored with mindless conversation. Women were allowed at the bar, but it was known that O'Neil preferred to run a club for gentlemen preoccupied with the art of drinking and keeping him amused. All that O'Neil asked in return was that they share their victory or humiliation with him. The juicier aspects of these situations were then incorporated into the folklore of the C.P. and passed along the next day to a thirsty mob of gossip-hungry O'Neilites. Once his superiority over his customer was firmly established, O'Neil was free to engage in probing their weaknesses, but he was so charming his customers were flattered by his sadistic meddling.

At night, the C.P. belonged to the people, musicians, and entertainment pushing O'Neil into the background. There was something about all the darkness mixed with gold, crystal, whiskey and the tinkling of the piano that people found irrisistible. Romance flourished; there was hardly a yard of space where you couldn't make out, and that included the toilet, store room, outside the back door, behind the ice cube maker, in the cloakroom, or under the piano. O'Neil claimed he could get a hard-on thirty yards from the action, in any direction.

Shepard Rifkin, our manager, was the only one who wasn't enjoying the Palace. He was taking it much too seriously, doing his job well, but lacking the flair of O'Neil. He always seemed too efficient and none of O'Neil's customers appreciated him. "He's ruining the business, mein Führer," O'Neil would plead with Fred. "When his customers ask for a second drink, he quotes them a few paragraphs from the goddam Yale University bullshit thing on alcoholism." Rifkin had to go.

Without him, O'Neil's financial situation improved. He took great delight in showing us how "other" bartenders knocked down on the boss, and when we occasionally would discover he was indulging in the techniques he so patiently explained, we turned a blind eye. Like our father, we were not in the business only to make money. We liked O'Neil so much, we really didn't care if he dipped into the register occasionally. Neither Fred nor I drew a penny from the Palace, much to Cutie's annoyance. "Let me behind the cash register and you'll see some profit." Her grim lips told us she was serious. There was a reason for this. O'Neil would come into the Galleries before work, smelling of expensive cologne, jingling the silver in his pockets to tease her into thinking it was his illegal gains. "I want to thank your sons, Cutie, for this new suit," he would tell her. Cutie was not amused.

The Crystal Palace was a stunning success. Couples came regularly, the way they might have gone to church in the old days, seeking absolution. They were people you always knew existed, but had never found. If it is true that culture is only alive in a town that has good bars, St Louis was heading for a renaissance.

12

During the fourteen months after I left the New York scene, so much happened that it could have been fourteen years. After the *Neurotica*'s castration issue, Legman was summoned to Washington D.C. to fight his case against the post office censors. He had an infected leg at the time, so he borrowed a wheelchair from an FBI agent (who he claimed was spying on him) and made an appearance before the officials. The wild fight I expected didn't happen. Legman told me they were quite polite, but nevertheless, they took away his right to receive mail. That was the ultimate castration to a man whose livelihood depended on it. He quietly buttoned his fly and fled to Paris. He was having a tough time. "Please send me money. My wife is sick and I'm going blind," was typical of his correspondence to me during that period. Fred and Paula were happy to contribute to my save the Legman Fund. I sent him a hundred dollars and he whipped back a letter that really stung:

"Received your money. If you think your bourgeois family can buy me off, you're mistaken. Art is something you businessmen will never understand. Throughout history you've been trying to buy your way into our lives . . . Don't think I'm fooled by your attempts to castrate the artist. Your society is dead . . ."

Finally, in the last line, he relented: "Thanks for the money." Poverty in Paris had merely sharpened his sting.

Holmes hit it big with his novel *Go,* getting enough

money from the paperback rights to buy his way out of New York. He dabbled in the glittering life that literary success gives to a struggling author, writing me about his three hour lunches with twenty four hour cynicism. He was good about keeping me in touch with what was happening to all our friends. Alan Harrington was in New Mexico nursing a bruised case of indifference. Ginsberg was in Tangiers, or was it Mexico? "Kerouac drunk last night; did Gore Vidal take advantage of him? . . . There's a suspected case of writers' block on West End Avenue at 92nd Street . . . proceed with caution . . ." Solomon was working for his uncle, a paperback publisher, trying to get Kerouac and Burroughs published. Brossard published his novel *Who Walk In Darkness* and sent me a copy with the dedication, "To a fellow conspirator." Both Holmes and Brossard's books were about the scene in New York while I was there; although I thought they got it right, it wasn't my scene. Almost the same cast of characters, but a completely different story. Would my story make a good novel?

I thought the line "You can't make it in New York and stay married" which turned out to be so prophetic, would make a good opening line for one. I probably would have forgotten about it if it hadn't been for a strange little woman who ran a writer's colony in Robinson, Illinois. Her name was Lorney Handy, the woman to whom James Jones dedicated his novel *From Here to Eternity*. One day when Jones was having dental rehabilitation in St Louis, he dropped by the Landesman Galleries to indulge his fondness for collecting porcelain. We immediately hit it off; he had read *Neurotica* while he was in New York going to classes in creative writing. A struggling writer and a struggling publisher, we'd both had a hard time in Manhattan and we exchanged rejection stories with relish. His "Hell, boy, when I walked the streets, everybody stepped on my shoes," summed up both of our experiences. When I told him I was thinking of writing a novel, he told me I should meet Lorney Handy and he promised to bring her around the next time he was in town. Meantime, Cutie managed to sell him a very expensive Meissen figurine of a Chinaman's head that wanted to talk.

"Why are you wearing all that jewelery, Mr. Jones?" Cutie asked him, "Are you a sissy?" Jones was loaded down with turquoise and silver jewelry, rings and pendants, he'd purchased in New Mexico. It seemed so out of character for the tough ex-soldier.

Jones looked at Cutie with the amused detachment of a man who is cocksure of himself. "Come out in the back room, Mrs. Landesman," he challenged her, "and I'll show you if I'm a man or not."

Cutie suggested I take him down for a drink at the Palace instead. Jones wasn't wearing a coat or tie, so on the way down Fred and I filled him with horror stories about what would happen to him if he tried to get past O'Neil in his Hawaiian shirt.

"Hell, there isn't a bar that I can't get a drink in, tie or no tie. I know how to handle bartenders. I'll bet you five bucks I can get a drink." Knowing O'Neil's opinion of men who wore jewelry, we figured it was a shame to take his money.

After about ten minutes, we went in to see what was happening. We suspected that Jones had been refused service and was too embarrassed to tell us. We thought he had escaped through the rear door back to his colony in Robinson; or maybe he was sulking in the toilet, waiting for me to come and rescue him. We almost walked past him, sitting at the bar, with a drink in front of him. Fred called O'Neil to the end of the bar.

"Why is that person," pointing to Jones, "being served?" O'Neil tried to apologize.

"You're right, your Excellency," he whispered, "I was about to turn him away when he ordered a double Chivas Regal." O'Neil's eyes pleaded for mercy. "I couldn't turn down such a smart drinker." He lowered his head awaiting forgiveness. Fred and I broke up.

"What's so funny?" O'Neil demanded. We told him about our bet and who his tie-less customer was.

"Oh, the son of a bitch," he cried out, snapping his fingers with glee. "Thank God I didn't throw him out," he said, whipping back to Jones to give him a free drink and tell him how much he admired *From Here to Eternity*.

On his next visit he brought Lorney with him. Over drinks at the Palace, she outlined her theories on writing, laying heavy stress on copying sections from the works of great writers like Hemingway. She told me she was an ardent disciplinarian, overseeing her colony of would-be writers with frequent lashings of criticism until they saw the light. When I told her my desire to write a book was hampered by a monumental writer's block, she smiled with the anticipation of getting me under her wings.

"You've got a novel in you, son," she gave me her hard, penetrating look. "You come back to the colony with us. I'll get that novel if I have to beat it out of you."

It would have been too impolite to laugh, so I turned to Jones for help.

"Lorney sure will. She's a tough old bird."

To show how tough she was, she threw her drink right in his face. She might have been offended by his use of the word, "old." She was drinking a Tom Collins and all the fruit in her drink landed on his bracelets.

"Aw shucks, Lorney, what did you wanna do that for?" Jones took it like a seasoned veteran.

The next time Jones came by, it was without Lorney. In the sophisticated atmosphere of the Palace, he loved to play the country boy, out on the town, getting as drunk as possible without passing out. But he was far from the country bumpkin he pretended to be. Keenly aware of the pitfalls of success, he wisely chose to remain far away from New York while he wrote his second novel, *Some Came Running*. He even used it as his excuse for not coming down to play with us more often.

"I start thinking about you guys two days before I'm due at the dentist. I get so plastered while I'm down here, I can't write anything for two days after I get home."

I thought Lorney's colony of writers was all bullshit; the

189

idea of copying the great writers really turned me off. But I liked her style—she was Barbara Stanwyck and Joan Crawford rolled into one great big small-time American, determined to show the big boys in the East she could beat them at the literary game. If Jones was any example, she hadn't done too badly. I understood what she was feeling; when I went to New York with *Neurotica* I wanted to piss on the Establishment too, but she was tough, and her chances of winning were better than mine. I told Jones that Lorney was OK, but I felt no need to join the colony.

"I started writing my novel the day after she threw that garbage in your face. It was an inspiration."

I read Holmes' novel *Go* and Brossard's *Who Walk in Darkness,* and I didn't think I could come anywhere near to their professionalism, but I dived in the deep end. Without any thought that what I was doing could ever possibly be published, I told the truth. My story was a very small canvas, an insider's view of the flotsam and jetsam of the intellectual life that I was a part of. All I had in the beginning was the opening line: "You can't stay married if you want to make it in New York," the title, *The Nervous Set,* and a regular schedule.

During the day I worked in the Galleries; in the evening after dinner I went to my study to write for three hours. By nine o'clock I was ready to join the party at the Palace with Fran at my side. I didn't tell anyone I was writing in the beginning and then, after I got into it, I couldn't stop telling people about it.

Meanwhile, Fran was handling the strictly routine jobs down at the Crystal Palace. Every morning she'd hop on the Olive Street trolley, let herself into the Palace, mix a large grasshopper cocktail for breakfast, and sit down with her adding machine to do her chores. Once in a while, Tommy Wolf, the resident piano player would drop by to work out some arrangements for whatever singer we had at the time. He was not the biggest attraction as a performer, but his knowledge of music, particularly anything obscure, was a source of delight to Fran who shared his reverence for the lesser known songs of Porter, Berlin, Hart, Arlen, Whiting, Mercer, and Wilder. Wolf was surrounded by jazz musicians who admired the way he sang a lyric or embellished a tune.

They talked in a new language that set them apart from the Palace's regular customers who didn't know what Wolf and his friends would be referring to when they talked about *pads*, being *hung up*, or *hip*; Fran couldn't hear enough of the language.

It was around spring, the season that Fran always felt left out of: "If April is the cruellest month, as T. S. Eliot claimed, how would you say the same thing in hip language?" she asked him. Wolf, at the piano, toying with a new version of *Polka Dots and Moon Beams*, shrugged his shoulders.

"How about, 'Spring can really hang you up the most' "? She hoped he'd be pleased with her little joke. He stopped playing.

"Say that again." And she did, a little less sure of herself.

"That'd make a good title for a song. Why don't you write a lyric?"

The idea was too far-fetched for Fran. She may have known all the popular songs of the past, but she'd never written one. Two days later she slipped a piece of paper in Wolf's pocket as he sat playing the piano, almost ashamed of what she had written:

> Spring this year has got me feeling
> Like a horse that never left the post
> I lie in my room staring at the ceiling
> Spring can really hang you up the most
>
> College boys are writing sonnets
> In the tender passion they're engrossed
> But I'm on the shelf with last year's Easter bonnets
> Spring can really hang you up the most
>
> All afternoon those birds twitter twit

I know the tune, this is love; this is it
Spring came along, a season of song
Full of sweet promise but something went wrong

Doctors once prescribed a tonic
Sulphur and molasses was the dose
Didn't help a bit. My condition must be chronic
Spring can really hang you up the most

All alone, the party's over
Old Man Winter was a gracious host
But when you keep praying for snow to hide the clover
Spring can really hang you up the most.

Wolf set it to music almost as quickly as she had written it. The tune was a bit advanced for her tastes, but she was afraid to say so. Wolf played the song that night to an enthusiastic audience, announcing that it was the "first collaboration between the boss's wife and the resident piano player."

Her line in the lyric about Spring being *"full of a sweet promise but something went wrong"* was an accurate account of what was happening to us that Spring: she was having an affair with the piano player and I was having an affair with the waitress. Our condition was truly chronic, as the lyric said, and no amount of sulphur and molasses was going to cure what ailed us.

Because I talked so openly about sex, marriage, infidelity, and other people's hypocrisy, I never recognized I was pushing Fran into a conventional life just like those I accused of being square. While I was under the impression that I was the only honest man around, I never levelled with Fran about my extra-marital adventures. Worse, I gave her the impression that I was this upright member of society who played according to the rules. I shifted any guilt I had about my liasons on to her. I made her feel that if she had any affairs, it was her responsibility if anything went wrong with the marriage. I wanted to have my cake and eat it too.

When Fran discovered she was pregnant again, this time she did it right: iron tablets, vitamins, weekly check-ups, everything that was expected of her. She even cut down on her visits to the Palace. It was a peaceful time, filled with family dinners, and a select social life that consisted of a few friends from the Palace who would come back to Fred and Paula's house to listen to O'Neil's refinement of the evening's happenings. Sometimes Fran would complain about so much bar talk. "Bar talk, bar talk; that's all they ever talk about". "Bartok?" O'Neil asked. "I never heard his name mentioned once in this crowd."

I was nearly finished writing *The Nervous Set;* she was happy with the pregnancy. We talked of getting our own house soon, and me not working so hard. We wanted to spend more time together, but there always seemed to be something or someone dragging us apart.

With new faces no longer at a premium, it was a treat to have an old one show up. Chandler Brossard blew into town on his way to a Mexican divorce. When the *American Mercury* became too vile, he quit its editorship to carve out a new life. With his good credentials as editor at *Time, The New Yorker, American Mercury,* two critically well received novels, and now a book on the state of American culture, he was applying for a job with the Government, to be its cultural editor. He saw himself as the head of a think tank dealing with heady issues. It was a great idea, but its chances of being formed within the Eisenhower administration were remote. To keep up his morale, it was non-stop party time for Brossard in St Louis. His monologues on life, literature, art, marriage, men in grey flannel suits, dazzled a small audience of Polish refugees and ex-German Counts—the cosmopolitan element of the Palace.

Two faces I could have done without were Fran's parents. I left Fran to deal with them alone. After a bout of drinking with Brossard, I returned home to see her in bed, her parents furious; she was having another miscarriage. Accusing me of deserting their daughter in her hour of

need, no amount of apology or explanation satisfied them.
I had a very depressed woman on my hands by the time
her parents left.

Watching Fran's deepening depression had a major
effect on the writing of the final scenes in *The Nervous Set*.
Originally, I was going to end it with the couple getting out
of New York, settling for the good life in a converted barn.
I realised it would never work; our own moves since leaving New York were living proof of that. I knew that black
thoughts were never far from Fran's mind. Her fascination
with death was a long-standing affair. Threats to jump out
of the windows when she was a teenager, crossing streets
in a style that challenged traffic, fast cars, pills, and destructive relationships were already part of her pattern.
There was only one thing that the girl in the novel could
do that would make sense: a suicide attempt. The heroine
in my book is left alone while her husband is out partying.
He comes home after another wasted evening convinced
he's going to play it straight.

> "Honey?" I whispered. "Honey, you asleep? It's me. I got
> something to tell you."
> When she didn't respond, I lifted her head, but it fell back
> before I had a chance to hold it. I began to shake her all over.
> I tried to pick her up, but couldn't get her more than a few
> feet in the air. She was like a limp wet rag, nothing held
> together. She fell back on her side and then I saw the bottle. I
> saw it was empty . . .

It was a scene that I could picture happening if things
continued to go wrong between us. This time we found a
doctor who took an interest in Fran. He recommended
that we try to have another child right away and made an
appointment for Fran with a psychiatrist that he was sure
she'd like. Within a few months, she was pregnant for the
third time.

Fran adored both her doctors. All their attention made
another pregnancy enjoyable. She acquired a self-as-

surance that I hadn't seen since our early days together. Her job at the Palace continued to interest her, but more important was her collaboration with Tommy Wolf. After writing *Spring Can Really Hang You Up The Most,* she began to put her life into her lyrics. Her work reflected that bitter-sweet approach that had become her forte: *This little affair just fills the bill/It doesn't mean much and it never will* was the perfect comment on her flirtation with Wolf. *It isn't so good it couldn't get better/It isn't so bad it couldn't get worse* summed up our marriage. The Landesman-Wolf song-book had about twenty five songs ready for the world, and a lot of left-over lines to work on.

13

That summer of 1954, I had high hopes that *The Nervous Set* would get published. Brossard was working with a bright editor at Rinehart on his novel. After spending the better part of a visit putting him down for his stupidity, naivete and general lack of smarts, he proceeded to condemn Rinehart, all publishing houses, the middle class, most other writers, the Establishment, the System and God. But he thought enough of the "incompetent" editor to leave my manuscript with him.

"After Brossard left me in my cubicle office," Gene Miller wrote, "I picked up the manuscript, read the epigraph on the title page *(What are you rebelling against? What have you got?)* and the first sentence *(You can't make it in New York if you want to stay married)* and got up and walked into Oliver Rea's office and told him we should give the author a contract even if all the rest of the pages were blank."

Miller read the book that night and wrote how much he wanted to publish it. The book had touched off something in his own life that he could relate to. At that time he was trying to juggle the lovely wife and two kids in the Connecticut home, a Parisian mistress with a mirrored bedroom on Fifth Avenue, his work at Rinehart, and about two fifths of booze a day. He wasn't making it.

The situation was complicated by the recent rejection by Stanley Rinehart of Norman Mailer's *The Deer Park*. "He didn't want to put his mother's name to a dirty book" Miller wrote when he sensed that all might not be as easy as he thought. "Your book is the kind that makes people like him and my editor-in-chief very uncomfortable; it reminds them about the truth about themselves and the world they live in."

Miller began lining up support from the other editors, but his best efforts to get me a contract ran into trouble. He got every editor, including the ones who usually worked on cook books and westerns, to vote for *The Nervous Set*, but when the editor-in-chief finally read it, it pushed all his panic buttons: "I think it's trash and I don't want to hear anymore about it."

So began the round of rejections and suggested changes to make the book palatable for the market. "Make the heroine more lesbian . . ." "Have the couple march off together to Connecticut, arm in arm" . . . "put some real violence into it". I wrote to Brossard of my disappointment. His answer that Rinehart had rejected his book of fiction for much the same reason didn't help me feel any better. I got an unexpected lift with the news that my book gave Miller the courage to say "fuck it" to the entire commuter marriage/publishing/Madison Avenue scene and move into a pad in Yorkville to start studying acting with Stella Adler. I put the manuscript in the old trunk, along with the *Neurotica* memorabilia: I needed a new project.

"Beat the heat with ASCA, the University of the Imagination. Free martinis served before, during, and after each lecture," launched a series of seminars on the more "important aspects of our culture." Called the Advance School of Cultural Analysis (ASCA), I printed up membership cards and stationery and sent out two hundred and fifty announcements to mainstays of cultural and intellectual life in St Louis, announcing the program of lectures to be given at the air-conditioned little cinema next door to the Gaslight Bar.

The response was predictable; a check from a public relations man for five dollars with an encouraging letter that ended with the ringing words, "keep 'em flying." I enrolled two unemployed sociologists, a waitress from the

C.P., a producer of kiddie shows on educational television, and a Polish count who was fascinated with my attempts to undermine the country. What ASCA lacked in quantity of membership, it made up for in quality, with lecturers from the ranks of the C.P.'s cocktail hour, and a few visiting 'professors' from out of town.

The offer of free drinks proved to be irresistible; the 'lecture hall' was SRO. The first talk given by Jim Harelson was called *Squaresville USA: A New Look at Main Street.* In the role of a straight-thinking, plain-talking successful member of the Chamber of Commerce, he gave his version of the small town cultural explosion. I had the words to a popular, corny song, *Hi Neighbor,* printed and put on the seats and led the audience in a chorus to set the tone for Harelson's lecture. It was our first and last sing-a-long.

Jack O'Neil's lecture changed drinking and tipping habits with his devastating attack on his customers. The 'Lord God,' a retired Chutney salesman and dedicated Anglophile, talked about the superior programming of BBC radio and offered to give any young matron in the audience the opportunity of listening to these programs with him any night they were free. "Candlelight and wine optional," he informed the restless women in attendance.

There were seminars on sports cars, a lecture by Tommy Wolf on *Modern Music and Nerve Endings,* the importance of wine in our culture, and the role of point-of-sales advertisements in an expanding economy. We were unable to present two lectures scheduled: *Abortive Attempts At Middle-Class Rebellion* and *How Deep Is My Funk.* The first speaker aborted in the early stages of a cultural pregnancy. The second speaker was in a helpless funk after a tidal wave of contemporary New York depression.

The series ended with my lecture, *American Culture is Here to Stay: How to Live With It.*

> American culture is here to stay. Get to know it, feel it, smell it, taste it, make love to it. Don't accept it by conformity. Don't reject it from snobbery. Don't try to improve it from guilt. Live

it creatively, spontaneously, fearlessly and, above all, imaginatively. The worse that can happen to you is to be called a phony.

The impact of ASCA created some new services, changed our drinking and sex habits, our musical tastes, our attitudes towards sports cars and the man from Main Street.

The one lecture that I had really wanted to give was *Abortive Attempts at Middleclass Rebellion*. It was my title, but I thought a real expert should give the lecture—a woman I was having a middleclass affair with. Married to one of the straight arrows of St Louis society, she had been in revolt since birth. Unfortunately, her husband missed the joke. To her everlasting credit, she aborted the lecture, but continued the affair.

Affairs by now were almost an epidemic. Everyone knew about them, but relied on the theory of safety in numbers. Nobody came out in the open to spoil the fun. Fran and I certainly talked about everything except our affairs. We just didn't want to know.

But more important than the affairs, the series caught the attention of the Director of the local Educational TV station who offered me the opportunity to bring ASCA, in a slightly different format, to his television audience, only marginally larger than ASCA's. Like me, he wanted to give culture a much needed break.

Off-Beat: An Excursion Down Cultural Bypaths opened with the theme music from *The Three Penny Opera*, the camera moving up my stove-pipe legs, past my daring black hopsacking suit, to a head shot of me: "Talk is cheap, so here I am."

Whether or not *Off-Beat* influenced future TV shows is debatable, but it certainly got an audience response. On the first program, O'Neil appeared in a chef's hat, mixing and stratifying the American salad! "For the great middle class salad, a touch of everything is needed," he began, throwing in bits of carrots, raisins, and apples—"you know how insecure they are," he added. He could hardly bring himself around to doing the lowbrow salad: his disdain for anything so loathsome was obvious. After concocting a mixture of truly repellent ingredients, he threw in bits of a greasy pork chop with the comment, "Now this is so disgusting, it's not even fit for a white man."

Before the show was over, the station's switchboard lit up like a Christmas tree with protests from a hostile audience. O'Neil was a racist, the station was Communistic, and "Who in the hell does Jay Landesman think he is?" The director of the station was overwhelmed with the reaction; no one had ever responded to anything they had put on in the year they'd been transmitting. He congratulated me and extended my contract for six more shows. Only the threat of having the station's budget severely cut stopped him from making *Off-Beat* a permanent fixture.

By September, Fran was in her ninth month without a hitch. The combination of a friendly psychiatrist and wise gynecologist was a success, so when the opportunity arose to buy a house two doors away from Fred's, we decided it would be perfect for a growing family. It was the first sign that we were growing up, no matter how hard we had fought against it.

We were in our new house only a few days when Fran began her labor. She was watching a movie on television and enjoying it so much she didn't want to leave before the end of the film. I was so nervous I started throwing up while she giggled at my anxiety.

"Listen," I warned her. "If you don't come with me to the hospital right now, I'm leaving without you."

We weren't home free yet. The baby boy weighed only four pounds and had to spend the first fifteen days in an incubator. Fran was released from the hospital without anything to show when she returned home.

It was a depressing start for such a joyous event, which didn't get any better when Fran's breasts dried up mysteriously. Against Fran's wishes, I named the child Cosmo, just to keep up the tradition Fred started by naming his children Rocco and Knight and Wyatt. Fran had a horrible fear that, with a name like Cosmo, he'd be beaten up in the schoolyard daily. She wanted to give the kid boxing lessons as soon as he came home. Cosmo rallied under the expert care of our pediatrician and was soon back in his mother's arms.

Everything changed once that happened. The temporary blues disappeared as Cosmo's smile lit up the house. Cosmo was Fran's new little friend, a constant companion that qualified her to join Paula and the other mothers on morning walks. Pushing the baby carriages along the familiar neighborhood streets, she basked in the compliments she received on producing such a beautiful child. Fran and I would fight over who got to change the diapers first, who hosed him down in the sink, who dressed him, and who could make him laugh the most. We were happy with our new toy.

Not that I needed one; I had plenty to keep me occupied. We had converted the six flats above the Galleries into twenty four studios, small but cosy, to create an atmosphere that would attract more sophisticated people into the area. Budding young entrepreneurs, inspired by our success and seeing the opportunities offered in nearby Bed Bug Row, began to buy up the empty or run down buildings and convert them into bars and restaurants, decorated in the turn of the century style the neighborhood had once been famous for. Nothing was planned or discussed in committee; nobody asked the city for money and no previous experience was needed. There wasn't a professional among the lot.

Jimmy 'the Picker' Massucchi, an antique scout famous for peddling zany collections of redundant artifacts from the back of his van, built a bar around his unsaleable collection of discarded telephone booth doors! It was a memorable day when the Picker sold three thousand croquet balls to an entrepreneur who was building a Dixieland Jazz beer parlour.

There was room for everyone no matter how outlandish their ideas. A Jewish civil engineer and his wife, collectors of Japanese folklore, turned a slum house into an island of Eastern enchantment, serving Japanese meals in a style the Emperor would have approved. Seeing this handsome middle-aged couple greeting customers in traditional kimonos with their ceremonial bow was only one of the many bizarre attractions on offer in the area, now called Gaslight Square. St Louis, never known for its night life, was showing signs of one. At least people were moving away from their television screens for the first time.

With Gaslight Square off to such a booming start, the Crystal Palace was no longer a novelty. Business had dropped off to the competition, but what saddened us most was the change in Jack O'Neil. Since his TV appearance, he'd become a minor celebrity. His customers, who couldn't get enough of him during the cocktail hour, began to take him to lunches that extended until he was due on the job. He would arrive back smashed and curse his malfunctioning speech with a contemptuous, "thank you, mouth!"

His relationship with his customers took on a conspiratorial tone that increased in intensity as the evening wore on. His sinister side would climb out of the cocktail glass and make anyone other than his regulars cringe with feelings of inadequacy. At the end of one series of hectic nights, O'Neil ran out of the bar shouting to the wind, "those orangutangs are driving me *muhula!*"

I knew it was time for him to go when one of his richest patrons began to fly him to lunch at the Chambord in New York and he started to miss the cocktail hour entirely, showing up a few minutes before closing time, tired, drunk, and with no apologies. His defection to the Gaslight Bar was inevitable, saving us the embarrassment of firing him. I knew he was going to be a hard act to follow.

On a trip to Chicago I found what I was looking for, the Compass Players, a group of improvisational actors doing business in a converted ballroom. Their founder, David Shepherd, had a dream of companies performing in nightclubs all over America. The Crystal Palace would be their testing ground with a new company under the direction of Theodore J. Flicker.

No one in the audience for the first night of the Compass at the Palace was likely to forget its impact. The stage was dark. Two of the players were planted at a table in the audience. They began to argue, until the audience was hollering for them to shut up. As the couple made their way to the stage, Flicker, a small, volatile man with a Mephistopheles beard, dressed in a black leotard, hopped onto the stage and shouted, "Freeze!" The lights went up on the performers. "What happens next?" he asked the audience. "You tell us."

They took the audience suggestions on topical issues or personal experiences of the most embarrassing kind and turned them into sharp, biting, satirical commentary on contemporary manners and morals that left no doubt something new was happening in entertainment in America. When they strolled off the stage at the end of the evening singing *Good Night Irene*, no one wanted to call it a night. (As a matter of record, the Compass Players went on to become one of the major influences in the theatre as well as the entertainment world.)

We were all in love with the Compass, especially its director Theodore J. Flicker. He was a human dynamo who never seemed to run short of ideas or ways to have fun. He entertained us even on his day off with Sunday brunches of lox and bagels and Bloody Marys in Paula's backyard, hovering over the guests like a Jewish mother, seeing that everyone was being amused.

After a few months, he brought Elaine May and Mike Nichols from the Chicago company to join the Palace Compass, and things on and off stage began to heat up. Nichols and May together at the Palace were nothing less than sensational. They were seasoned performers, masters of improvisation, able to turn a flawed idea into an inspired sketch. They were so good, they eventually threw the company off balance, leaving the other members out on a limb. Flicker suspected that they were using the Compass to prepare their own act, indifferent to the success of the company. He considered Nichols a threat and after many warnings to him to stop hogging the action, Flicker came to me with the problem.

"He's ruining the show. You've got to fire him."

I was stunned. "There are those who think he is the show," I replied.

"That's just what I mean. It's all Nichols and May. When he saw how confused I was, he put his arm around me. "Don't feel so bad about it. Everybody I fire becomes famous."

All my attempts to dissuade Flicker from such a suicidal act were futile. "What excuse should I use?"

"Tell him he has too much talent."

Flicker capped it with a big smile.

Nichols was so pissed off, he and Elaine flew out of St. Louis the day after I told him his services would no longer be needed. They opened as a duo a short time later and the rest is history. When Flicker heard about their success, he came over beaming.

"Didn't I tell you we were doing him a favor by firing him?"

The departure of Nichols and May marked the end of the Compass at the Palace, but Flicker stayed behind. When he came up with the idea of a production of *Waiting for Godot* in our little bar, I had some reservations. Although we had trained our audiences to accept almost everything we put before them, giving them a dose of Beckett with their bottle of Budweiser was revolutionary. It would not only be the first time a full scale play was done in a bar, but also one of the first performances of *Waiting for Godot* outside of New York.

The audience loved it. Every night for the next eight weeks it was SRO. The phenomenal success started us thinking in terms of bigger productions with our own theatre company. Then Flicker came up with a package of ideas and figures that was both innovative and exciting: we would move the operation to the growing Gaslight Square area and build a theatre that would seat three hundred people who could drink during the show. For thirty-two weeks we would do original and experimental theatre with an Equity company of our own under the direction of Flicker. The rest of the time, I would produce cabaret, revues, and bring in some star attractions. We all agreed it was going to be financially risky, but we were in perfect agreement that there was a need for this to happen. What New York didn't have the nerve to do, we'd do here in the sticks. More important—I had found a new career.

It was an exciting time for all of us. I was going to be a real producer, and Fran was in the last stages of another pregnancy. Her parents' invitation to spend the summer with them in Connecticut gave our relationship with them another chance.

Cosmo was the star of the show. His grandparents' indifference to us melted away with his laughter. It gave me great pleasure to discover her folks were human after all. Bringing Cosmo into their lives gave Fran the feeling that at last she had done something her parents approved of unreservedly. The beautiful surroundings, the early morning walks in deserted country lanes, and the uncomplicated country life had me back in shape within a week. I was itching to get back to civilization, an urge cured by a week-end in New York.

New York had changed since we were there last. The San Remo bar where Fran and I spent our courting nights had turned gay. My old house was still there, but the little man in the pee-stained underwear wasn't. The corner news dealer who sold *Neurotica* was disappointed to hear that I had become another business man. "Oh well," he said, not wanting me to feel too badly, "it happens to the best of them."

Ginsberg was a celebrity. Beatniks were becoming socially acceptable; there was money to be made renting them out for parties. Kerouac had just published *On The Road;* it had a lead review by Gilbert Millstein in *The New York Times.* Holmes was working on a novel about jazz, happy in a new house in Old Saybrook, Connecticut. Brossard was working his way up *Look* magazine with his penetrating and sardonic essays on the rich and famous. He confessed that the only pleasure he got out of life was writing outrageous plays. I encouraged him to stay with it by telling him that one of these days I'd produce one of his least outrageous ones. It cheered him up considerably.

P. J. Clarke's bar still put ice blocks in the urinal, but the elevated train running along Third Avenue had disappeared. Marshall McLuhan had been taken up by *Life* and *Time* in spite of the nasty things he had said about them in *Neurotica*. The artist from whom I bought the 'Davy Jones' sculpture had commited suicide.

The changes in New York were too much even for Fran, and we returned to St Louis with a sense of relief. It didn't last long. The old Crystal Palace was dying and the wake was held nightly. But it went out with style with a month of tongue in cheek entertainments ranging from Kenneth Rexroth reading from his translations of early Chinese cantos, to jazz, and a spectacular act from artist Ernest Trova. Every night for a week, Trova, with his brush and blank canvas, would battle with the Little Walter Westbrook Trio—sound against colour—that ended in brilliant abstractions and equally exciting music by the trio. At the end of the evening, the painting was given away to the person who came up with the best title. There was never a title that summed up the experience better than *Six Million Colors in Search of a Primary*.

The last guest performer came unexpectedly out of the past. Gene Miller was passing through town with the seventeen-year-old bride he had married while they were both doing a season at the Margo Jones Theatre in Dallas. He had only been in town a few days when he got an offer from another repertory theater in St Louis to take over a lead with only three days notice. He was in good shape then, able to handle any contingency that came up, but by the end of his contract, he was a mess. Instead of moving on, sparing us the sight of him going down into the bottom of countless bottles of brandy, he stayed on hoping we would find a place for him at the Crystal Palace's new operation. When he suggested that he do a reading of classic bits from Hemingway, Faulkner, Fitzgerald and Kerouac on the C.P. stage, I thought it would be the perfect note to close the party on.

Miller recited with such reverence his excerpt of Fitzgerald's *Crack Up,* there were tears in his eyes, and the audience felt they were watching an artist falling apart before them.

Miller stayed around hoping that the Crystal Palace would be his new home, providing work for him and his wife. He misread our efforts to provide him sanctuary while he got himself together. Hanging on desperately through the interminable delays in getting the new Crystal Palace together, his behavior became increasingly erratic. One morning he was seen running up and down Gaslight Square shouting, "They promised me the doors would be left open."

We got him to a psychiatrist who told us to get our friend on a plane. "The State of Missouri is not a good place to go crazy in." Confused, a little hurt, he chose Los Angeles as the natural place to go nuts in, offering no resistance as we bundled him on the plane that same day. For the record, it was the Crystal Palace's first genuine casualty, but not its last.

From Bedbug Row to Broadway

Meet the happiest businessman in St. Louis read the caption on the cover of *Pageant* magazine in 1958. The feature was called, *RICH FULL LIFE IN ST. LOUIS, MO.*

Three of the luckiest and most amazing people in the world are the Landesman brothers, who have discovered it is possible to do what they like and make it pay.

There followed a double-page picture of me being wheeled in a wicker invalid's chair around our swimming pool and a six page picture story on Fred, Gene and me and our families, concluding with:

Well-liked and respected by their fellow St. Louisians, the Landesmans are, despite the unconventionality of their lives, by no means bohemians. They are devoted family men who are not so rich that they don't have to work—and fairly hard—to make a living. Their secret, and the moral of this story, is that it takes talent plus a measure of wisdom to make money doing the things you would like to do to make money.

The other articles in that issue, A SPERM BANK FOR SURVIVAL ... A NUN'S STORY IN PICTURE ... WHEN SHOULD YOU LIE TO YOUR MATE? ... PLUS DEODORANTS: EXPENSIVE NONSENSE?—rounded out the kind of fare mass circulation magazines used to boost sales. The happiest businessman theme was what they printed for laughs. They knew nobody would believe such a family existed, and they were right. The birth of our new son only contributed to the illusion of the "happiest businessman." Underneath all that respectability was a middle class Jewish boy, son of Cutie, still trying to escape.

The *Age of Splitsville* was upon us; after decades of everyone playing the marriage game by the rules, rocketing divorce figures made the headlines. Instead of "You can't stay married and make it in New York," it seemed more accurate to say "You can't make it at all if you stay married." The race was on to discover a new kind of basis to make marriage work. It threatened to become a growth industry: Agony Aunts were breaking down under the pressure, psychiatrists offices were Standing Room Only, and Marriage Counselors were emerging as folk heroes. While suburban couples were throwing their keys under the rug, motels were becoming the new Valhalla of wrecked marriages. There was even a rumor that President Eisenhower's marriage was in trouble.

For me there was only one way to go, onward and downward. After a lifetime of breaking the rules, it was going to be fun making up some new ones. My prescription was a steady dose of infidelity, taken at regular intervals. It was like vitamins; you knew it wasn't going to do you any good, but you had to keep in training.

It left me very little time or energy to spend on finding a site for the Crystal Palace Cabaret Theatre, a problem that was fortunately solved by the death of an antique dealer in the heart of Gaslight Square. We'd already tried to buy him out of the three adjacent shops he owned, but without success. His death left our way clear to open our theatre and for Fred to create his masterpiece.

The Crystal Palace that emerged was a cross between a church and a movie palace, without the reverence. The walls and ceiling were painted fire station red, casting an unearthly glow over the proceedings, while the air of decadence was completed by a 50 foot mural of church stained glass, lit from behind, and complete with 'in memoriam' notices. The especially designed huge crystal and brass chandeliers added the necessary touch of frivolity.

"If they don't like the show they can always look at the chandeliers" was Fred's motto. The only problem we had now was finding plays that could compete with the decor.

A mountain of plays produced nothing good enough to launch a world premiere, and then I remembered my old friend Chandler Brossard. I wired him immediately to send us his most comprehensible play. It was about circus life, but not the sort of circus you could take a kid to. Among the odd assortment of characters it featured a Zulu with a bone through his nose delivering Shakespeare in a Yiddish accent, a circus strong man who couldn't lift a flea, but could break a heart with a smile, and the circus owner, an honest man who couldn't stop lying. It was alternately shocking and tender, a combination of absurdities, exactly the kind of play that challenged an audience more than the producer.

It was a gala premier with the cream of St. Louis society and cultural life in rapt anticipation and ready to be pleased. The polite applause at the end was more, I suspected, for the decor than for the play itself, and the mood was softened by the novelty of theater-going-while-you-drink. The box office groaned under the weight of unsold tickets, but I was proud that the first production hadn't compromised.

After another world premier, an adaptation of Dostoevsky's novel *A Friend of the Family* by a friend of Flicker's, Peter Stone, we decided to return to Beckett for some comic relief. *Endgame* was another box office disaster, with one leading critic suggesting that I should pass out knives of throat cutting size and bottles of brandy so that the audience could take their choice. It was hardly a money review. I couldn't understand why audiences didn't want to see two old people living out their lives in a couple of garbage cans. It seemed like real life to me.

After three non-commercial plays in a row, with another scheduled, we were facing financial ruin. Something drastic was needed to stave off disaster. Flicker's solution was certainly that. It sounded like a line from *Babes on Broad-*

way: "I know what we'll do, gang. Let's put on a musical." He proposed using the Landesman-Wolf songbook as the basis of a show.

Fran and Tommy had come a long way in their songwriting collaboration since the days he stood in the rain by the stage door of a Mel Torme concert, clutching a handful of lead sheets to lay on him as he emerged. Recordings of *Spring Can Really Hang You Up the Most* by Ella Fitzgerald, Sarah Vaughan, Jackie Cain, and others had established them as a serious song writing team. Fran was flattered by the idea and when Flicker asked if there was any book she'd like to base the show on, she didn't think for long. "Jay wrote a pretty good book some years ago that I'd like to use, if you can get him to show it to you."

Flicker had once threatened to make a musical out of Machiavelli's *The Prince,* but time was running out so he asked for my manuscript. Its history of rejection was so painful I'd tried to forget the work, so it came as a pleasant surprise on re-reading that it seemed to hold up well. In fact, it seemed timely. Since the publication of Kerouac's *On the Road,* he had become a media personality, albeit reluctantly, and was making a mess of it. My novel predicted the whole scene so accurately I was impressed. Kerouac was, of course, only a fringe figure in the novel, as he had been in our lives, a symbol of the archetypal Beat character who becomes famous and then sets about destroying himself. Aside from me and Fran, the main character was Legman and the effect he had on our marriage during the *Neurotica* days. It certainly captured the atmosphere of those early Beatnik days in the Village, but I couldn't, by any stretch of the imagination, see it as a musical. I gave it to Flicker very apologetically, saying, "It's nothing . . . a cheap little exposé of my decadent days in the Village." Flicker looked at me as if he believed me. "I understand," he assured me.

The next morning Flicker arrived at the house with the manuscript under his arm. "Let's have a cup of coffee at the Rex Cafe," he said. I couldn't understand why he didn't just hand over the script and forget all the bullshit about being sorry, etcetera, but at the Rex he said, in his most sombre voice, "You're going to faint when you hear this." He drifted in to his rabbinical voice, tapping the cover of *The Nervous Set*, "This is it, my boy. It's going to make us all rich and famous."

Before I could caution him that anything he said might be held against him, he was outlining our writing schedule and putting out his hand for the golden handshake. I shook it. If I wasn't so well known in St. Louis I'd have thrown in a kiss.

We worked on the manuscript night and day, that is, I would write a scene at the Galleries during the day, give it to Flicker at night at the Palace, and in the morning he would return a completed draft and I would start the next scene. Flicker, Fran, and I went over the complete Landesman-Wolf songbook, picking out those songs that would fit the story. It was quite easy—all of Fran's lyrics were about her life with me, and many of them were of the *Nervous Set* period. Any new lyrics needed to fit the action she dashed off in record time, but time was running out.

Because of his work on *The Nervous Set* Flicker had to drop out of the lead role of our next production *Clerembard*. We needed a leading man for that and more importantly, for *The Nervous Set*, but it had to be the right person. At Fran's suggestion Flicker flew to New York to talk our friend Felix Munso into joining the company to play both roles, the tyrannical, impoverished Viscount Clerembard and Yogi-Legman. Offered the Equity minimum, Munso, a dedicated Trotskyite, was adamant, "I never let my enemies exploit me; why should I let my friends?"

I had written the part of Yogi with Munso in mind, but my frantic phone calls and promises that this "would be the making of him" fell on deaf ears. Fran was determined he should play the part. She'd written a lyric that was a possible show stopper; she thought if Munso didn't sing it the song would die, and probably the show would die too. Her first phone call softened him up, but it was the third one that convinced him that if he didn't come she'd probably die as well.

Even an embittered Trotskyite has a heart: Munso was on the first plane out of New York. Relieved that the problem was solved, there was something about his attitude that was more cause for concern than jubilation. Munso's reputation as a trouble maker was legendary in the theatre; he even bragged about it the first time we met. "When I played opposite Michael Redgrave in *Tiger at the Gates*, he tried to destroy my performance, but I emerged triumphant." It was, perhaps, great party politics, but now that he was going to be a member of a company of young actors, I wasn't so sure we could afford that sort of integrity.

Flicker called the cast together for the first reading of *The Nervous Set*. He read all the parts and Tommy sang all the songs. The script was very similar to the original novel; Legman, Kerouac, Holmes, Broyard, Sobolof, and the millionaire were all there, plus the parties and the pressures between Fran and me, as we tried to hold a new marriage together. When Flicker finished the reading, there was a dead silence. Fran and I looked at each other, not knowing what to think as we saw our private life go public. We retired to the bar for a much needed drink. Munso was the first person to come up to us; his face was so solemn it led us to think we had laid an egg.

"I can't believe it," he began. "I never thought you kids could write anything so sophisticated. It's definitely Broadway material."

One by one, the actors came over to congratulate us. Everybody was full of love, respect, and admiration, to say nothing of surprise at what we had created.

At rehearsals, Munso was nothing short of brilliant. His timing, his comic flair, and his rich baritone voice were an inspiration to the others in the cast. Munso, as nasty Viscount Clerembard at night, was another story. One of the actors, Barry Primus, playing the role of the moronic son of the Count, overplayed his role in an attempt to get the audience's sympathy, a ploy that did not go unnoticed by Munso. Little things began happening on stage that weren't in the script. Primus would leave his shoes in the way of Munso's entrance or something equally insignificant. To an actor with Munso's perfectionism, it skyrocketed into another case of a fellow actor trying to destroy his performance. Munso struck back, lightly at first, unnoticed by the audience, but not by the actor when it called for physical contact. Munso resorted to his 'Redgrave technique' and boxed his ears soundly at every performance.

Naturally, Primus complained bitterly to Flicker to stop "the madman's antics" before he went completely deaf.

Munso's reaction was immediate. "He'd better not mess with me. I've battled with giants. I've had a six foot-four faggot chasing me around the stage with a sword. I'm not about to let that little squirt get away with ruining my performance." In spite of Flicker's attempts at peace-making, the feud continued. Primus began to underplay his role in an attempt to pacify Munso. It merely fueled Munso's sense of professionalism, leading to threats of "not being able to work with such amateurs."

We couldn't understand why Munso was destroying the play and endangering our close relationship. He was a guest at our house for breakfast, lunch, and dinner and tried to generate as much sympathy as he could with his stories of how the cast was out to destroy him. Fran's attempts to reason with him were ignored. When I would try to soothe his ego, he countered with a demand that I support him in his fight against the enemy. Before I knew it I was involved with a one man Trotskyite splinter movement.

As much as we loved him, we wouldn't interfere; instead, we tried to minimize the trouble and talked with him in terms of all the future projects we were going to do together to make us rich and famous. It had the opposite effect. His performance in rehearsals never lost its brilliance, but he began to bicker with Flicker over the thinnest of excuses until it became impossible for Flicker to function as a director. Munso's reading *The New York Times* during rehearsals was hardly morale building. After repeated warnings, Flicker came to me with his own ultimatum: "He's got to go."

I consulted with Fran who I thought still had some credibility left with Munso, now that he felt completely isolated by the rest of the company. All she was able to report back was Munso's disappointment that she had betrayed him by "siding with the capitalist exploiters" that we had become. I released him from the cast of *The Nervous Set*, but he had a week to run in *Clerembard*.

This set off a whole new turn in Munso's tactics. As Equity deputy of the company, everything from now on had to be according to the rule book. He looked for petty violations to substantiate his case against us when he would bring us up on charges before the Equity board. When he claimed the blankets we furnished the actors with had less than the wool content that the rule book demanded, I knew he was going for 'the final solution' to our theatrical future.

We knew he was out to wreck us, but we didn't know he had a hot line to God. After a bitter argument with Flicker, he threatened to destroy us once and for all. An hour after we all left the Crystal Palace, a tornado struck Gaslight Square, damaging many of the buildings, including the Crystal Palace. Luckily, it was not enough to stop the next night's performance.

Inspired by the disaster, Munso created a minor one of his own onstage that night by physically attacking the actor he'd accused of trying to destroy his performance. The play was held up until this chap recovered from the onslaught. We had survived a tornado and we weren't about to let an actor bring us to our knees. I decided to fire him and Flicker agreed to take over the part even if he had to do it with a book in hand. The next morning I came back unexpectedly to tell Fran of my decision. Munso was having a late breakfast. Fran was looking like a agonized deaf-mute as Munso harangued her with his defense.

"Are you enjoying your breakfast?" I asked him.

"Of course. Fran's a wonderful cook". He said it as if nothing had ever happened between us.

"I'm glad, because it's the last meal you'll ever get in this house." Fran lowered her head, knowing what was coming next. I said it very calmly.

"You're fired." He gave me one of those 'what-took-you-so-long' looks, but didn't stop eating for a second.

Fran was upset about what Munso had tried to do to the Palace, but miserable about what he had done to her dreams about *The Nervous Set*. What he was doing to our marriage I never suspected until some time later on.

The Nervous Set opened on March 4, 1959. It was an instant success; even Fran's folks, who came down especially for it, were impressed. I remember a large luncheon on Frank Moskas' riverboat, moored on the levee of the Mississippi, with the cast and all the people who had helped make it such a great show toasting one another and the musical's future. Fran's father turned to her with a compliment: "Just think if you had worked at your piano lessons you could have done the music, too." Cutie was pleased with the show, but complained about how badly the cast was dressed.

Variety's man in St. Louis gave it a review that attracted the New York producers immediately:

> *The Nervous Set*, a locally-written musical comedy, has premiered at the Crystal Palace saloon theatre to ecstatic packed house enthusiasm . . . *The Nervous Set* deals with the beat generation, sometimes tenderly, sometimes spicily, sometimes hilariously, but always entertainingly . . . Mrs. Landesman's lyrics and Tommy Wolf's music are polished to a fine sheen, either on the tender, Spring Can Really Hang You Up The Most, or the ribald chant, How Do You Like Your Love? The show has some twenty tunes, tailored to the assorted beatniks,

squares and snobs who populate the three acts . . . The musical numbers punctuate a tragi-comic scene that shifts back and forth from square Connecticut to beat Greenwich Village to Manhattan's tony Sutton Place . . . The appealing hero and heroine are storm-tossed between the wacky world of the editor's milieu and the sane domesticity the girl craves . . . although there are some shining moments of pathos, hilarity is always just around the corner . . .

So it looked like clear sailing all the way to the big time. But there were complications. I had signed a contract with Flicker at an early stage of our collaboration stipulating that, if the show went to Broadway, he had to direct it. At the time, I saw nothing wrong with the clause. He had done a magnificent job of whipping the book into shape, for which he got co-author credit, and his conception of the show was brilliant. Broadway producers, Alexander Cohen and Saint-Subber, who rushed down to see the show, didn't think Flicker's direction was that good and would not accept him as part of the package. David Merrick called to say he was on his way down and to do nothing till he arrived, but there was someone on the scene who would take the show with Flicker as director, Robert Lantz. All he wanted was a few changes in cast and a new ending. "Broadway is not ready for a musical ending with a suicide," he told us. I didn't agree.

"But they're the professionals," Flicker and Fran kept telling me.

"They're talking in terms of an original cast album," Fran screamed at me.

I told them both to cool it and let's see what Merrick would offer us.

Lantz, a charming Hungarian agent who was associated with the films *The Quiet American* and *I Want to Live,* wanted to make our show his debut as a Broadway producer. He was very convincing and assured us he would make it a success. I told him I couldn't do anything until Merrick saw the show. Then Lantz played his ace card. If we signed with him now, he would produce the show immediately after it closed at the Palace. That didn't mean anything to me—the longer we ran that show at the Palace, the more money the Palace would make for future productions, so why hurry? No matter how much pressure they put on me to sign, I refused. I felt that Lantz wasn't the right man for the job.

I explained to Flicker and Fran that if he took the whole show exactly like it was to Broadway, he'd be much more likely to pull it off, but if he started to tamper with it to meet some kind of mythical Broadway formula, we'd be in trouble. They kept repeating how professional Lantz was and how the professionals know what's best. I went so far as to give Lantz an oral agreement, not binding on either side, but it was enough to make me call off Merrick, who was really pissed off. But he wasn't as annoyed as I was.

The phone calls from New York started to come in from Lantz. He had Goddard Lieberson, the head man at Columbia Records, interested in financing the show. Would Tommy come to New York and play them the score? Tommy did and they loved the songs. He returned full of enthusiasm for Lieberson. I made a few calls of my own. One of them was to Janet Rhinelander Stewart, who was working for a Broadway producer/agent at the time. I told her my problem and asked for advice. After hearing my side of the story, she said: "I have two words of advice for you. Don't sign!"

Lantz called Fran: "Columbia Records is prepared to do an original cast album under the personal direction of 'God' himself. Time is running out," he warned her. I tried to explain to Fran that if they made those changes, the show would flop on Broadway.

"Listen, Jay, if you don't give me this opportunity, I'll never forgive you. What do you know about show business? They're the professionals. Leave it to them."

Strong stuff, I thought, stated with conviction. One of Fran's tough girlfriends mentioned that she had connections in East St. Louis with gangsters that would take care of Flicker with no fuss: "You could put it down as a legitimate pre-production expense". Fran could have strangled me with her own hands, she was so furious about my delaying her entrance into the Hall of Fame. Somewhere I got the feeling that she wanted to get to New York even if it meant walking over my dead body. Flicker's agent began to call Fran, always with the same message: "Get that crazy husband of yours to sign those contracts."

Everybody was putting on the pressure; I turned to Fred for support. If the show left the Palace, we'd never find another to replace it and make the kind of money we were taking in at the box office. We even had to do a matinee to accommodate the demand. People came back two, three times to see it. At one of the matinees, I saw Martha Gelhorn's mother, a grand dowager on the St. Louis society scene since the turn of the century. She was seeing the show a second time. I asked her what was there about it that made her come back and see it again.

"It's the story of my life," she said.

I was more convinced than ever not to give in to Lantz and Fran.

Fred was sympathetic. He realized that *The Nervous Set* had saved the Palace from financial ruin. He was grateful for that, but wouldn't stand in the way of it going to Broadway, even if it meant closing at the Palace.

"Listen, Jay," he told me confidentially, "if you hold it up from going to Broadway, you'll have a crazy woman on your hands." He paused, then added: "for life."

I got his point. I was weakening fast. There was absolutely no one to support me. In the end, I gave in and signed, reluctantly.

Maybe I was wrong. They were the experts. I was just an antique salesman.

15

Trova came to the rescue with a project that took my mind off my troubles. He wanted me to be properly dressed for the Broadway debut with a specially designed *Nervous Set* suit. He and I spent days with the best tailor in St Louis, going over materials and designs; he wanted a Broadway look, but with refinements. The buttons of the sleeve were a special jet black ebony that had to be sewn in an overlay line; the trousers had what he called a "Trevor Howard pleated front" and a "George Raft back" with a belt buckle. The fly had buttons: "Makes less noise in the cinema," claimed Trova. It could have been a gangster suit of the Twenties, but Trova's refinements gave it a contemporary look. The material was a dark blue, soft-wool pinstripe, with padded shoulders and a 1920's orange Parker pen in the breast pocket, I looked like a promising model for the tailoring of the absurd.

The musical was scheduled to open at the Henry Miller Theatre, New York, May 11, 1959. The comedy of errors began long before that date. Why this Hungarian entrepreneur wanted to do *The Nervous Set* in the first place I never understood: "It is my job to explain America to the Americans," was his explanation. Lantz wanted to change the name of the show to *Like Tomorrow*. I won that round, but he insisted upon changing the cast leads. I lost that one. I had some buttons made up that simply said, *The Nervous Set*, which everybody loved, but he thought they were corny.

Fran, unknown to me, got Tommy to request her presence in New York on the pretext of writing some new songs. She began to see the show's transfer as her ticket back to the Big Apple, Felix Munso, and more Broadway shows. Everyone was telling her how great she was as a lyricist; the show, they insisted, was bound to be a smash hit. I was totally ignored once I signed those contracts. The cast was in a high state of excitement, but the leads didn't know they were going to be replaced. I kept the show running smoothly and licked my wounds during the intermissions.

Fran came back with the news that the hit song of the show, *Spring Can Really Hang You Up The Most*, was out of the show because the producer couldn't work out a satisfactory arrangement with the publisher; it seemed like a stupid move, but it was a fact of life. Without that song, the script needed some rewriting, so Fran and I drove to New York earlier than we intended to.

Driving into New York in our convertible Packard, with the prospect of a hit on Broadway and the car radio playing *Everything's Coming Up Roses*, I thought of that trip out of New York seven years earlier in the old touring car, heading for St. Louis, with nothing to look forward to except settling down in the shop with Cutie. Fran and I were no closer now, in spite of the two boys and other good things of life we'd enjoyed together. She was still looking over my shoulder for someone else.

We got a suite in the hotel opposite the Henry Miller just to see the signs that had already gone up announcing the show. Although nobody's name was in lights, it was still a big thrill for us to see "book by Jay Landesman and lyrics by Fran Landesman." Had we finally done something our parents would approve of?

The next day I sat through my first rehearsal and my heart sank. The actress chosen for the lead was three inches taller than the hero and twice as tough. I thought it was very clever of Flicker to disguise this physical incongruity by directing all their scenes together with the

221

hero always standing on a piece of furniture or she sitting down while he stood; they certainly couldn't afford to be seen erect together. The heroine was supposed to have that vulnerable quality that made her suicide at the end believable, but the heroine was so ballsy it would have made more sense if the hero had committed suicide. It might have seemed petty of me to give such significance to this detail, but it only showed the producer had a peculiar sense of humor, or perhaps he saw *The Nervous Set* as a musical of the absurd.

I also found it odd that nobody noticed the heroine couldn't sing in the style a jazz musical demanded. I made a last desperate plea for the original girl to play the role, but Lantz thought there must have been some hanky-panky between us for me to push her career so intensely. "Your husband's favorite actress has no talent, my dear," he told Fran. The fact that the producer and the director had not decided on an ending for the play three days before it was to open said something about their talent. I stopped going to rehearsals—it was too painful to watch.

In the morning Fran and I would have breakfast with her folks. In the car on the way to their apartment I would have to stop at Central Park and 59th Street and throw up. While trying to keep some food down, I would unload all my doubts to the folks, but they couldn't understand. By this time even Fran had a sneaking suspicion that I was right, but still did nothing to support me. The only thing that cheered us up was the rumor that *Gypsy* was "in trouble," and it was opening the same week as we were.

Fran and I had dinner together but they were gloomy affairs. Even being with our old friends gave her little pleasure; she gave the impression that she was off in a dream somewhere. Usually she would split right after dinner, saying she had some shopping to do. One evening Harelson asked: "Is Bloomingdale's open at one o'clock in the morning?" Everybody knew what he was talking about. Fran was seeing Munso as much as she could, leaving me to find solace with the old gang at the bar. I always got a few laughs out of the routine of the forgotten man: "Give me three sticks of wood, a can of sterno, and I'll hit the road for hobo heaven."

There were three preview nights and at each one the show had a different ending. Flicker was Mr. Panic by now, a little the worse for all the dexedrine he'd been taking. Lantz kept reassuring all of us that "Ve are five minutes from success." After the second preview, we had a conference. Fran was lying on the floor, completely out of contact, when someone came in with the news that Stu Ostrow, who was handling the music publishing for Frank Loesser, had just become a proud father. Fran woke up enough to say, "Who the fuck cares about that at a time like this?" then collapsed again. I wished I could have joined her. The ending we had seen was so dumb, I thought they would be forced to go back to the original one, but no, they'd think of something. As writer of the show, I was the last one they consulted. I had no idea what was going to happen on opening night. I left them to work it out.

A big contingent of St. Louis friends showed up for the premiere, eager, excited and all dressed up in tuxedos and long evening dresses. Half of Gaslight Square was there, including Jack O'Neil; it looked like one of his cocktail hours. Seeing all the familiar faces with their loyalty and faith in the musical made me feel worse about letting them down.

Joseph Pulitzer, the editor of the *St Louis Post-Dispatch*, a big fan of *The Nervous Set,* and one of the investors, was looking good under the bright marquee lights and I went over to say hello. While I was there, Kerouac swerved toward us with a brown paper bag around a bottle waving in his hand. He had just come from a screening of Robert Frank's film *Pull My Daisy,* which he had appeared in. He looked awful, weaving in and out of the first nighters, an act so surrealistic it put me in a good mood. I never thought Kerouac would show, but Holmes had seen him at the screening and told him about it.

"What's this all about, Jay?" Kerouac asked. "Have you

maligned me in some way with this show? Who's this dude?" he said, offering Pulitzer a swig from his bottle. When I introduced them, Pulitzer looked Kerouac over, stepped back a pace to avoid Kerouac's ferocious breath, and asked the big question.

"Where's your tie, Mr Kerouac?"

Pulitzer took a long swig from the bottle and handed it to me. I didn't know who needed the whiskey more, but I too took a long swallow and returned it to Kerouac, who proceeded to do a few takes on Pulitzer's fancy dress shirt. Everybody was watching Kerouac's moves as he staggered around Pulitzer and me, sizing us up as if he were about to back us in a fight. I was terrifically pleased that he had shown up. It was years since I'd last seen him—he'd dropped by the old *Neurotica* pad with a signed copy of his first book, *The Town and the City,* a gesture that surprised and touched me.

"You'll like it," I said, putting my arm around his shoulders to support him through the lobby. He put on a little extra show of drunkenness that caught the attention of the theatre manager who came over to us, very excited.

"I'm sorry, but this gentleman can't come into the theatre."

"Why not?" Kerouac asked belligerently, waving the bottle in his face. "Ain't I dressed properly?"

I took the manager aside and explained who he was. "He's the original beatnik," I told him. "I'm the author of this show and he is my guest. It's a good piece of publicity to have him at the opening, don't you think?"

He looked Kerouac over, arched his eyebrow, put his little finger under his lower lip and said: "It would make a better publicity story if I barred him," and led us to our seats.

Kerouac sat next to me and immediately went to sleep.

The part of Kerouac was played by Larry Hagman, as clean cut and handsome as Kerouac used to be when I first met him. He played it with a southern accent, not unlike the one he uses today for the role of J.R. The audience was very responsive as first night audiences usually are since they are made up of friends and backers. Just before the end of the first act there was a song called *Fun Life* that had the lines, *"Let's just have fun/Let's not be serious/Shakespeare was a hack/So we read Kerouac."* When they came to his name, I swear to God, he woke up, turned to me and said: "Hey, that's pretty good, man," and promptly dozed off again. At the intermission, he joined Holmes and me for a drink in the bar across the street, but we couldn't keep his attention. He ran off into the night and didn't come back for the second act.

I found Fran hiding somewhere in the theatre and together we said hello to Janet Rhinelander Stewart who was talking to Richard Rodgers. Rodgers was extremely gracious, complimenting Fran on her "clever lyrics." There was one line in a lyric early in the show that was a put-down on everything about New York: *"No matter how they rave now/Larry Hart is in his grave now/And whoever takes Manhattan is a square."* He told Fran that people who came to the previews were outraged with that line and they called him up to tell him so. "I don't think it's disrespectful and I know you kids didn't mean to knock Larry." Fran was very touched by Rodger's approval. During the second act, Miss Rat, as I called Fran during this period, and I were standing in the back of the theatre, too nervous by now to sit. If there was any laughter, she would give me a painful smile. At the end of the show we exchanged pained expressions in absolute silence.

"You will come to the after-theatre party?" I whispered as the curtain came down.

"Do I have to?" she replied.

We'd gone back to congratulate the cast after each of the three previews and neither of us could face a fourth performance in the dressing rooms. I stayed around the lobby where there was an air of doomed gaiety about the place. An old man who looked like a permanent 'go-fer' was hawking the sheet music to *The Ballad Of The Sad Young Men* and *Travel The Road Of Love* without any takers. Most

225

of the people who had seen the show in St. Louis just shook their heads as they went by and a few brave ones came up to me with "good show, Jay," but I knew their hearts weren't in it. Thank God we didn't have the after dinner theatre party at Sardis, where they put your table next to the toilet if you've failed. Instead, Flicker chose a nice Jewish lobster restaurant where he used to eat on credit during his student days. I walked to the place with John and Shirley Holmes, trying to explain to them what happened to my show; Holmes thought it was terrific with all its faults and the portrait of Legman extremely funny.

At the party, I went over to Cutie, who would certainly give me some credit for having arrived on Broadway.

"It's not the Muny Opera," she said, referring to the St. Louis outdoor civic theatre that she could relate to. "It was better in St. Louis," was her final comment before she resumed her lobster hunt.

When the first paper arrived, a wave of repressed excitement hovered over the party. It was Brooks Atkinson's review in the *New York Times,* and in those days it was believed that a good review from him was enough to make a show. Someone began to read it aloud to the hushed audience. It was a rave review, only complaining about the false ending. We couldn't believe our ears. The crowd, stunned at first, applauded madly, congratulating one another on the turn of events. Toasts were lifted to the success we all so desperately longed for. It seemed to happen in slow motion, like a dream. Fran thought someone had slipped in a fake review as a cruel joke. The actors were stunned. We hugged and kissed and fell into waiting arms all over the place. For the next ten minutes the world was ours. Maybe those plans that Fran and I had of moving to New York and writing more shows, living in a penthouse, hanging out with Betty Comden and Adoph Green, and having drinks with Leonard Bernstein would all come true.

When the Herald Tribune arrived, my brother-in-law read Walter Kerr's review. From the opening line I could tell by his voice that it was going to be a bumpy ride, but I didn't expect us to be shot down like mad dogs. Our hopes collapsed as the other papers arrived. Each review was worse than the previous one. "This theatre-goer found himself out in left field. Man, he didn't dig a lick of *The Nervous Set*" was one of the kinder ones. "*The Nervous Set* makes me wonder if I am really an old poop," said the Hearst critic. "One of those rumpuses that will either irritate you or fascinate you. It irritated us enormously." "The cast should have their mouths washed out with soap for singing Mrs Landesman's lyrics." "The cast should be sprayed with roach powder," said another.

The strongest line in all the lyrics was in a song that Yogi sings: "*Have you ever loved a pheasant/Have you ever eaten peasant?/You may find that it is pleasant for a change.*" This was Broadway, the big-time sophisticated N.Y. audiences and critics—this was 1959. Were we out of touch? Our little spoof, tongue-in-cheek, beatnik musical was evidently taken seriously by them. The worst review came from Felix Munso. I overheard him tell Fran that Kerr's review was a rave compared to the one he would have written.

In the morning, Fran and I jumped up early to see if, by some miracle, there was any action at the box office—we could see right out of the window the crowds passing by the theatre without a look at what was playing. We crawled back to bed with heavy hearts; there didn't seem to be any reason for getting up at all.

Columbia Records, who had put up most of the money for the show, decided to keep it running and do the original cast album even before *Time* magazine gave us an excellent review. Richard Rodgers, hearing the show was in trouble, called up Lantz offering to give us a rave quote to use in the advertising. My old contributor to *Neurotica*, Leonard Bernstein, who was also a good friend of Lantz's, staged an impressive demonstration by walking out in the middle of the show with his entire entourage.

The show's publicist tried to promote some interest, but the best she could come up with was an interview for Fran and me in a third rate restaurant for transmission over an FM station after midnight. She was really pushing things when she got the bright idea of having Richard Avedon, then the hottest photographer around, do some shots of Fran and me, for what purpose I'll never know.

The Nervous Set was tagged as "that Beatnik show" and nothing was more unpopular than a beatnik in 1959. Rent-a-beatnik had come into full play by then, and Kerouac's public performances, usually grotesque, didn't establish any sympathy for them so anything that faintly resembled one was considered 'un-chic'. The idea of someone bothering to satirize them was inconceivable.

On our last day in New York, the cast recorded the show under the production of Goddard Lieberson. He thought Tommy and Fran were extremely talented and wanted the album to prove that he was right. Fran and I were there, but I felt superfluous; she was called upon to do lyric changes and editing and generally encourage the morale of the cast. She did her best, but her heart was somewhere else. By the lunch break we were feeling like outcasts, estranged from the actors, and from Flicker and Lantz. As we were sitting in a booth alone, Lieberson came in and joined us in our exile. It was a touching show of loyalty and affection for Fran, but no amount of 'God's' good words could cheer her up. Fran was itching to split; she had done all she could to help the leading lady get through seventeen takes on *The Ballad Of The Sad Young Men.* Flicker rushed over to her, furious that she was leaving.

"If you leave now, I'll never speak to you again," he warned her.

"I'm sorry to hear that," she said very coolly. "I'm going to miss you, Ted."

I left soon after, but I had no place to go.

That Sunday, the *National Enquirer,* a paper notorious for starting trouble between couples, carried a news item about us going "phtt": "She wants to try for the big time in New York, while her husband wants to go back to his small town life," was the quote. They weren't far wrong.

Fred and Paula picked up two very unhappy Broadway rejects at the St. Louis airport. The show hadn't closed, but only a miracle would save it, and those were rare on the Great White Way. When we arrived at our house, we all got out except Fran. She sat in the car trying to summon the strength to go inside. "I guess I have to," she said at last.

She waited around all summer for the call everybody told her would come, but evidently Broadway was doing all right without her. There were one or two consolation prizes: Marya Manes, one of the few critics we respected, wrote a piece on Broadway and mentioned that *The Nervous Set* was more fun and had better songs than most of the shows that season. When the Broadway cast album came out, it got a better review in the *New York Times* than the *Gypsy* album. But still no calls came; the only calls were those made to Munso by a very lonely and disappointed lyricist. Promises had been made. None had been kept.

Sometimes I would come home in the afternoon to find Fran on the phone or on the bed, crying. Then I found a letter addressed to Munso lying on the bed, unsealed. It was the kind of letter that, left lying around, told a husband he'd have to do something about the situation.

"If you're serious about Munso, you ought to see a lawyer."

Instead, she called Munso, who told her it was "bad timing," much to her relief. She really didn't want to split from me and live with an unemployed actor, no matter how romantic it might look on paper. I didn't think she'd be that dumb either. She put Munso on hold.

For being such a good girl she deserved a present and I gave her one: a new musical we could work on together. Both of us had read Nelson Algren's novel *A Walk On The Wild Side* and recognised its potential as a musical. It had my favorite theme: the Horatio Alger myth, in reverse. The hero comes to the big city and goes down the ladder of success. It reminded me of my own attempts to conquer New York and become a "world shaker" (Algren's term), ending up beaten by the system, just as Algren's hero was.

On a hot Sunday, we drove up to his summer house in Gary, Indiana. I would have thought the proceeds from the Hollywood sale of his *The Man with the Golden Arm* would have purchased more than a little shack on a dirty river in a steel town. But his little house was cosy, if sparsely furnished.

Algren had been playing a new recording of *Spring Can Really Hang You Up The Most* by his favorite singer, June Christy, so he was in the mood to talk about the show. He took us to a Greek restaurant and, by the time the check came, we had a deal: I would collaborate on the book with him and he would collaborate on the lyrics with Fran. Tommy Wolf, whose music he really liked, would do the score. We were heading back to Broadway, only this time we couldn't miss. We were working with a master who knew his way around a verb.

Fran and I spent a week on Fred's farm, mapping out the first draft of *A Walk On The Wild Side*. Fran was never so happy as when working on a project. We worked beautifully together, feeling close and friendly as we helped each other whip the script into shape.

When we had a first draft of the musical ready, Tommy flew in from the West Coast with a complete score, and we met in Chicago to do a reading for Algren and his friends. When they heard Tommy's romantic score, their enthusiasm soared.

The next day, after Algren had read my script, his enthusiasm faded. He said it wasn't what he had in mind. I had used his novel as the basis for the script, not realizing that he had another book in mind that he never wrote. Since he was collaborating on the script, it was his turn to work on it—"run it through the typewriter," as he liked to say. Although his interpretation was completely different from mine, it was his baby, and Lord knows, he was a professional!

What he returned was the scenario for a Wagnerian opera.

He believed life had to be lived first before you could write about it. "Part of the trouble with today's writers is that they all try to play it safe. You can't sit in a glass cage and write. You have to be out there among the people." He showed us what he meant, taking us around to an old bar run by some ex-carnival friends of his where we met "his kind of people." That bar was so exclusive they kept it locked during opening hours lest some stranger come in. The regulars there had names like "Chicken Neck Herman" and "Dog Face Sal." The proprietor and his wife were battle-scarred veterans, too "real" for the likes of Fran and me. Algren seriously suggested to me that they play the role of the couple who run the Spare Nobody Bar in the show. The whole place seemed to be populated with characters straight out of Algren's books. I thought it was a sensational idea; fortunately more practical heads prevailed.

That didn't stop me from hiring a jazz singer who never acted in the theatre for the lead role of Hallie, the whore with a heart of gold. I received a letter from Stella Brooks, whom I saw at a party in Greenwich Village in 1949 during the *Neurotica* days, demanding I give her the part. "It was made for me, baby," she wrote; "I've lived all my life preparing for the role." She had heard about the show through a friend in jail, jazz pianist, James Blake, who was a good friend of Algren's. All three of them had been corresponding for years (Blake later wrote a book about it) and Algren agreed she would be perfect.

When she arrived in St. Louis, she looked perfect, she sang perfect, and we congratulated ourselves on such perfect casting. For the male lead, we cast Bob Dorough, another jazz singer who had never acted before in his life. He had the perfect background for the role of the poor white boy from Southwest Texas. He could play piano, sing, arrange music, and had the perfect accent, but unfortunately his vegetarian vibe wasn't quite right for the part of a Texas stud performing arduous feats of sexuality in a New Orleans whore house. His authenticity and musical contributions were so enormous, I conveniently overlooked the problem.

After a week of rehearsals, tears, sweat, and trouble, Stella Brooks felt she couldn't cut the role and asked to be replaced. In spite of her having menopausal hot flushes on stage, I thought she was terrific and encouraged her to see it through. Her hysteria was just what we were looking for; unfortunately, she couldn't channel it to the role. It turned into hostility directed against me. "Let me go home, back to the sun. Quit torturing me!" she screamed. She was replaced by a professional, wholesome actress who could do all the right things, but wasn't dirty enough for the part.

Algren reworked the book, making the hero out of a minor character without any legs, who spent his time going in and out of rooms with low-knob doors. The show opened to a stunned audience. Pimps, whores, criminals, dopers, beggars, cripples, drunkards, illiterates, and the legless man on wheels sang and danced their way through a bizarre, downbeat evening that made *The Threepenny Opera* look like a Christmas pantomime. The show opened with a song about the depression, and it didn't get any more cheerful, although it had great scenes of heartwarming disasters and inescapable confrontations between good and evil. It was too strong even for the Crystal Palace audiences.

After running a week, Algren polished it up so that it was even more downbeat. I called David Merrick to come to see it and to my surprise he said he would. He arrived on the night of one of the worst blizzards St. Louis had seen in fifty years. They were still shovelling snow from the entrance of the Palace when Merrick and his girlfriend arrived. The cast gave a magnificent performance that night. I had packed the house with afficionados of the Palace and everything was going smoothly. Fran and I watched Merrick's face throughout the show, but he wasn't giving anything away.

After the show, Merrick asked to see the cast. We took him to the basement dressing rooms where he thanked the actors for giving such a wonderful performance. He told them how much St. Louis had changed since he grew up there, how delighted he was to see something like this happening in a town he had always despised. To have Broadway's biggest producer give such praise to their performance gave the actors a badly needed shot in the arm.

We went upstairs to sit around the family table with a few drinks and some clever chat. We did not discuss the show. Instead, we took him on a grand tour of Gaslight Square, stomping around in sixteen inches of snow. He thanked us for showing him such a good time, but it was getting late and he had to get back to the airport. Checking with the airline, there were no planes leaving St. Louis that night; we invited him to stay over with us. Nothing would induce him to stay. "Listen," he told us confidentially, "I don't even fly over St. Louis for fear the airplane will develop engine trouble and have to land." Finally we drove to a bus station and sat with them till they could get a bus to Kansas City where he might get a flight to Las Vegas. To see Merrick and his lady in mink drink coffee out of cups designed for Algren's skid row buddies was a sight. But give credit where it's due: he'd come a long way for such a short walk on the wild side.

At the bus station, we thanked him for coming down to see the show. He didn't say anything for a minute, looking away, as if his attention was distracted. But it wasn't; he was trying to break it to us gently.

"It's a very good show," he said, boarding the bus. "Jean loved it, but it's not my kind of musical."

We waited until the bus pulled out, waving goodbye.

"Well, what do you think?" Fran asked on the way home.

"I don't think he liked it, old girl."

But we loved our crippled crew and had faith that someday, somebody would take them to their heart.

The next few weeks the production got better and better. Some nights it ended in total silence; some nights the actors were booed. The actor who played the pimp was so disheartened by the audience's hostility he could hardly get through the performance. But the show had its fans. Our resident millionaire offered to subsidize it for as long as we wanted to run it. But audiences were alienated by Algren's message and refused to come.

Two flops in a row left something to worry about. As a consolation prize, we decided to take our first trip to Europe and join Fred and Paula who were in temporary residence in Rome. Unfortunately, another pregnancy looked as if it might mess up that plan. Fran was adamant about not cancelling the trip, yet she didn't want to risk a miscarriage overseas. I thought it would be a shame not to go through with the pregnancy. Cosmo and Miles were such "good uns", Alfie, their nanny and guardian angel, could have handled a half a dozen more. Fran didn't feel that way. She got the name of a disqualified nurse from a girl friend and had an abortion. She became infected and at the hospital, the doctor said she was a very lucky girl to survive.

She couldn't have cared less.

Stars of Tomorrow

We had a couple of days in New York before the ship sailed for Le Havre. As usual, Fran disappeared with Munso during the day, leaving me to drink with the boys. We spent time reminiscing at Radulovich's new place, the Cafe Renaissance, about the good old days when laughs didn't cost a thing. All of our friends came down to the ship to see us off with the usual champagne and forced gaiety, but Fran seemed reluctant to participate in the bon voyage festivities. As the ship pulled out of New York, past the Statue of Liberty, I couldn't help thinking of a lyric in *The Nervous Set: "So the lady with the torch can soak her head."* She was in that kind of mood—bitter and cynical.

I tried to be as cheerful as one could in the cabin class of a floating Hilton, the S.S. United States. The maitre d' had the good sense to seat us at the only table for two in the dining room. Any ideas we had that ships were romantic were short lived; there was no one we could even exchange a few lies with. They didn't have paper party hats on their heads, but they looked like they should have.

Walks around the deck with Fran gazing intently at the waves, only reminded us never to travel by boat again. Fran's depression was so acute, she said it was a wonder the ship didn't sink with the weight of her heart. We landed at Le Havre with no expectation that things would get any better. We did the sights of Paris like ordinary tourists, but on the flight to Nice to see Legman we were prepared to be victims; I didn't know what kind of reception we would get.

He had heard about *The Nervous Set* and my "maligning" his character and made it plain that he hadn't forgiven me, but for old time's sake would see us. We rented a car, drove up the hills to Valbonne and found him sitting in his field waiting to welcome us. It was an incredible piece of land, lying between the Alps on one side and the Mediterranean on the other, his house in the middle of a picturesque olive grove. Naturally, there wasn't any electricity, gas, toilet, or heat. Being summer, it wasn't so bad.

"Where do you shit?" I asked. He gave me a big grin, indicating his satisfaction at my discomfort.

"Anywhere!" he screamed. "Isn't it wonderful?" adding, "It's good for the land."

Since we hadn't planned to stay overnight, Fran didn't panic.

It was a beautiful, sunny day, and Fran took full advantage of the sun. Legmans' wife came out to say hello and dashed back in the house. Taking off her blouse, Fran stretched out on the warm grass next to Legman, who kept insisting she get more direct exposure; he helped her off with her clothes, one piece at a time, while he condemned my attempts to be a playwright, a husband, a playboy, businessman, and "finking out on the culture." It was fun to see the old boy still operating with so much style.

I had brought him a copy of the original cast album. Although he didn't have anything to play it on, the picture of the actor who played him, on the cover with a long cigarette holder, looking like he needed a shave, did not go unnoticed.

"Did you have to make me look like a fag?" he asked.

By the time he got through telling me how difficult it had been since he left America, Fran was lying on her stomach, completely naked. He planted a daisy in her ass as a finishing touch to an accomplished performance. "You're still too good for this bum," he said, pointing to me.

We wanted to take him and Beverly to dinner in Valbonne. Beverly declined, but Legman was glad to get out of the house. He ordered us a profound French meal and some expensive wines that made him so mellow he told us about his long awaited book on oralgenitalism; it was with a big American paperback publisher and he was sure it was going to make him rich and famous.

His big work, *The Rationale of the Dirty Joke,* was still in progress. He almost said something nice about our days together, but couldn't bring it to the surface. Instead he told me the FBI was tailing him and pointed to a suspicious-looking guy in a raincoat taking pictures of the village square. Some things never change, as I told Fran on the drive back to the hotel in Nice: "His paranoia is in as good a shape as ever."

Back in our hotel suite that night, we felt a little guilty about the luxury of it all. The hotel's bathroom was larger than Legman's whole house. It contained a choice of basins and a huge white porcelain tub; the towels were as big as sheets and softer than down. After soaking in a scented tub of blue water, we wrapped ourselves in the towels and stood out on the balcony with a drink and a cigarette and a lot of fantasies, looking over the yachts moored in the bay. What play were we in? *Design For Living* or *Red Peppers?* I had a hard time fighting off memories of sweating it out with Legman back in the old days, with his balls hanging out, a string for a belt, and words of defiance for a world that was ignoring us both. Had I become the sort of man I used to put down? Was I still yearning for another Legman to come into my life?

We both looked at the moonlit sea. The only light on the street came from a large neon sign advertising a bar called 'FELIX'S'. Fran tried not to notice it, but how could she not?

The next morning, the sun was out in full force, lifting her spirits considerably. The thought of seeing Fred and Paula later that day contributed to our having a very animated conversation in a waterfront cafe. We talked so much, and probably so loud, we attracted the interest of two Americans at the next table.

"Excuse me," one of them turned to us. "We're having a bet about whether you two are married. I said you couldn't be because married people never have anything to say to each other over a meal."

When we told them we had been married for ten years, his reply was: "There's hope for us all."

We joined tables and discovered we were all in show business, travelling around Europe to forget our recent flops. They had come from London where their show closed to deafening silence, just like our beloved *Wild Side*. They were, however, wild about London. "It's the city of the sixties," they said. "If it happens at all, it'll happen there." We definitely added London to our itinerary.

Fred and Paula's beautiful villa on one of the hills overlooking Rome could have been on anyone's list of great ruins of Italy. Wild lilac trees scented the magically overgrown garden, a perfect Henry James setting that made us feel for a brief time that we belonged there.

Fran and I had many years of experience in games where people were the entertainment, but we never saw anything like the streets of Rome. It was one, big, glamorous, naughty Gaslight Square, full of people looking like stars watching those who were stars. As Cutie would say, "Who's watching the store?"

Paula said we knew more people in our two weeks in Rome than she and Fred had met in their six months. It was easy; all you had to do was enter a room glowing with confidence: gesturing and talking fast helped. At a restaurant we sat down with a table of twelve strangers and came away two hours later with ten new friends and a possible lover or two. Guitars were passed like pasta, and passes were made with the music. A beautiful boy sitting next to Fran was kissing a beautiful girl next to him and holding Fran's hand under the table. We didn't know a word of Italian, but we were familiar with the body language. We soon learned to thrive on a diet of Chianti and attention. Rome was a playground for children and we fitted in perfectly.

We went with our new friends to crumbling palaces to hear the young Mussolini play a kind of Fascist jazz on a jumbo Steinway or to little clubs to catch Chet Baker do the real thing. Fran had her picture taken with her head on the lap of a lion in a public gardens, while the old poets shouted *bravo!*

Before we left, we relented about sightseeing and did a quick trip around St Peter's. Fran took one side and I took the other, establishing something of a record by covering it in seven minutes flat. People were still the best attraction, we decided.

People were the number one attraction for us in London. Asking the Dorchester Hotel's hall porter where the Bloomsbury Set hung out, he smiled, but didn't give a hint as to how out of date we were. Sizing us up as a couple of lost americans, he recommended Chelsea. By accident we walked into the Markham Arms on Kings Road and we thought we were back in a Greenwich Village bar of the early Fifties. The accents might have been different, but the conversation was early Beatnik. When I mentioned Kerouac and Ginsberg, they knew more about them than I did. The angry young men were well on the way to the English marketplace, but it was the American Beats they were buying. We felt so at home we succumbed to all the traditional tourist attractions and enjoyed them. The highlight was the rental of a limo and driver to take us out to the country for a typical English dinner at a typical English Inn that made us feel like typical tourists, but we didn't care. We were impressed with every minute of our sojourn in England, even the weather. Our friends were right—it looked like the city of the sixties.

Our trip may have begun on a depressing note, but by the time we got back to St. Louis we were in high spirits. It was rare for both of us to be up at the same time, and being back with the children and the beloved Alfie gave our life a certain order, at least for a while. We spent time with the children, doing the rounds of birthday parties, car pools, and big family picnics.

In spite of our best efforts to corrupt them at an early age, they were all turning out to be normal American kids; there were nine little Landesmans, enough for a baseball team, but thank God none of them liked sports.

By the time a man reaches the age of forty, his children can usually answer the question, "What does your father do for a living?" None of the Landesman children could. Starting out with an identity problem in the forties, I had moved from antique dealer, publisher, editor, novelist, playwright, TV personality, entrepreneur, theatrical producer to urban renewal expert. When Cosmo's teacher asked that question, his answer was as good as any: "bigshot," he answered triumphantly.

Gaslight Square was growing at an unbelievable rate. It needed a lot of attention if it were not to be infiltrated by the quick-buck operators who were itching to get a piece of the action. I formed a loose organization to keep the professionals out. No strippers, no hustlers, no clip joints, and no sleazy premises were the only standards set. Local politicians were beginning to be impressed with the way we were handling the area; the police were pleased that there were no signs of trouble in a place that was surrounded by urban decay and racial tension. I petitioned the city to change the name of the area officially to Gaslight Square and talked the local gas company into restoring the original gas lights.

Jane Jacobs passed through St. Louis and later gave the Square an approving nod in her classic book on urban redevelopment, *Life and Death of the Cities;* urban planners began to come down to look us over, pick our brains, and ask us to help them build similar areas in their cities. And they were the professionals! Jimmy Massucci was hired to help a group of Chicago entrepreneurs create an 'Old Town' in an area similar to ours. I was invited by the city fathers of other municipalities to make surveys of possible sites for development. Had I been more professional I could have made a fortune in the advisory business, but I was too honest in my reports. They couldn't understand the easy-going, game-playing approach to rehabilitation.

Overseeing the Square, developing our other growing enterprises, and producing at the Crystal Palace left me little time to work in the galleries. I tried to replace Cutie, but it didn't work. She refused to be squeezed out and made life miserable for any "strangers" I brought in. She remained unimpressed with anything I did outside the galleries, treating all my extra activities as more examples of my congenital irresponsibility. Like any good Jewish mother, she cautioned me against the evil-eye that befell those who strayed from a mother's good advice.

She wasn't all wrong. The antique business wasn't the only thing I was neglecting; there was Fran who, after giving up Munso without finding a replacement, was feeling abandoned, especially by me. In a way I had; but abandonment was too strong a category. She was with me nightly, holding forth at the family table as before, participating in the warm, close relationships with the people who worked at the Palace, whether bartenders, waitresses, actors, or performers. At the end of the evening, unwinding with more drinks, there were sure to be some new alignments, always of a sexual kind.

Nobody was ready for the one I made with a five-foot-ten waitress called Pete. Some wit said "It was very smart of Jay to hire a waitress who could double as a bouncer!" but that was the least of her talents. She could carry a tray full of drinks through a crowded room with the grace of a Pavlova. Pete was a philosophical Hell's Angel without the bad breath, treating every customer with benign contempt. "Get lost, jerk," was her standard put down to anyone who doubted her authority.

Customers warmed to her brisk style, egging her on to more outrageous behaviour. She developed her own coterie of fans who came especially to the Palace to be insulted.

To those who really appreciated her foul language, she was never at a loss for words. "This fucker comes up to me and sez, 'dis drink is awful', and I sez, 'drink it, you fucker, it'll do you good.'" After she finished work, she'd sit around with all of us, glowing with life and excitement. "Honestly, you guys," she would say with a fetching smile, "it was a great night; my cunt was so moist all evening the busboy had to follow me around with a mop." It may not have been the style of Janet Rhinelander Stewart, but it fired my imagination! Her presence was a nightly event; you never knew what she was going to come up with next. If she had been a budding actress, I would have made her a star.

For a girl from a poor Polish background, whose only reading matter was a hairdresser's magazine, she had a remarkable insight into human nature. She knew the secret of handling an affair with me and winning over an unsympathetic Fran, who, never having accepted my theory of embarrassment as a source of pleasure, couldn't understand my attraction to Pete. To her, Pete was just another dumb broad, a walking embarrassment with a foul mouth act of limited appeal.

Our affair was taken for granted by everyone but Fran, but that changed when a plot by a jealous member of the family table misfired. "Look Fran," he told her one day, "in the last five years Jay has been having it off with everything that moves. My friend Richard is really interested in you. Why don't you give him a break?" The news that she had a secret admirer was a pleasant surprise, but the revelation of my unfaithfulness was a bigger one. She was so happy to find that I wasn't the moralistic, monogamous family man she had imagined me to be the last ten years of our life together, that she confessed to her long standing affair with Munso. "I guess we're both rotten to the core, but at least I don't have to carry around all that guilt of feeling that I was the bad, bad, bad girl and you were Mr Goody Two Shoes."

Surprised as she was by the extent of my adultery, there was no punishment to fit the crime. Since we were both sexual criminals, it was unlikely we would do anything to turn each other in. One good thing came out of it: I could no longer pretend that I had the exclusive right to the double standard clause in our marriage contract. Another thing: I couldn't expect Fran to take off my shoes and have a tall drink ready for me after an adulterous day at the office.

With our new found honesty, we both found Pete a positive asset, especially when Fran discovered she could cut hair. Her presence around the house was never intrusive—she made herself useful in doing those little things that Fran found to be a chore. Pete's greatest quality, refusing to take any role too seriously, lifted Fran out of the doldrums. To Pete, there wasn't any cause for Fran to be depressed; she wasn't losing a husband; she was acquiring a chauffer, a social secretary, a hand maiden, baby sitter, and sympathetic pair of ears.

With Pete and me it was all physical. Experienced in matters of sex far beyond her twenty years, there were times when I thought of myself as an innocent. While she spent a lot of time cheering up Fran during the day, her nights were devoted to exercizing her imagination in bed with me. It had all the promise of a future ménage a trois, something we used to giggle about when the lights were out.

My career as an adulterer was much more successful than that as a theatrical producer. The theatre season was critically acclaimed but financially disastrous. I was fighting against the tide by bringing original plays to an audience more interested in playing than plays. But I couldn't resist experimenting; that was what we originally created the new Crystal Palace for. Doing Mailer's *Deer Park*, Shaw's *Don Juan in Hell*, Ionesco's *The Chairs*, Beckett's *Krapp's Last Tape* and Brossard's quirky one-acters was simply more challenging, and a lot more fun.

The crowds coming to Gaslight Square had changed considerably. They didn't want to be educated; they wanted to be entertained. Producing the cabaret season was a lot less difficult and a lot more financially rewarding.

My highly satirical revues were always well received, especially when they were topical. *Love, Money, and Fame,* a theme everyone was interested in proved to be almost as successful as *The Nervous Set. Hostilities of 1961* captured the changing mood of the times. *New Directions* pointed the way to the future.

No one represented that change more than Lenny Bruce. There were those who said the Palace would die with his act, and there were those who saw it as a courageous piece of booking. But I had seen him in a basement club in Chicago on his way up and knew he was a genius. It was a shock to my nervous system to pay three thousand dollars to Lenny Bruce in the days before he was really famous, but I took a chance.

When he arrived at the St. Louis airport, I spotted his mohair suit and fifty dollar shoes at twenty yards. What I didn't recognize was the fellow with him, also in a mohair suit. In those days, you heard of the mafia controlling the entertainers, and for a moment I thought Bruce was being 'protected'. He was introduced as "my friend." It turned out that his friend was really his minder. Bruce had just "kicked" he told us, and he brought Frankie to help him stay that way.

Bruce played a lot of clubs on his way to the top, but he wasn't prepared for the Crystal Palace. It was part of my job—and the one I liked the best—to introduce the guest artists. It gave me the opportunity to try my hand at performing. Unfortunately, some complained the introductions were getting longer and longer, and there were some, usually the waitresses, who said they lasted as long as the act. But that's a lie. I stayed only as long as the laughs came. My introduction of Bruce required delicate timing. On opening night I kept it mercifully short, but managed to earn a few chuckles. Bruce acknowledged the introduction and applause, picked up the mike and walked over to the far edge of the stage to get a better view of the wall of stained glass, looked around at the chandeliers, and shook his head in amazement.

"This looks like a church that's gone bad. First they started with bingo, then they thought, 'what the hell let's sell a few drinks,' next month they bring in the strippers. I've never worked in a church, but I'll try not to let it inhibit me." He didn't let his audience down. The dirtier he got, the better they responded. By the last week of his engagement, I was doing introductions that lasted a good five minutes, garnering some solid laughs. When I tried to stretch it to ten, Bruce plucked the mike from my hand and cocked his head in my direction:

"Died, didn't you? You got a few laughs in the beginning, 'Say, I like this comedy bit, why should I pay that schmuck three thousand dollars a week?'"—imitating the voice of a typical Jewish club-owner-gangster—"And then, bang, you know you're dying and can't get off. Your material?—right down the toilet, eh, Jay?"

He was right, of course; how did I have the nerve to try to be funny with Numero Uno on the premises? I tried to get off before I died, but there was something so satisfying about holding a microphone in your hand and having the freedom to say anything you wanted to—I could have done some Jimmy Stewart impressions—and nobody was going to give the boss the hook.

The fact that I didn't fit his conception of a night club owner worried Bruce. I made him nervous. "Jay's over-bred, baby," he told Fran one night. "Let's you and me go on the road. We'll send him a little money now and then."

Bruce was one of the few people who ever played the Palace that put up a barrier between the artist and the owner. "The motivation for work is bread," he told me. "That's all that matters." If he'd really meant that, he'd have wound up a rich man.

Bruce's engagement at the Crystal Palace was a howling success, but more important, he was the inspiration for my debut as a performer. In one of our revues I played the role of cynical commentator reviewing a fashion show.

"That dress the tall one is wearing is made entirely of lint saved from somebody's navel," was one of my more subtle lines. At the end of the evening, the audience cheered madly. Nobody was more surprised than I. The greatest accolade came from the drama critic of the *St. Louis Post-Dispatch:*

> It was apparent that the loud laughter Landesman received went to his head. I'm afraid that last night an incurable ham was born and in gaining a comedian, we have lost a producer.

When the Palace bought out the last remaining old time neighborhood bar next door, we put in a little stage to do late night cabaret with no-name talent. It was an attempt to recreate the relaxed atmosphere of the old Crystal Palace and catch the overflow from the crowds waiting for the big room act to begin.

Phyllis Diller was playing in the big room to overflow audiences twice nightly. Every man, woman, and child who saw her show came away with that satisfied feeling of superiority. I don't know if she inspired her fans to leave the dishes in the sink and become a comedian, but she certainly gave me something to think about.

One night during her engagement, when nothing was going on in the annex, I got up on the stage and started talking. Introducing myself as "The Mystery comic," for the next half hour I explained to the audience my theories of humor.

"Anybody could get up here with a few well worn jokes and make some of you laugh. That's not my intention tonight. I'm here to take the laughs out of comedy. I'm here to make you cry. You may think I'm not funny now, but on your way home or if you're sneaking off to some motel, you're going to laugh hysterically. You're in on an historic occasion—the birth of subliminal humor."

My material consisted of stories of the heroic failures of my childhood, some rank Cutie material, and a description of the plight of post-industrial man in an increasingly consumer world. I exited to complete silence.

"What was it all about?" customers asked the waitresses.

"We don't know. He owns the joint."

I became quite confident performing in front of a live audience to absolutely no feedback. If I had any gift at all as a comedian, it was for easing people into acknowledging the fact that things were as bad as they secretly knew they were and providing a way for them to enjoy it. I gave them a better understanding of the importance of accepting humiliation as a part of everyday life. It obviously was not succeeding, not even among fellow comedians.

One night I asked Phyllis Diller to catch my act after her show. She sat through my confessions in stony silence. After it was over, I rushed over to her table and asked her how she liked it.

"Listen, honey," she made one of the faces she used when talking about her husband, whom she called "Fang"; "your act needs work. I don't think the American people are ready for you yet."

I continued to do the mystery comic bit until the waitresses went to Fred with a petition.

"Get him off that stage or we quit. He's emptying the room and we're not getting any tips."

Yet, there always seemed to be some nut in the audience that appreciated me. One of them came back night after night.

"You must really like my act," I said to him, "I appreciate your support."

He seemed pleased.

"What is it you like about me?"

He looked a little embarrassed. "I don't believe what I'm hearing. I'm just curious to see how much rejection you can take before you crack up."

It was only because I was getting so much acceptance that I could afford the rejection. Even Cutie admitted it. She said the sisters in the Sisterhood of her local Hadassah club would often come up to her and say how proud she must be that her son had done so much for St. Louis. My name appeared regularly in the gossip columns and my picture was frequently on the cover of the local what's-going-on-in-St. Louis magazines. The mayor, civic leaders, and the social, artistic, and professional leaders of the community were impressed with the way Gaslight Square was becoming such a big tourist attraction and, as I requested, they changed the name to Gaslight Square and installed the old gas lights. Even the police were partners in our drive to keep the area clean. I couldn't even get a ticket for speeding.

"Hey, Jay Landesman," the cop said after stopping me zipping through the park at an outrageous speed. "I really should give you a ticket, but you've done such a nice job over on the Square, I can't. My wife and I really enjoyed Phyllis Diller."

I made sure he got tickets to her next show.

The Landesmans were becoming so respectable we began to feel guilty. Our children were going to private school; we were asked to parties given by the swells. When I told Cutie that we were going to dinner with one of the families that founded St. Louis, she didn't believe it.

"Don't kid yourself," she said disdainfully. "They just want something appraised for nothing."

The respect and recognition I got in the night club world led to my election as vice-president of an organization of nightclubs, formed to raise the standards of entertainment nationally. On visits to other clubs in New York, either to look for talent or impress them with my own, I acted as if they were, indeed, my own club. I moved around them like a humming bird, lingering at a table of agents or performers long enough to let them know who I was. Working a room, as it was called, was a fine art. One night at the Blue Angel, I began doing my maitre d' bit, seating the customers with the customary "how many in your party?" to the amazement of the owner and my entourage of assorted sycophants.

These were valuable trips, a constant source of new talent and agents who were handling it. Irwin Arthur was the only agent I took seriously. Called the "Prince of

Darkness" because of his sometimes shady dealing, he was always trying to get his favorite acts work. Unfortunately, they were never the name acts that put bums on seats.

"You've got to see this one, Jay, she's the funniest thing since Martha Raye. Have I ever lied to you? Believe me when I tell you this broad is the next big star." I asked where I could see her act. It turned out she'd never worked a nightclub, but she had appeared on the Jack Paar TV Show and, according to Arthur, "broke it up."

"She's just your style, crazy, and cheap, and I'll give you options when she's a star. Get her now while she's available. Her name is Barbra Streisand."

"What an awful name. She'll never make it with a name like that."

Arthur smiled. "The name is nothing. You should see the nose! Ah, but when she sings, you forget the face. She sings the kind of stuff you like, obscure numbers nobody ever heard of. She'll even do your wife's songs. The kid can do anything."

I was interested, but couldn't afford to show too much— his price would leap at any sign of acceptance.

"My name is a household word compared to hers," I said. That comment brought his price down to a reasonable one hundred and twenty five a week with two options. The eighteen-year-old singer with a nose and name problem hadn't worked since her appearance on the Paar Show, which wasn't a good sign.

"Trust me," he pleaded. "The kid's going to make it. How could you go wrong? Paar wants her back."

We made the deal. I had a plan for using her on the same bill with the Smothers Brothers, a much bigger name since they, too, had been on a recent Paar Show. The Prince of Darkness came up with a comic, Marc London, who had also just done a Paar Show. Their TV exposure was the only thing they had in common; building on this theme, I created a little revue type format that I called, *Caught in the Act.*

249

It was the Smothers Brothers who were the stars of the show. Inspired by them, Streisand began to do their sort of patter, but with a Fanny Brice accent that left something to be desired. Her raps between numbers went on as long as my introductions. I thought her heavy Jewish material detracted from the mood and delivery of the subtle songs that followed. Trying to be a comedienne as well as a chanteuse was a very ambitious act for one so young and inexperienced.

After a few nights of this, I called her into the office for a little fatherly advice.

"Why don't you do the show like on opening night? You can't improve on that performance. Everybody loved you. All your terrible jokes are ruining the effectiveness of your songs. My advice is to cut them out."

"I get bored doing the same thing every night."

"You've been in show business two weeks and you're bored already?"

I found myself imitating her Brooklyn accent. I was beginning to like her.

"You think I'm funny when I talk in your living room," she replied. "I talk the same way on stage." She started to get that petulant, deprived-kid-from-Brooklyn look.

"That's the trouble," I told her. "The stage is no place to be natural on. It's a glamorous moment that shouldn't be tampered with."

She moaned at my explanation. "I want to do Shakespeare. I'm really an actress."

Infuriated at her presumptiousness, I gave her a little innocent push that she made into a drama, falling over a couple of chairs and landing on the floor spreadeagled. She really was an actress!

While I tried to be some kind of father figure to her, Fran was more like a sister. Both being from New York, both being Jewish, and both being children at heart, they giggled their way through shopping tours, trying on everything and buying nothing.

Cutie, an acid critic of all my productions, wrote on the

back of the program of *Caught in the Act:* "This got a wonderful reception. The house just vibrated with laughter and applause. I didn't like it. The young girl talked too much."

It was one of those rare occasions that I had to agree with her.

17

The exodus to the suburbs was underway with all the signs that urban blight was taking its toll. The school next door to the galleries had been desegregated to the point where it was all black, except for a few white children, including ours. Miles, while still in kindergarten, had developed a colored accent that we all thought was cute. We had taken Cosmo out of private school because he complained about his "snobbish classmates who talked funny." He was socially precocious. We used to take him with us to Jack O'Neil's cocktail hour at the Gaslight Bar where he would sit at the bar and engage in conversation with everyone he knew, and a few he didn't. O'Neil would take elaborate pains to mix him a 'Kiddie cocktail', serving it to him with all the style he reserved for a favorite customer, but in an aside to us, he let go his feelings: "The little fucker is bad for business." Everybody made a big fuss over him, particularly Pete, who would pretend he was her boyfriend.

Fred and Paula's surprise defection to the suburbs was a blow to both of us, but particularly to Fran. Paula was no longer available for delightful morning walks with the children through the leafy neighborhood. Even those impromptu, after the bar closed parties at our houses stopped. The loss of that family unity escalated Fran's depression. There was also the feeling that her career as a song writer had come to an end. There was no one to collaborate with on any projects. Pete was the only source of relief. She would come over to the house and pull Fran off the bed and take her out of the house on any excuse. But it was only shallow therapy.

By now, I considered myself an expert in choosing the right psychiatrist. I had put so many of our friends into therapy that I got to know who was permissive and who was effective. There was our personal family psychiatrist, who played with us at the Palace and was always invited to our parties. He was familiar with all the details of our sordid life. Though he thought I had played a minor role in the break up of his own marriage, he didn't hold it against me. When he welcomed Fran back on the couch, she warned him to put in a large supply of Kleenex.

My affair with Pete was at its height, yet it didn't occur to me that it interfered with anything that Fran and I had together. Nothing could shake us as a couple. Not even Pete. She was my back up team, helping me to look a smart thirty and feel like a reckless teenager. Emotionally, we were both about twelve years old.

She was my barometer of public taste. She could tell before opening night if the attraction we had would be popular. "It stinks" was one of her more subtle phrases. The minute I attempted to do some arty production, her "Don't do it, you fucker, you'll die with that act" saved me from many a fiasco. She was totally in touch with what the common man wanted, but I fought against giving it to him. I wanted to give them another play of my own.

I started on it, but put it aside when Martin Quigley came to me and Fran with a proposition: help him write a full-scale musical for the St. Louis Municipal Opera. To us, the Muny Opera was the graveyard for Rudolph Frimmel and the *Desert Song* type of operetta. For Quigley to ask the couple who wrote the musical of the Beat Generation to write an operetta seemed eccentric. Since Quigley was the most successful eccentric in town, we listened.

There were many people who listened to Quigley in St. Louis and paid handsomely for the privilege. He was the ace public relations man for the St. Louis Police Department and Anheuser-Busch, but we knew him as one of the guys that sat on the curb with us at 2:30 in the afternoon, talking baseball scores and Gaslight Square problems. We listened to him at the cocktail hour at O'Neil's doing his Will Rogers' observations on life in a Brooks Brothers shirt. Author of several successful novels, he still liked to take chances. Writing a cavalcade of early St. Louis was an idea that he had been toying with for years.

We suspected he had a twist to the idea and weren't disappointed when he told us: "Kids, this is going to be a great spoof of the concept that progress makes life better." Quig was a former newspaper reporter on the old *Kansas City Star,* a place where you learn to be cynical early in life.

The Muny Opera was the pride and joy of St. Louis, an outdoor theatre seating 15,000. How he thought we were going to get away with a cynical musical about the suffragettes and the early automobile industry never crossed his mind. "They'll love it, kids. When the old-maid suffragettes sing 'There's Nothing Fair About It', the sexy young women in the chorus counter with a song 'Who Needs The Vote?'; while the hero sings, 'I've Got My Eyes On Tomorrow,' the old St. Louis establishment sing, 'Progress Will Ruin Us Yet.' I tell you, this is going to be a lot of fun. We'll get a half-dozen vintage cars on the stage—*Molly Darling* will be a show like they've never seen before."

His enthusiasm was infectious. He insisted we use Tommy Wolf, the super-cool composer, to write turn of the century music, a piece of optimism we didn't challenge. It was quite a project to be doing on speculation, but we knew that Quig didn't undertake anything without the odds being stacked in his favor. Our tastes, to put it mildly, were on the decadent side; could we clean up our act enough to write a family musical for the masses?

What should have been a happy collaboration misfired. While Fran was writing the light-hearted lyrics the show required, her heart was heavy. The lyrics were flowing, but so were the tears. She tried to communicate her loneliness by withdrawing from Palace activities, even though it was the place she got the most attention. When I suggested she go to visit Tommy and Mary Wolf in California to finish the show and get a little sun, she reluctantly agreed.

She called several times from California, wanting to come home. My insisting she stay until she finished only contributed to the feeling that she wasn't wanted back in St. Louis. She began to imagine she was losing me. Nothing could have been further from the truth. Although my affair with Pete retained its passion, there was never a moment that I ever thought of separating. Pete was fun, but marriage was still a serious business.

A letter from Flicker, who had taken the Compass Players to London, was waiting for her when she came back. It was a conciliatory letter, admitting he had made some mistakes with *The Nervous Set*

> Sitting here on this little hillock of success I find that I am able to pick and choose which of the projects I will be doing, and it seems that I have interested a producer in a London version of *The Nervous Set*. If you are a very good girl, I will fix it up for you to come over, sans husband and children, to live it up for a while so that you can pick up the local flavor. I owe you a silver plane now and you are the only one out there in St Louis I would send for. Stick with me, baby, and I'll give you the stars. Love, Ted.

That cheered her up for a few minutes, but Flicker's plane never arrived. Fran was in pain. She couldn't understand why, if everybody told her how great she was, nothing was happening. Where was the call from Broadway or Hollywood? Meantime, she was doing a show for the Muny Opera in St. Louis! Even if the show was a smash, where was that going to get her? It only made her feel more like a victim of what St Louis playwright, William Inge, used to call "The St. Louis Syndrome: If people in the arts succeed in St. Louis, they have to become suspicious of the value of their success. If they were really good, why weren't they in New York?"

That was a point of view that I had fought against ever since I left Manhattan. I was in St. Louis to avoid "The New York Syndrome." My trying to tell her this only seemed to make her sadder. How do you get across to a talented girl that a call from Darryl Zanuck isn't the answer? Even a write up in *Esquire* by the esteemed music critic George Frazier didn't help:

> Talking about style, Comden and Green are delicatessen, for Christ's sake, and, as for Leonard Bernstein, you can have him tax free and gift wrapped. But if it's style you're looking for, then listen to the wonders that Fran Landesman and Tommy Wolf have wrought.

When the publicity began for *Molly Darling,* our photographs appeared in the local papers looking like bereaved victims of some tragic event instead of the proud parents of a future one. Watching the rehearsals, we were appalled at how they had cut any subtlety or irony that our script called for in order to develop the large production numbers audiences expected of a Muny Opera extravaganza. Instead of the lavish scenery one expected of such a period piece, we were treated to black and white flats in the style of the New Yorker cartoonist, Saul Steinberg. Nothing worked except the authenticity of the vintage cars as they paraded across the stage.

The one satisfying thing that came out of the show was the fact that the children loved it. I thought for a moment that I had at last given Cutie something to be proud of. Just to make sure, I called her attention to the lead editorial in the *St. Louis Post-Dispatch* that pointed out what a civic asset I was. It was not to be.

"It's a flop," she said, without any explanation.

As usual, she was right.

I went back to producing the kind of shows that I knew something about—satirical revues that anatomized the taboos that still existed in marriage, the family, careers, sex, politics, and success. One of the most successful was *Stars of Tomorrow,* with the nervous, analytical Woody Allen; a shy, short, red headed man with a pale green complexion almost obscured by his large, horn rimmed glasses. He was here to break in his act as a stand up comic, but he had his doubts.

Before the show, he'd pace up and down in the dressing room muttering, "I hope they're going to be nice. I do hope they're not going to throw things." I surrounded Woody with the talented harpist and ancient musical instrument historian, Tom O'Horgan, the jazz singer, Irene Kral, and a six piece Afro-Cuban band. There was so much talent on that stage, the audience wouldn't notice if Woody was any good.

He was the most nervous performer I had ever seen, but also the funniest. I didn't understand why he was torturing himself working as a comic for two hundred and fifty dollars a week when he made thousands a week as a writer of comic material for others. The audience didn't throw things but they found his delivery understated. His material concentrated on his being the world's biggest loser in personal relationships. To those of us who understood his plight, he could do no wrong, even if he stammered a little. "I can't seem to find myself. Does it look like I'm coming over as your average neurotic boy next door? It's all a mistake," he'd cry to me, "I wish I'd never left New York."

After each show, he would put in an emergency call to his New York psychoanalyst from the public phone on the wall between the men's and ladies' rooms. Anybody waiting to use the toilet (there was usually a queue) would be treated to the intimate confessions of a patient to his analyst. Sometimes it was even funnier than the material he had done on stage. The laughs from the toilet queues encouraged him somewhat, but he would have preferred to be back on the couch instead of on the phone. "For one thing, it's a lot cheaper than these long distance phone calls," he explained to me.

On a really bad night when he felt his performance had made the world forget about sunrise, he would call both his analyst and his girlfriend, begging either or both of them to come out to St. Louis to save him from committing suicide on stage. I encouraged him to develop the suicide line in his act.

"It would be better than Lenny's pissing on the audience and a lot more hygienic," I told him.

At the end of the first week he didn't want to accept his salary.

"No, Jay, I haven't earned it. I was lousy. Keep it. I'll try to do better next week but I think I'm hopeless as a comic. Give the check to the Afro-Cuban band; they were a lot better."

I insisted he take it if only to help defray his phone bill.

"I suppose you're right," he said, pocketing the check. "I'm ashamed of myself for not being able to hold out against the phone company."

Although we tried everything to make him happy—I shortened my introduction, saw to it that he had New York-type pastrami sandwiches in his dressing room after a show, and even offered him the use of our family analyst—he refused to enjoy himself. Before the week was out, he talked his girlfriend into coming out to watch his slow death. Her presence required twice as many phone calls to his therapist.

Woody should have been an inspiration for me to bring back "The Mystery Comic," but I wasn't the competitive type. Inspired by his reverence for the loser, I built a special room in the basement of the Palace to attract back the people who thought we had gone too commercial. I gave them poets, expresso, and Viennese pastry, and a setting out of a Berlin twenties cabaret—a background of two plaster heads eight feet tall with jewelled tears stream-ing down their cheeks—but all we attracted were other poets and their girlfriends without a dime to spend.

When that failed, we opened a summer outdoor garden of delights with stained glass hanging from the trees and hanging lanterns over a barbecue pit. We built a dance floor and put in a rock band to entice the younger people who were flocking to the area.

For the first time the entertainment places were actively going after the visitor's dollar and regretfully, the Crystal Palace was no exception. There were now over twenty clubs and bars offering everything and anything that would attract the crowds. A Roaring Twenties nightclub presented an old time floor show with chorus and all the employees dressed up as gangsters. There were nightly mock raids by 'FBI men' and those fingered would be sent to 'jail'—a booth with bars where they drank champagne on the house for being such good sports. Music began to blare from loud speakers up and down the Square. Scotch bagpipers from the Irish pub, O'Connels', were almost dignified by comparison.

The professionals were moving into the area at an alarming rate and we were unable to stem the tide. The old timers would meet to discuss the invasion, but could not come up with a solution. The new kind of people that the Square was attracting wanted the novelties the newcomers introduced. Who were we to dictate what they should see? They were giving honest entertainment, and they even joined us in our determination to keep the Square 'clean'.

I became a sort of Lone Ranger of the entertainment world, riding into any trouble spot to straighten out problems that success was bringing into our little community. One of my jobs was to protect the image of the Square. Together with the Mutrux Brothers, Jimmy Massucci and Sammy Deitsch, we offered our services to any of the new entrepreneurs who stayed within our prescribed guidelines. We wouldn't tolerate any hustling.

As a result of our vigilance, the Square was a bigger attraction than the Cardinals Baseball Team. My old friend, Chandler Brossard, who was now a senior editor at *Look Magazine,* came down to look around with a vague idea of doing a story on the Crystal Palace. With the development of Gaslight Square, he decided to do a story about the new cultural scene I was attempting to establish as a continuation of my pioneering days with *Neurotica* in the late Forties. He tried to sell me as an "originator and perpetrator of a lot of ideas that permanently changed and charged the American cultural scene", but cooler heads prevailed at *Look Magazine*. He was unable to sell the story. It was left to *Time* magazine to do it. They saw Gaslight Square as an American success story. Under the caption NO SQUARES ON THE SQUARE, their team of reporters summed up what had happened:

> In the gazeteer of US nightlife, St. Louis has never been placed high. With the exception of a night at the Symphony or Municipal Opera, most of St Louis spent its evening the way much of the rest of the U.S. did: watching television or drinking beer in somebody else's living room. But now all that is changed. St Louis finally has a place to go at night and the place is Gaslight Square . . .

> A three-block oasis of nostalgic frivolity where some fifty gaudily atmospheric taverns, cabarets, restaurants and antique shops are packed together in fine, fin de siecle jumble, it combines a sort of Disneyland quaintness with the gaiety of Copenhagen's Tivoli Gardens and the innocent naughtiness of Gay Nineties beerhalls . . .

> Last year, this casbah of culture and whoopdedoo earned more than $3,000,000 for its investors and property values tripled over the last four years . . . Jay Landesman has been voted unofficial mayor of the quarter. Says Landesman grandly: "It means nothing. I'd rather be king." . . .

After that accolade, there was only one place to go and that was *down*. Yet there was no obvious signs of the Square's approaching demise. There was so much interest generated by the *Time* article we became the number one attraction in town. I became unofficial spokesman for the Square, accepting invitations to speak at the local Chamber of Commerce, Kiwanis, and Rotarians. I even spoke before various Parent Teachers organizations. "Build more parking lots" always got a round of applause.

All doors were opened; all social barriers downed. Fran and I were invited to dinner parties at the St. Louis Country Club where few Jews, if any, had even been before. Ann and Louis Werner, St. Louis's jet-setting couple, gave us a taste of high life in a French Chateau on the Missouri river where everyone dressed formally for dinner and the gentlemen had brandy and cigars while the women retired to separate rooms afterwards.

Fran could never understand why I accepted their invitations. She found such evenings incredibly tedious. How could I explain to her that after years of serving time in the Galleries and the Palace, reading about them in the society columns, and hanging their chandeliers, I was now enjoying their hospitality.

The first signs of trouble came with business falling off in the Annex. There were those who said I was a genius, but there were those who thought I was lowering the standards of the Square when I turned the annex into the first 'Twist Room' in the West. Even more sensational was the fact that I had become the Grand Master Twister, demonstrating the new dance craze with Pete, who wore a black fringed dress that swayed counter clockwise to her shakin' hips, urging the spectators watching us through the window to step inside and have some fun.

We drew crowds of 'mad twisters' to the exhibition area that overflowed into the aisles. Passers by looking in from the street formed a traffic obstruction. I was a good twister, but Pete was an inspired one. Together we 'Ponied' and 'Mashed Potatoed' our way through the night to a never ending stream of compliments.

Pete no longer did waitressing. She was exhibit number one now, drawing crowds every night with her frenzied antics on the tiny stage. At last, she congratulated me on my new attempt to please the fuckers instead of trying to educate them.

The policy of lightening the fare at the Palace was extended to the theatre. As the columnist Bob Goddard wrote of the first show of the year, in *Variety:*

261

Jay Landesman, producer of the revues at the Crystal Palace cabaret theatre in humming Gaslight Square is at it again. This time it's an old time mellerdramer, *Letta Ripp,* complete with villains to be hissed, sweet young country girls, slinky sirens and holier-than-thou heroes. Altogether it spells hilarity.

Although packed houses were the rule, reviewers' use of phrases like "king size laughs a mile long" and "the laughs come thick and fast" made me cringe. The author of the show, a Madison Avenue ad man, actually timed the laughs, working like a human computer. He figured there was a laugh every four and a half seconds, establishing some kind of world record for an original musical. But I never laughed once, even on the way to the bank with the night's receipts.

Running Dry/Running Off

It was obvious even to me that the Crystal Palace could no longer afford to experiment with serious theatre. If laughs were what they wanted, I would give them a season of controlled hysteria. The idea was sparked off by a phone call from Lenny Bruce asking for a date. It was a different Lenny from the cool, calculating, $3500-dollar-a-week, dope-free, mohair-suited cat who had played the Palace earlier. After his bust at the Gate of Horn in Chicago, where they arrested the club owner, there were very few offers for Bruce's controversial act.

He was willing to work for half his price. Rumors that he was pissing on the audience as part of his act didn't bother me. I was beginning to feel like pissing on them myself, without getting eighteen hundred a week for the privilege. My unconscious resentment at the way I'd been deserted left me feeling exactly like Lenny. He told me it meant a lot to him to get the date at the Palace; it meant a lot to me to have him back. Together, we might do something about straightening out the squares.

Picking him up at the airport this time, I nearly missed him. Instead of the mohair suit, he was dressed in a long, black, collarless jacket, looking like a young Nehru. On the drive back to my house, I got the Lenny Bruce version of constitutional law and briefings from the Supreme Court's last three decisions on the obscenity laws. Obviously, I was dealing with a lawyer who used to be a comic. My experiences in trying to fight the obscenity law with Legman were nothing compared to what Bruce was engaged in. His fight was a struggle to the death. With right on his side, he was sure to lose. Bruce seemed to have taken on some of the characteristics of Legman. He felt secure in victory because he had incontrovertible proof that he was right. I didn't have the heart to tell him he was on a losing roll.

His obsession with justice went hand-in-hand with a self-destructive return to drugs. The first thing he did when we arrived was to pull up his sleeve and show Fran and I how to get the maximum high by jacking off the blood in the needle while it was in his arm. He was using Delauden instead of heroin, but the effect was the same. Once the ritual was over, he relaxed enough to join us on the bed for Sunday night TV and take-away Kentucky Fried Chicken, with the kids running in and out of the room. We were like any other ordinary American family enjoying the Ed Sullivan Show. Instead of a six-pack, we shared a couple of joints.

It was a new Lenny Bruce we were dealing with. On stage, his act was a strange mixture of constitutional law and some very dirty talk. He was still attracting large crowds, but of a different kind. Along with the die-hard Bruce fans, there were many in the audience who only knew of his reputation and wanted to see what all the fuss was about. They were straight sensation seekers. Lenny didn't disappoint them: he still threatened to piss on the audience.

"Piss on them, Lenny," I encouraged him.

"There's always some loony in the audience egging me on," he said sadly, but he changed the subject.

I was at the box office one night when I noticed the prosecuting attorney of St. Louis buying tickets to the show. He was accompanied by his two teenage daughters. I had a vision of them squirming in their seats while Lenny did his come-a-thon. After that, all of us would be on the way to jail, the Palace stripped of its liquor license and Gaslight Square down the toilet.

I greeted the attorney warmly, congratulated him on his

adventurous spirit in wanting to see Mr. Bruce, but advised him against bringing his daughters.

"You know, Lenny does a great show, nothing too far out, but why don't you and your daughters be my guest next week for the Smothers Brothers. I think they'll like that a lot more."

Luckily he agreed.

Lenny had written a pamphlet, *How To Talk Dirty*, and he sent a thousand copies of it in advance to the Palace. The cover showed a naked Lenny seated on the crapper. He wanted me to sell them in the lobby before and after the show. We had them displayed prominently, but there were few sales. He became paranoid about my not pushing them.

"It's an important book, Jay," he warned me. "You're not plugging it properly."

The next night I took an armful and hawked them up and down the aisle like the old-time candy salesman in a burlesque house: "Get your *How To Talk Dirty* sampler here while they last. Guaranteed to give you the thrill of your life. Money back if not satisfied. Ladies and Gentlemen, see Lenny Bruce in his naked grandeur. No American should be without this handy guide." When it became obvious to Lenny that I was setting him up, he told me to cool it. He got the point.

Bruce packed a lot of action into his two weeks. There was always a line of groupies who wanted to give him something to remember them by. Meanwhile, he and Fran had progressed from playing footsies under the family table to meeting down in the dressing room for something more intimate. One night, the fun turned sour when he gave her a shot of Dilauden right through her knitted skirt, straight into her ass.

Pete came up to tell me Fran was sick and wanted to go home. I had no idea what had happened until she told me what Bruce had done. She threw up in the car all the way home. Pete laughed, but I did a slow burn thinking about what a dumb thing for Fran to let happen. I had a vision of her becoming a junkie. At least, I could salvage a little prestige out of her misfortune by telling people it was Lenny Bruce who "did it to my poor, junkie wife."

About the only thing Lenny and I had in common was dancing. He would join Pete and me in the Twist room after his show, and the three of us would give exhibitions of the proper way to do the 'Madison' and other variations of the twist. Bruce was a natural dancer and we would both throw ourselves into the performance. People were used to seeing me dance, but the dancing Lenny Bruce was a sensation. It seemed to be the only thing that gave him any kicks during his engagement, yet the dark circles under his eyes looked like bruises by the time he left us. His act had not gone over very well. His lectures on jurisprudence failed to captivate the audience and they left feeling cheated out of the real Lenny Bruce. There was no need for Fran to open up a sore point by asking him if he still felt that "bread was the motivation for work." But Bruce didn't mind. He understood Fran's 'I wanna be bad' role and played upon it every chance he had. He liked her distant look and once, from the stage, he said: "Ah, the boss's wife is in the house tonight. I recognise that heavily sedated laugh."

One night, it was all set up for Fran to go off with Bruce for an after-hours session. I had suspected something was up and my way of handling it was to get drunk. I arranged for Pete to take me home. Fran changed her mind at the last minute without any prompting from me. Her instinct for self-preservation must have gotten the better of her. Or perhaps she knew that she'd lose him as a friend if she made it with him. He always told so many jokes about the wives who were always trying to get him into bed. For all his crusading, Bruce was, underneath it all, an old fashioned Jewish puritan. When Fran occasionally let go of a "fuck" or two, he'd disapprove.

"Don't use that kind of language; you sound as if you've been hanging out with hoodlums."

This from the man who tried to teach the world to talk dirty!

It was a relief to follow Bruce with the cleanest act in showbusiness—the Smothers Brothers. At least, that was the image everyone in America wanted to believe. Their gentile sibling rivalry was a tonic after the nasty alienation of all those Jewish New York comics. In real life, it was the Jewish comics who were chasing the shiksas and hitting the booze. With the Smothers it was the opposite; they were the family men and more 'chicken soup' than the Jews. Their strong sense of family loyalty and rhythm fitted in perfectly with our little community. After a particularly long stretch on the road, living and working with faceless people, coming back to the Crystal Palace was like coming home. They felt a part of the Palace's success and took a great interest in the growth of Gaslight Square. They participated in all its functions, making friends with the other establishments' owners.

It was no wonder that the Smothers Brothers were considered the Square's patron saints. Whenever they did guest shots on national TV, they mentioned us when they could slip it in, saying what a great place Gaslight Square was. They had three albums in the charts the last time they played the Palace. They could have commanded three times the amount of money they were getting from us. Yet they came back to the Palace to change into something comfortable and mix.

I had the same feeling of 'going home' when I went to New York nightclubs. By now, I wasn't looking for talent as much as I was hoping to see old friends who had played the Palace. When we saw Lenny at the Blue Angel, he was in terrible shape. In his dressing room, we watched him warming himself with a hair dryer instead of shooting up. Finally, Bud McCreary popped his head in:

"Lenny, are you coming down or do you want me to send the audience up?"

Lenny told us he hated to do a show when he knew people like us were in the audience who knew all his material. "You won't think I'm funny anymore," he explained. Sitting in the audience that night, he didn't get many laughs. He rambled on about his problems with the law until someone shouted out:

"Hey, Lenny, why don't you do the prison bit?"

Those requests from the audience pulled him up tight; he hated doing the sketches that had made him famous. He tried to explain to the audience that he couldn't do that tonight because "Jay and Fran Landesman are sitting in the audience and they run a fabulous club and I've played it a couple of times and they know all the material." Then he did about ten minutes on the Crystal Palace and what a crazy place it was, and how crazy we were, and how he used to do twist exhibitions, and my long introductions . . . by the end of it, thanks to Lenny, I was a celebrity. Even if it wasn't true, I acted like one.

On that trip, while at the Bon Soir, we ran into Barbra Streisand. She wasn't working there, but hung around with other unemployed artists to remind agents they were 'available.' She pleaded with me to have her back at the Palace.

"If you don't," she warned me, "Tommy Smothers said he'll never play your place again."

I knew she'd had a little romance going with Tommy while they were in St. Louis, but I didn't think they were still tight; it had been a year since she played with them at the Palace. Nothing much had happened to her career since then, in spite of the efforts of The Prince of Darkness to make her a star. The option I had on her contract was running out for lack of exposure.

She was carrying a brown paper bag of ripe plums, offering them around a table already crowded with other singers and an army of empty cocktail glasses. Her generosity was amusing, but hardly bookable. She was being very serious offering the plums around and telling everybody how talented she was in spite of her temporary unemployment. Fran thought she was adorable, but I kept wishing she'd cool it.

"Look, kid," I said, annoyed at her attempt to take attention away from me. "Can't you see I'm busy talking to some important people?"—pointing to the agents in mock seriousness. She offered me one of her plums.

"You better take me back before I get too big to play your place," she said.

We laughed at this far-fetched suggestion.

"And I'm going to record *Spring Can Really Hang You Up The Most,* too, so you better be nice to me."

Fran was the only one who believed she'd ever get a chance to do anything again. Her "that's great, Barbra," only encouraged her to stick around. When it came time to move on to another place, she followed us like a stylish bag lady with no place to go.

I had a lot of people to see when in New York. I always saw Klonsky and Broyard for a drink at some Village bar. No matter how hard we tried, we could never recapture the excitement of those early Village days. After our brief meetings were over, we both thought: "Thank God we only do that once a year." When Kerouac was in town, we always managed to meet. Holmes would keep me in touch with his movements and his constant battle with his mother or with the booze. I gathered his visits to the City were never happy ones for him. On this occasion, he showed up for drinks along with Janet Rhinelander Stewart and some other old friends, looking and smelling like a survivor of a three-day binge. Anybody looking like they represented respectability was a natural target for his abuse. With drunken bravado and a humiliating need for attention, he began to attack Janet.

"My name is Jack Kerouac and what do you do for a living?"

"I'm independently wealthy and socially prominent. What do you do?"

For the first time, Kerouac was stuck for an answer. Later, when Janet heard we were driving up to Connecticut with him to see Johnny Holmes, she warned us to stay downwind of him if we wanted to enjoy the ride. When we decided not to make the journey, we heard he got so disoriented while in New York, he ended up taking a taxi to Holmes' place.

Our best times in New York were spent with Jim Harelson and our friends from the Crystal Palace. Smoking the weed, watching television, hanging out in P. J. Clarke's and the Cafe Renaissance, putting down anyone dumb enough to take themselves seriously, we managed to have a great time without any 'names' in attendance. Jim Harelson, Gerry Gadarian, Gene Miller, Ed Medard, and Brad Cunningham were all in their middle 30s, but were still playing at being young men. They were the inspiration for Fran's *The Ballad Of The Sad Young Men:*

> All the sad young men
> Sitting in the bars
> Knowing neon lights
> Missing all the stars
>
> All the sad young men
> Drifting through the town
> Drinking up the night
> Trying not to drown
>
> Autumn turns the leaves to gold
> Slowly dies the heart
> Sad young men are growing old
> That's the cruellest part
>
> While a grimy moon
> Watches from above
> All the sad young men
> Play at making love
>
> Misbegotten moon
> Shine for sad young men
> Let your gentle light
> Guide them home again
> All the sad young men.

Fran had a tender spot for all the sad young men. They were the lovers of her early years and she hung on to the illusion that romance, no matter how disappointing it could be, was better than the reality of settling for me. She had never forgiven me for taking her away from New York, but the fact that I was apparently enjoying the success bestowed upon me "by a bunch of small town sycophants" was a much more serious problem. It would surface whenever the discussion of success came up. When she got tired of arguing, she would hum a few stanzas of *I'm Bidin' My Time* to let me know that she'd have her success in spite of me.

Seeing her so unhappy, I began to feel guilty about Pete. It never occured to me that having these affairs would ever be detrimental to the marriage. I thought that Fran and I had an understanding, a kind of gentleman's agreement, that our affairs were taken for granted. Such risks went with the territory of marriage. To those of us in the business of entertaining, it was just another occupational hazard; some contracted 'bar burn-out,' others looked upon getting laid as a fringe benefit. I even talked myself into believing it was marriage building. After a hard day of making love and telling lies at the local motel, it was good to get back to the peace and serenity of a conventional homelife and make-believe contentment. In the drive to be a misfit, having affairs was a quality much prized, but not for women. So what if someone got hurt? We had a family psychiatrist on retainer that we could send a broken heart or a broken marriage to for mending.

Before this affair became a serious problem, in a rare moment of insight, I decided to break it off. I sent Pete to New York. If I couldn't enjoy her anymore, my friends there would have the pleasure of her company. This left a big space in my life that I filled with afternoons of self pity and heavy drinking.

Once, when I was too drunk to dial, I asked the operator to do it for me. When she told me in that nasty telephone manner that she couldn't, I flipped. (That was in the days before operators wished you a nice day).

"I'm sorry, operator," I said in a very controlled, hysterical voice, "I don't have any digits to dial with. I'm a veteran. At home I have a special instrument to use, but I'm calling from the funeral parlor where my mother is laid out. Won't you help me?"

She was still suspicious. "What is the number you're calling from?" She wasn't going to let me get away with it. "And your name?"

I told her most of the folks around here call me Lucky. "Sunny Lucky, with a 'y'," I added, "but you can call me Sunny."

The bartender and assorted customers were cracking up at my little joke. When the phone rang, the bartender answered "Rindskofts Funeral Home" in his best sepulchral voice.

"Is there a Mr. Lucky there?"

I got on the line again and listened to a very repentent Southwestern Bell telephone operator, who was now only too happy to complete the call for me.

Taking on other identities had been my alternative to the practical joke, a form of activity I always considered undignified. Wearing masks was my way of getting on top of the other person and testing his credentials. Nothing was sacred and everyone was fair game.

I never realized the extent I played this game on Fran from the beginning of our relationship. I had posed as a rebel with a cause during our courtship—the iconoclastic *Neurotica*, my commitment to living outside the establishment, my flamboyant lifestyle, the glamorous people I surrounded her with in New York was all part of the picture she fell in love with. After a decade of marriage I had strayed so far from the original portrait, I was practically a stranger to her. There was no longer any cause that she could identify me with; there was only a very successful business man, a big-shot, fawned over by people she thought intolerable. Where was the man she thought she had married? It was a dangerous situation, loaded with dynamite, near to exploding.

What was worse than my inability to communicate with

Fran, was my inability to be honest with myself. I still saw myself as a rebel who could beat the system on my own terms. Wasn't I still taking chances with my marriage? Wasn't I still creative? Was I not a success? I was still a 'dutiful' husband providing a luxurious life for my family. Never, at anytime during our marriage, did I have any desire to change partners. Fran was a permanent fixture in my operation. Unfortunately, I treated her like one. If it was defective, it wasn't my fault. Get it to a doctor for repair.

Even an appendage gets lonely. My withdrawal was unintentional, but the effect was damaging. When her depression became acute and all her psychiatry was giving her no relief, I asked her what those damn doctors were doing for her? She said, sadly: "Nothing. All I do is cry and blow my nose." Now I felt helpless as well as resentful. The money didn't matter. Her ungratefulness for what I had given her, did.

One evening, I didn't show up for dinner and didn't phone either. I was having too much fun. To call up and say I wasn't coming home would have spoiled the good feeling of being such a bad boy. Knowing full well where I was, a furious Fran appeared at the bar. Her demand that I leave with her at once only made matters worse. Feeling humiliated in front of my buddies, I grabbed her by the hair and dragged her out of the place, into the alley nearby, where I exploded into violence. Hitting her, I screamed: "You made me give up Pete, what else do you want from me?" She tried to tell me that Pete had nothing to do with the way she felt, but, blinded by rage, I ignored that. I continued to hit her until she collapsed. I took her battered body home and called her psychiatrist.

"You better get over here. I've just beaten up Fran."

He was over in a flash. He examined her briefly, but from the catatonic look in her eyes, he thought she was more than physically damaged. He arranged for her to be taken to the psychiatric ward of the Jewish hospital. Examination there disclosed two sore ribs, a swollen face, and a black eye. When I visited her the next day, I couldn't believe what I'd done. The psychiatrist told me that he was going to have her stay for some further examinations. After two nights of confinement in a ward with old, crazy people, she begged me to take her home. She had planned a party for that weekend and didn't want to miss it.

Upon returning, she seemed almost cheerful, examining her bruises in the mirror and experimenting with Erase to cover black and blue souvenirs. She appeared at the party, skillfully made up, her ribs taped, but there was no disguising the fact that she had been in an 'accident'. That night she got the sort of attention she had been longing for, even though the price was high. Although I was deeply ashamed of what I had done, at least it brought our deep hostility into the open. Now it was a time for reconciliation.

The psychiatrist came up with a complex formula that sounded promising. He was working with a psychoanalyst and woman psychologist on certain cases and finding that three heads were often better than one in dealing with some difficult patients. His suggestion was that the two of us see all three of them once a week and that Fran continue seeing him twice a week. I thought that this might be an interesting, if not a pioneering approach, to group therapy. I appreciated his sense of humor when he added: "You can fool one of us all of the time, some of us some of the time, but you can't fool all of us all of the time." After he told me what it was going to cost, I told him at those prices I wasn't in a position to fool anybody.

We were all a little nervous at the beginning of the sessions. I had some doubts about the psychoanalyst. He was an occasional visitor to the Palace, where his behaviour under the influence raised a few eyebrows. The woman psychologist was tipping the scales at a smart 200 pounds, which didn't suggest that she was too well balanced. Fran's doctor was the straightest of the bunch, but he had recently undergone a messy divorce. Put that trio together with two fuck ups like us and the chances of success looked pretty slight, but at that point we were willing to try anything.

As the sessions progressed, I became one of the therapists, alternating between judge, prosecutor, and jury. Fran was victim, defendant, and perennial juvenile delinquent. Since I wasn't under pressure at the beginning of these trials, I enjoyed the weekly meetings, always managing to make a strong case for myself by declaring my 'rights' from the start. I would have gotten away with it, too, if it hadn't been for old Fatso. All my attempts to make the life we were leading sound practical didn't fool her. She wanted to know why Fran was not consulted more often. Fran brightened up with this new ally and became her part-time prosecutor. At first, I resented her new role. I had always made the decisions in the family. My excuse was Fran's refusal to take any responsibility for her actions. When I described how I handled everything from the family finances to the family infidelities, the psychoanalyst thought that was very interesting and made repeated dents in my rationalizations. What exactly was Fran doing that made me so insecure, they wanted to know. "Me insecure?" I asked incredulously. They smiled. Before I knew what was happening, it was me who was on the ropes. Fatso joined in with relish. The psychiatrist was enjoying his role of referee.

Fran was a good in-fighter. She told them about her affair with Munso, explaining how guilty she felt about being so bad until she found out that I was equally bad and how relieved she was to know I wasn't the goody two shoes she always thought I was. She revealed even more intimate occasions: our three-way scenes with our various lovers; and before I had a chance to confess some smart indiscretions of my own, she told them of her slide into nymphomania:

"On one beautiful day, the snow falling softly in the morning, Jay and I made love. When the weather turned balmy, I dashed out of the house to spend the afternoon with the Yummy Kid. I was back in time to give Jay a beautiful dinner and then, while he was at the Palace, I had another lover for the evening. Three men in one day! I felt like I was sliding into total sexual depravity. The next day I had a giant hangover of guilt."

Even I was surprised to hear there was so much life in the old girl.

Fatso smiled at her true confessions. "What a lucky girl," she said. "There's no law against it."

That became Fatso's favorite phrase and Fran's passport to a guilt-free existence. Fran and I had both been having affairs. We both knew it, but we never really levelled with each other.

We looked forward to those weekly meetings with the doctors. They gave us a new kind of confidence in our attempts to live outside the rules of marriage. Not only did we feel we were sexual pioneers, we felt we were made for the job and now had the tools to do it successfully. Each time we left their offices, we felt closer together.

"Now, with all this honesty between us, I think we ought to renegotiate our contract."

I agreed. "What took you so long to ask?"

To celebrate our new-found freedom, we invited Fred and Paula to have lunch so we could tell them of our breakthrough.

"Say it isn't so." Paula nervously fanned herself with an imaginary fan. "You've torn the mask away before, Jay, but in the name of sanity, I beg you, don't carry this thing too far. Leave sleeping dogs like me and Fred lie!"

We considered them our best friends so we spared them nothing.

"It's the only way a marriage can work," we insisted.

Fred was sitting back, taking it all in with the calmness that was expected from him. We had all talked about sexual freedom many times during our soul-searching, living room games. All agreed that it was an ideal philosophy, but like Communism, it would never work.

"You two ought to try it."

Paula had stopped making any pretense of eating her

lunch, ordering instead another martini. "No, thanks," she cried. "Not in my lifetime. Keep affairs to yourself. It's the only way to survive. At least for old squares like us."

Fran's enthusiasm for the new credo was unstoppable. "We tried it the old-fashioned way, and we tried ignoring it. Neither worked." We must have sounded like two characters out of a soap opera: "Can a handsome young couple from a respectable bourgeois background find happiness in the arms of other lovers and still have anything left over for each other?" Paula thought we were crazy to mess around with our lives like that. I must admit it felt a little shaky in the beginning. I thought I had been in control of every detail of our lives since the day we got married, and it was a hard concept to give up.

Fran began to cultivate her own group of friends. Faces whom I disapproved of in the past were now a part of our social life. I had actually forbidden some of them to enter the house, but with our new set up, that was a thing of the past. I even began to enjoy their company, amused by the gossip and intrigues they had to share. I welcomed them at the family table and eventually some became part of the family. One was an ex-hooker who was having a bizarre relationship with our resident millionaire bar customer. A dedicated masochist, his pleasure came from giving her large sums of money upon demand without expecting anything in return except castigation. The worse she treated him, the more generous he became. She felt she was doing him a favor.

"It gives him so much pleasure, how can I deny him the opportunity of making me rich?"

When the millionaire's wife invited Alan Watts to come to St. Louis to conduct a seminar on *The Art of Zen Living in a Complex Society,* we were ready to welcome him with open minds. We paid a small fee to participate, but all formalities were dropped. The three days with Watts seemed more like a pajama party than a serious workshop. Watts had a great act. Charming, funny, permissive, he made Zen as easy to understand as a comic book plot. I suggested to him that if he ever wanted to take his act into the show business arena, I'd book him for a two week gig at the Palace. After a few rounds of double vodka on the rocks, we recognized each other as fellow conspirators. Twisting away on his last night in town, he moved around the dance floor like a happy Japanese monk.

"It's all show business," I told him when he awarded me his personal Zen seal of approval.

Fran confessed to him a certain exclusivity in her view of life.

"You said we shouldn't discriminate, but can you really avoid it?"

Watts looked down into his drink, hoping that the melted ice cubes would give him a clue. Finally his answer came.

"I have to admit it, Fran, that there are a lot of bores in this world."

In our search for futher enlightenment, we got involved with Timothy Leary and Richard Alpert when they arrived in St. Louis to give a lecture on their recent experiences with LSD. We took them up on their invitation to visit their headquarters in Millbrook, New York. When the time came to drop acid, Fran backed out. I took it with Leary as my guide. Nothing happened. I was very embarrassed.

"Nothing?" Leary was perplexed. He had given me the same acid that they had all been getting off on. He called in Alpert for consultation. They suggested a booster shot of DMT, but by then I was too suspicious of the whole trip.

"You must be one of those rare people who are too transcendental to be affected by LSD," he concluded.

There was another experiment going on in our own backyard that Fran and I knew nothing about. As we pursued our explorations into other methods of survival, Masters and Johnson were conducting their sexual experiments at Washington University. We may not have been as scientific, but we were getting some interesting results. Jealousy, for instance, seemed to disappear from our life.

Against all the odds, we decided we could have our cake and eat it too. After all, we were only doing openly what many in St Louis were doing secretly. With the three doctors behind us, we were the only ones that had a license to practice.

19

When word got around the Square that I had signed Gypsy Rose Lee for a two week engagement, a roar of disapproval went up among the proprietors. They lived in mortal fear that the strippers would some day invade the Square and it would be all over. That I should be the first to bring them in was, they said, an incredible act of betrayal. Gypsy Rose Lee's image as Queen of the Strippers was still very much alive, in spite of the fact that she had not shed anything more than a glove in twenty years. The hypocrisy of it all concerned our audiences; where once we required coats and ties for admission, in the race for the buck nobody cared what customers took off.

Once again I was needed to prop things up in the Twist Room, which was starting to fade. I tried a number of unique acts, including a young black Yoga disciple who meditated on a bed of nails while another stood on him, chanting. It was impressive, but not a crowd pleaser.

"Can you eat glass?" I asked them in desperation.

What the Palace needed were new friends as well as a new act. A patron's group to help foster new shows and spark local talent was organized. After much publicity and hard work, we found that only a handful of people responded. Then we began to offer the shows free to civic, cultural and educational groups just to cash in on the drinks. One of the programs we offered was *An Evening with Brecht and Weil.*

It was an attempt to recreate the atmosphere of the old

Berlin cabaret during the last days of the Weimar Republic; we felt it was an appropriate symbolic gesture commemorating our own dying days. Unfortunately, it was sponsored by the local B'nai Brith. Since the show was sung in the original German, the audience, predominantly Jewish, walked out *en masse*. They were shocked that we would present such a bill of fare while the memory of six million Jews murdered by the Germans was still fresh in their minds. They weren't the only ones who didn't like it. A young critic on the *Post-Dispatch*, eager to establish his reputation, chose the Crystal Palace as his target for abusive reviews. No matter what we did, his bitter attitude turned audiences against us. It was the first sign of the backlash of criticism that Gaslight Square was about to be subjected to.

When a visitor to the Square was mugged in an adjoining area, the newspapers gave it front page space: MUGGING IN GASLIGHT SQUARE. Not only was it inaccurate and unfair, it was signing our death warrant. People had always felt safe on their nights out on the Square. Now, for the first time, they were alerted to be 'on their guard.' After the mugging, there was concern with the rapidly decaying neighborhood that surrounded us. There was no way to stop urban decay and racial tension. Our attempts to have more police patrolling the area only dramatized the situation. It wasn't obvious at first, but we proprietors knew we were under attack. Our organization was helpless in trying to tighten standards.

The new breed of visitors were looking for a different kind of excitement. They were no longer interested in atmosphere. The Youth Culture was emerging. We had become the Establishment. Street action became more colorful than some of the acts presented in the entertainment places. Audience participation was in full swing. Mitch Miller's sing-along influences were to be heard up and down the Square. I'd watch from the door of the Palace the newly-arrived revelers to the Square start to clap and sing to the music of Dixieland Jazz from the Golden Eagle fifty yards away. I never realised so many people knew the words to *St. James Infirmary Blues.* The race for the customer's buck was on in earnest now. Jimmy Massucci's prophetic words that "greed was going to be the ruin of the Square" were ringing true. If there had been an audience for an amusing, colorful, tuneful piece of entertainment, Quigley's satirical musical on public relations, *The Raspberry Queen,* would have run for a year. Unfortunately, it lasted only eight weeks. After it closed, the Crystal Palace went dark for the first time. It would have stayed that way if the Prince of Darkness hadn't called to sell me what he called the "hottest act in showbusiness."

"Bubie, listen. I know how you feel about the Palace. I love what you guys have done out there. It's a class operation, but times are changing. Would I handle anything like belly dancers in the old days?"

I was shocked. The guy was trying to sell me belly dancers? That was the first step to hiring strippers. I would die rather than bring them into the Palace.

"Listen to me, Bubie. Belly dancers are packing them in here in New York. And have I got a class act for you. Believe me, I've never steered you wrong before, have I?"

"I'm listening," I said coldly.

"This one is an artist, I'm telling you. She's the best in the business. Class act. Beautiful. She'll pack the place. You'll love her."

He went on for five minutes about her pelvic charms. I was weakening.

"How much?" I asked. The price he mentioned seemed reasonable, especially since it included her own native musicians. "I'll call you back." My heart was pounding. After all the talk about keeping up the standards of the area, would I be the first to bring in the strippers?

The Prince of Darkness didn't let me down. Habeba and her oud thumping musicians were indeed a class act; ethnic qualities, too. Nothing to be ashamed of, in spite of the disapproving looks of the other proprietors. It was a sensational act. Night after night, I would be out on the sidewalk, hawking Habeba's charms like an old carnival barker.

"Step right in, Ladies and Gentlemen, and see the new sensation of the art of belly dancing. She's Little Egypt, Theda Bara, and Marilyn Monroe rolled up into one package."

After the initial novelty wore off, subsequent belly dancers proved less of an attraction. I couldn't go any lower and bring in the strippers. The Palace went dark for the second time. Then, comedian Irwin Corey dropped by on his way to the West Coast. He had played the Palace before with great success. He couldn't believe what had happened. His pathological compulsion to work would not let him see the Palace dark.

"I'll do a show tonight and split the door with you."

I told him he was mad. "You can't get an audience in fifteen minutes."

"Wanna bet?"

I resisted. I couldn't see the great artist who had played the best (and some of the worst) clubs in America for over thirty years standing outside the door hawking his own appearance, but he didn't give a damn about dignity. I should have known. He had built his whole act around denigrating dignity. It was going to be an interesting experiment. He hurriedly dressed in his baggy pants and long, flowing tail-coat and tennis shoes and battered top hat, the trade mark of his profession, and stood outside the Palace calling the faithful home.

"The world's greatest authority will be performing in fifteen minutes, at reduced prices."

Within half-an-hour, the Professor had enough people in the theatre to give a show. It was one of the best of his career and possibly the longest. I knew it was going to be our last. The Square was still jammed with traffic, but it was over for us. The place that had sparked the whole area into a multi-million-dollar industry was its first casualty.

Never had a bubble glowed with such colors or burst so quickly. Never had a heart broken so completely. There was pressure on me to step down and turn the Palace over to those "who knew how to get the audience back." Negotiations began with various groups of people who were sure they had the right formula for success. We finally hammered out a deal to rent out the Palace to one of the other entrepreneurs in the Square. I watched with a certain amount of satisfaction as the new operators brought in acts they thought would revive the place. None of them were successful. They brought in big names of the past, doing shows that went out of style long before I did. I could have told them, but they never asked.

What started out as a party ended up as a tragedy. The Three Fountains went up in flames. Jack O'Neil died waiting for a game at his bridge club. The Palace was dark. Jimmy Massucci went blind. The first murder in Gaslight Square took place in the winter of '64.

After twelve years of producing shows, I was creatively exhausted. Without the Palace, I didn't see any future for us in St. Louis. I couldn't go back to the antique business with Cutie. I didn't want to be trapped in the real world. We began to think of places we could escape to. New York was a possibility; Fran was, by now, a recognized songwriting talent, collaborating with Alec Wilder, one of the most respected composers in the business. There was no doubt that she could promote her career if she lived in Manhattan. But what would I do? There wasn't a big demand for my talents. I revived the idea of us living in Connecticut, in the barn, Fran working at her career, and I would become a country gentlemen with no visible means of support. Fran didn't want to take the chance—her parents were still a hazard. Then I got a fantasy of going someplace exotic, like a Greek Island, leaving the commercial world behind.

"All I want to do is watch the flowers grow."

I tried to make it sound romantic, but the idea of communing with nature gave Fran the horrors. "I don't want to go anyplace where they don't speak English" was the other demand she made.

England seemed to be the perfect answer. The children could go to school there without any problems. There were no medical bills to pay in Great Britain. There was theatre there; perhaps Fran and I could get something going again with our plays. I had finished my play about Stella Brooks; I had a very amusing script of a musical based on *Dracula* by local talent with lyrics by Fran, and there was always the possibility that I could get *A Walk On The Wild Side* produced; even *The Nervous Set* was a possibility. Fran could find another collaborator to write songs with. The music scene was very much alive in England with the arrival of the Beatles. We could live cheaply over there.

Once again, I was breaking with the family that was such an important part of my life. I had only been on my own once before, when I went to New York with *Neurotica,* but then I was single, without family responsibilities. Without the income from the Crystal Palace, it might be tough. I still could get enough to survive on from our partnership, but I felt it unfair to Fred to leave him with everything to take care of and still draw money. Fran's folks, who had never grown accustomed to the idea that we were still married, offered to underwrite our stay in England for a year. As grandparents they were perfect, but Fran and I were still "brats" in their books, which made their support at our time of crisis a complete surprise. I suspected they thought it would do their grandchildren some good to see another part of the world. We took them up on their generous offer.

When the newspapers heard we were going to London, they wrote it up as a news feature: LANDESMANS TO LONDON FOR TALENT TUNE UP. Quigley wrote an article about our leaving that presented a fairly different picture:

Now Jay and Fran Landesman are leaving town, and their going marks the end of an Era—the Era of The Crystal Palace and High Style. They are leaving with no boo-hoos, no bitterness, but with a little sadness and a touch of puzzlement. They are not leaving for a better offer. They are leaving us to get away from us and take a look around another town . . . What are they worth to us? What did they cost that we were not willing to pay? All of us, those who love them and those who are saying good riddance—have been enriched by them. We become a little more drab as we wave goodbye.

"St. Louis isn't a place. It isn't a city," wrote Bob Miller to us many years later. "St. Louis is something that happens to you once in a lifetime when you are just right for it and then it never happens again." I knew it was over. I would never return.

When it came to saying goodbye, Alfie dressed the children as if they were going to another party. Fran and I had done nothing about the house, leaving it all in Fred's hands, to dispose of it and the contents any way he saw fit. Saying goodbye to Cutie was going to be the hardest part of leaving.

"Well old girl, you'll be happy to know that the psychiatrists have given us a clean bill of health and we no longer need them."

She looked at me with an expression of old fashioned Jewish contempt.

"So what did you learn from all those fancy doctors?" The corners of her mouth twisted upwards, exposing her two gold incisors.

"They told me that you loved me best of all the children."

Her hand shot out, striking her forehead in the classic gesture of frustration.

"Why didn't you ask me? I could have told you and saved you all that money."

I picked her up and waltzed her around the Galleries for the last time.

"You're right, Cutie, but look at all the fun we would have missed."